The Oleanders of San Leon

The Oleanders of San Leon

ANDY UPCHURCH

TATE PUBLISHING
AND ENTERPRISES, LLC

Published by Tate Publishing & Enterprises, LLC
127 E. Trade Center Terrace | Mustang, Oklahoma 73064 USA
1.888.361.9473 | www.tatepublishing.com

Book design copyright © 2012 by Tate Publishing, LLC. All rights reserved.
Interior design by Nathan Harmony

Published in the United States of America

ISBN: 978-1-62024-467-8
1. Biography & Autobiography / Personal Memoirs
2. House & Home / Do-It-Yourself / General
12.09.10

With original art by Charlotte Callison

Acknowledgments

Many helped in the writing of this book. Some in big ways, some in little ways.

I'd like to thank Vicki Atkins for her sharp, unforgiving eyes, Rene Armstrong for her helping hand and guidance, and Charlotte Callison for her wonderful art. I'd also like to thank JJ, Pat, Julie, my publisher, and the myriad others: you all helped me achieve my dream.

Dedication

To my wife Vicki, who challenged me to stretch, and to grow.

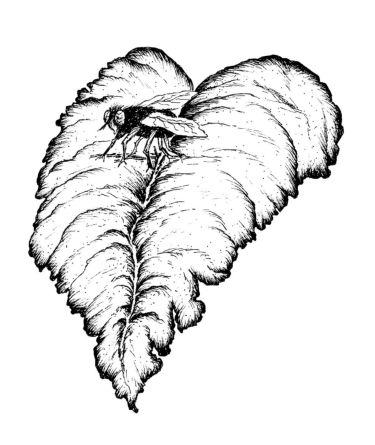

Table of Contents

Foreword

An oleander is a flowering bush. "The Oleanders" in this book, however, refers to a place, not shrubbery. It is named this because of the profusion of wild oleander bushes found growing there. This is in the style of some of the smaller Caribbean islands, where the houses have names instead of street addresses. The Oleanders is located in a rural area known as San Leon, located on the coast of Texas.

I grew up in Arkansas and became a musician and sailor. I migrated to coastal Texas where I lived aboard a sailboat. I later got the notion to build a house, even though I had never built one before and had no construction skills.

The book draws from each of these life experiences. It contains a smattering of stories, snippets, memoirs, and a yarn or two. They help explain who I am. They describe the chain of events of how I got to coastal Texas. They are all loosely related and connected in some way to how the Oleanders of San Leon came to be.

Building your own house—have you ever wondered what that would be like? Just for the adventure of it? To end up with a place to live when you were finished and save money by doing it yourself? A house you could be proud of and show all of your friends?

This is the story within the story. I did wonder and I did have the desire, but I had basically no carpentry knowledge that could help me build a house. What I *did* have was an interest, some extra energy, and a stubborn streak. These qualities seem trivial when compared to *concrete* building skills such as framing and roofing, but they turned out be the very qualities that brought me through a great adventure, and led me to the completion of a real house.

This is not a "how to" book that one would buy to learn all about building houses. It's not like what one might see in a program on cable TV. It's merely the story of how one person with a bad coffee habit and too much time on my hands did it.

Everyone has gifts, talents, and skills. Mine included music, sailing, and computers. What knowledge do these areas have to contribute to building houses? Precious little!

What makes a person want to build their own house? For me, it started off as a project and a challenge. It became an exercise in perseverance and a labor of love.

Every day, people complete immense, complex projects, certainly more so than building a small house. These people have discovered the keys to success. Two of these keys are *vision* and *tenacity*. I learned a valuable lesson in vision and tenacity. With them, I found that I was, as we all are, able to do anything we set our minds to. Vision and tenacity are necessary for a task like this one. Patience and humor help, too.

Out of the experience of building the house, I gained a sense of accomplishment. If you are reading these pages and thinking about a similar project, this story will offer strength, courage, and hope. The yarns and snippets will provide comfort and enjoyment for you along the way.

Preface

Oleander; o-le-an-der (ō'lē an'dər) (n) 1. A tropical flowering shrub of the Apocynaceae family, genus Nerium featuring clusters of white, red, pink, or yellow flowers and narrow, evergreen leaves. The sap of the oleander is said to be slightly toxic.

Oleanders are thought to have originated in northern Africa, the Mediterranean, the Persian Gulf, India, and China. They were introduced to Europe as ornamentals in the fifteenth century. They were brought to the West Indies by the early Spanish colonists where they proliferated easily. Oleanders were first brought to Galveston, Texas, from Jamaica by Joseph Osterman in 1841 as a gift for his wife.

Due to hybridization, there are more than two thousand varieties of oleanders in the world today, and they may be found on every continent.[1]

"They never said it couldn't be done—
they said it couldn't be done… by me."

Chapter 1

The Bulldozers Roll

"If you obey all of the rules, you miss some of the fun."

—Katharine Hepburn

Well, not bulldozers by the strictest sense of the word. More like lawn mowers.

Saturday morning I rolled out of bed all full of purpose. This was a big day. For I was going to do battle with the tangle of undergrowth—*my* tangle of undergrowth.

I donned long pants—something I hate to do in Texas in August—grabbed some water, and drove away from Kemah—a town on the Gulf Coast where the sailboat on which I lived was moored. I was headed down the coast to little San Leon about fifteen miles or so away. I stopped to pick up the lawn mower I was borrowing from my friend, Fran.

I was excited. My adventure of building a house was beginning! Never mind that I had never built a house. Never mind that I didn't know how to use a nail gun. I was not worried. The only thing I had to worry about that day was clearing a building site. Time to get started.

San Leon is a sleepy little place. From the out-of-the-way and neglected lots I had just bought on which to stage this adventure, you could see the water and smell the salt air. These sights and smells flooded in, along with a few dozen mosquitoes, as soon as I parked and opened the car door. I had to park on the road; you couldn't drive onto the land for all of the brush. I soon learned a brand new dance: the *Mosquito Mambo* (swat, half-turn, shimmy, swear, whirl, swat again).

This piece of coastal prairie for all I knew had never been cleared. It was well upholstered with thick scrub growth and stunted trees, all laced together in an impenetrable matrix of luxuriant vines. In some places you could walk; in other places you couldn't even crawl. It all awaited me this morning. It lazed in the sun as insects droned. I could already feel the heat starting to build.

I got my bundle of metal stakes, machete, and gloves, and headed into the underbrush to mark my territory. No, not like the male bobcats on TV nature shows. What I mean is I wanted to locate the surveyor's pins and mark them with taller, more visible, metal stakes. This would provide a little visual definition and give me a better idea of what I was in for. The cool, glinting steel of my two-dollar machete felt good in my hand, gave me courage, and made me feel real big.

Slashing and whacking with my machete I whirled and flailed like some demented flamenco dancer, assaulting the undergrowth. Three of the pins were easy to find because the land is on a corner and the pins were more or less visible from the street—they had been marked by the surveyor with fluorescent pink tape. The fourth pin took some crashing about in the brush to find, but I finally did. One of the pins was right in the middle of a luxurious poison ivy grove. I waded in, nonetheless, trying not to touch anything, and hammered my stake into the ground. Feeling clever and smug, I immediately took a break to wash up.

The best I could do here was to splash a little soap and water from my gallon milk jug onto a towel. Dumb me—anything less than an immediate, full-fledged shower and change of clothes was completely inadequate for poison ivy. Indeed, these words were written the next day as I languished on the verge of calamine shock. You know, sometimes I think I can get a poison ivy rash just by looking at it.

Back to task. After planting the corner stakes I stepped back to survey what God had created and placed under my custodial care.

What a mess! Time for the lawn mower. I started her up and boldly headed for, apparently, where no man had gone before. I'm sure that once the lawn mower saw what it was about to be asked to do, it would have turned and run the other way, if it could. I brought the lawn mower to bear on the first mound of brush, and it immediately gagged. *Brrrrrap, cough-cough, sputter,* recover, *sputter,* silence. Drat—killed the motor. Not to worry. I patiently started her up again and resolved to take smaller bites.

Job one was to mow a path around the perimeter of the lot. This took nearly half a day. I then cleared a spot by the road, big enough to park a car, and turned my attention toward the interior—the wild state of which ranged from riotous growth to stark death.

There were lots of oleander bushes growing in and among the rabble. Oleanders are pretty tropical shrubs with white, pink, yellow, or red flowers. They grow all over the Caribbean as well as many places in the southern United States. Glad I was to have them! Their presence puzzled me though. Oleanders, while ubiquitous in San Leon, are ornamental and not, as my sister says, "indignant" to the area.

In other words, they must have been planted there by somebody. Did this mean that there used to be an old homestead here once upon a time? Might I come across the foundation of a house hidden from view in the undergrowth? I resolved to save as many of the oleanders as I could. I had been thinking that I needed a name to call this special place. The perfect name suddenly leaped out at me. I would call it "The Oleanders!"

This is in true island style. On some of the smaller Caribbean islands and Bermuda, the houses have names instead of street numbers. Numbers aren't needed. Most everybody knows everybody else there. This is not so far-fetched when you consider an island may only be ten or twenty miles long. So, you have houses with names like *Gulls Rest,* or *The Breakers,* or *Widow's Walk*—very quaint. Their names are often prettily painted on small signs, or on the houses themselves. This place would be forever known as "The Oleanders."

Someday a sign would proclaim this. Of course, being in the United States, I would also need a regular number address as well.

Enough blathering, back to the mowing. I mowed a path to my new marina. That's right, marina! Or at least, if you could call one ruined ski boat and a couple of large, abandoned boat dock sections in the middle of the woods a marina. It was included in the cost of the lot. How lucky could a guy get? There I go, being pretentious. Still, I could tell my friends I just got a new boat. Never mind that the boat had a tree growing up through it.

I went into a leafy thicket and established a field latrine, dubbing it, "St. Louis," for no reason in particular. I then mowed a path to the "Shady Glen" back in the southeast corner, skirting the "Black Hole of Calcutta," finally rejoining the property line on the backside. The "Black Hole of Calcutta" was a pit about fifteen feet across and half filled with water and junk. The pile of earth that had once filled it sat like a small hill next to it. As I worked my way around it, I kept a sharp eye out for gold doubloons and human remains.

This mowing was tough going. My borrowed lawn mower, an economy department store model, was woefully inadequate for the job. I found we worked better if we went backward, performing this sort of tango, wherein I crashed backward a few paces and pulled the protesting lawn mower after me. It was in this rather "galumping" fashion that we worked through the terrain.

When we gained the property line on the other side, I stopped for a drink and a rest. I picked up my gallon milk jug of ice water to take a mighty draught, and…it was only a third full. It had a leak. *Caramba!* Off to the Quick Stop for a Coke, some lawn mower gas, and a burrito.

Truly, I didn't want to tear up Fran's lawn mower. I had seen a lawn mower shop just two blocks away, if a shack with several rusty lawn mowers sitting around in various stages of wholeness can be called that. I decided to go there and inquire about whuther (a real word in some rural places) I could borrow one for a couple of hours and pay for my time.

I found the proprietor sitting in the front seat of a car, probing the depths of a pint of whiskey. Normally a scene like this would be alarming, but the amount of rust on the car, along with the broken windshield, assured me that this plastered driver wasn't going to imperil anybody's life on the road, or at least not with this car. Four flat tires confirmed this.

It turned out he didn't rent out his inventory, but he'd sell me one. I tried to start a couple of them—all dead. When it dawned on him I might be good for some money, my new best friend disappeared and returned with a lawn mower that had large rear wheels, a perceived asset. This lawn mower was reasonably all there, which was more than I could say for the owner, even if it was missing its air cleaner, and the engine cover was held on—honest—with baling wire.

Well, she just started right on up and purred like a kitten. That is, a purring kitten with someone standing nearby rattling a box of silverware. But it ran. Twenty-five dollars made her mine, and back we went to my lot. Guess an extended service contract would have been out of the question. People would laugh when they saw this decrepit machine, but I cared not. Within it, like me, beat the *heart of an adventurer.*

Bones

*"Outside of a dog, man's best friend is a book.
Inside a dog, it's too dark to read."*

—*Groucho Marx*

What a great day! The next thing to happen was that I got a dog. Or should I say I found a dog. Good, he could keep me company. This dog would not bark much. I didn't even have to catch him. He stayed put when I told him. He would make a good watch dog…

Oh, all right, I'll tell all. While mowing, I came across…bones. Real bones. Timidly poking lest I be gotten by a *duppy* (a colloquial name for ghost in the Caribbean), I made a tentative determination that they weren't human bones, but those of a small dog. What do you know? I had a pet. My new dog didn't come when I called, but he wouldn't always be trying to run off either. Nor would he disturb the neighbors or chase cars. His name? Bones!

The day grew long. I mowed another path or two, enlarged the parking lot, and then called it a day. By then it was hot, brutally hot. Hotter than a June bride in a feather bed! Even my retinas felt sunburned. Time to beat a retreat. I started thinking about finding someplace quiet, dark, and cool—the boat. The Kemah Bums were going to be raising hell at the Hoagie Ranch that evening. The Kemah Bums were a small local band that rather irreverently played tropical music around the waterfront, and I was the piano player. I needed to have some energy.

I parked my new purchase underneath a bush. If somebody stole this poor lawn mower overnight, they could have it. After one last visit to St. Louis, I drove away tired, but happy. I couldn't remember when I'd enjoyed mowing so much. A great adventure was beginning, and it was off to a great start!

"Bones"

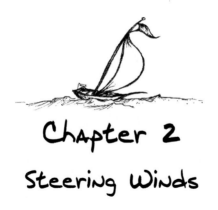

Chapter 2
Steering Winds

"If you surrender to the wind, you can ride it."

—*Unknown*

My life has been governed by two major *steering winds*: music and water. Each played a role in bringing me to The Oleanders of San Leon.

For the Love of the Song

I took piano lessons from an early age. My teacher had taught my mother many years before, and by the time I came along, my teacher was, bless her heart, not a spring chicken anymore. Ancient though she was, she was very good to me. I didn't particularly enjoy practicing since it kept me from being outdoors. However, the time I spent on lessons and practicing when I was young gave me a head start in music that served me in good stead later in life.

I participated in music programs throughout public school. I went on to major in music in college at North Texas State University in Denton, Texas. After graduation I went on the road playing with various groups, including a stint with an Elvis Presley tribute band. Those were fun times! After a couple of years I grew weary of traveling and decided to settle down in Dallas, where I had developed some musical connections. Dallas is a great city. There was lots of work there and lots of fun to be had.

The Water

"If it wasn't for low life I'd have no life at all"

—*Gene Rutt*

The second steering wind that has shaped the course of my life is this: I love the water. I always have. Oceans, lakes, rivers—all water. I even like taking long baths! I have a particular affinity for salt water, and that is what eventually led me to San Leon. I can trace this paramour back to its origin.

I grew up inland, in the wilds of Arkansas. When I was about eight years old my family took a driving vacation to the panhandle of Florida. Right then and there commenced a love affair between me and the sea that continues to this very day. I loved the sand, the sea gulls, the salty air, the surf, the land crabs, and the palm trees. I can remember being depressed for days after we got back home. From then on, I knew that someday I would live close to it.

In the meantime, where we lived there were rivers and lakes in every direction, just waiting to be explored. We fished, swam, camped, canoed, and water skied. I learned to sail then, too, in little eight-foot Styrofoam boats. I wasn't a very good sailor, but I liked it. Sailing was to take on more significance in my life as I grew older.

I yearned to return to salt water. There were a few more vacations—New York to visit relatives and to the Texas Coast. On each of these trips I was in heaven. I spent every available minute in and around the ocean. Later, when I went to college in North Texas, I was glad that, if not on a coast, I was at least closer to one than I had been in Arkansas. This allowed trips to the beach over spring break and such. That suited me fine! I could worry about actually living on the coast later. Until I was able to move south, any money I was able to set aside for travel was used to get to the beach.

When I graduated from college and went on the road playing music, we sometimes found ourselves playing in coastal areas. At those times I would rise early to walk the waterfront and see what there was to see.

To me, a natural complement to this affinity for water was sailing. While in college, I had friends here and there who had small sailboats, and we would occasionally go sailing. Sailing as a sport started to grow on me. For the cost of a six-pack of beer, we could spend a whole afternoon zipping across the water, capsizing often and generally having a ball. Later, when I got tired of the traveling and settled down in Dallas, I again started thinking about sailing. I had never forgotten how much I enjoyed it, and when I got a little money ahead, I bought a small sailboat, just to see if it was as fun as I remembered. The answer to that was a resounding "yes."

I found myself sailing more and more, whenever I could work it into my schedule. There are sailing waters all around Dallas. The only downside to living in Dallas was that it didn't have a coastline, but then, that's not really Dallas's fault, is it?

Up to this point, I was enjoying a full life that consisted of playing music with all sorts of bands, and sailing. After a few seasons of sailing the little boat, I graduated to a sixteen-foot catamaran. Those are the boats with two, long, narrow hulls or floats, a trampoline for a deck, and entirely too much sail. They are light and fast; the true sports cars of the sailing world.

Talk about fun—when you point a catamaran out to sea and trim the sails to catch the wind, you must jump on quickly, lest you get left behind in a cloud of spray. You tumble onto the rearing boat in a wild tangle of flailing ropes and sails. You try to quickly sort yourself out and get your bearings as your craft leaps ahead. It doesn't care if you're on board or not. By the time you glance back, the point from which you started is already far behind. When a catamaran is sailing at speed, one "shoe" comes up completely out of the water. It's like a carnival ride!

Imagine, blasting along, spray flying in your face. All of a sudden, grandly, majestically, the hull you are perched on rises up in the air as if by magic. You are now in a precarious balance of wind and water. You carefully play your two wildcards of sail trim and your own weight. You're riding a rocket, barely in control, and flirting with disaster. One flinch could mean capsize. Few things have thrilled me more than that catamaran. It only whetted my appetite for…more sailing. How I wished I'd had a catamaran when I was in college. I'll bet I would have been more popular with the girls!

Up to this point, music was still the primary focus for me. I regarded my ratio of music to sailing to be 75:25 percent. Over the next couple of years, this ratio started to change. It became about 50:50 percent. Then it was 25:75 percent, the opposite. I began feeling resentful, having to leave the lake early on a perfectly good sailing Saturday to change into a tuxedo and go to play piano somewhere.

Time for a Change?

"The pessimist complains about the wind
The optimist expects it to change
The realist adjusts the sails."

My musical career was going well. At one point I was playing twelve to fourteen times a week, often twice a day. I was saving money, but boy, that was a lot of playing. There wasn't much time for anything else. Not only that, but it's hard to be creative when playing so many hours, and it's a challenge to keep from becoming stale. I was being what I set out to be—a career musician—but certain factors began to emerge that somewhat cooled my zest.

First, many live music venues were switching to discos that played "canned" music, reducing the amount of available work. Second, music creation and performance was becoming more and more electronic. One musician armed only with a computer could sound just like a full band with background vocals, brass, string parts, everything.

I must admit it sounded nice, and I could appreciate the technology that made this possible. I could also see that this was, in fact, a way for many talented musicians to keep performing, but what about all of the side men? High quality sound and technology aside, the music was not completely *live*. I preferred live music played by live musicians. I still do.

Finally, I concluded that luck must have been the biggest factor for success in some performers because it sure didn't appear to me that there was much talent involved.

To still the growing inner conflict I was experiencing, I made the anguished decision to find another occupation. I chose software development, an emerging, exciting, and ostensibly profitable field. Music would no longer be my livelihood. It would still be my creative outlet, but its role would change to become a fun and occasionally profitable pastime.

Software development could bring better pay, better hours, stability, and security. Stability and security can be hard to come by for a working musician. Not that I was all that materialistic, but things like owning a home someday, a new car as the need arose, etc., had their appeal.

As in the old joke, "What's the difference between a musician and a large pepperoni pizza?"

Answer: "A large pepperoni pizza can feed a family of five."

Enough said?

Therefore, I returned to school to study business computer systems, after which I began my new career in software development. I still performed with bands on weekends. With more income rolling in, I could pick and choose when I wanted to play music and have more time on the weekends for sailing. *Woo-hoo!*

I was still living in the Dallas area. I sailed more and more, both on my own boat and on friends' boats. Plus, I was reading everything I could about sailing. After a few wild seasons with the catamaran, I began to think about owning a larger boat, one on which I could spend the night.

I started looking at sailboats. While I was looking, I heard about a used, twenty-seven-foot Catalina for sale and decided to have a look. When I saw her, she was propped up on stilts, neglected, and unkempt. Her bilge was full of black, foul-smelling water, there were lots of dirt dobber nests on the ceiling, and her bimini, or shade awning was a dubious pile of sticks and canvas. She was dirty inside and out.

I scarcely noticed these things. What I did see was a nice-sized salon down below and a spacious forward berth. She had an aft berth, as well, that would make good storage. She had an inboard diesel, desirable for a sailboat; electronic instruments; wheel steering; and a roller-furling jib that allowed the sails to be rolled in and out like a window shade. She could sleep a family of four. This boat would do! It was love at first sight.

Some would have shaken their heads and walked away. I, however, saw real potential. I saw a freshly scrubbed deck with crisp white sails hoisted against a bright blue sky. I saw refinished, gleaming, teak wood trim and a clean, orderly interior. I could imagine blustery, fast rides and tranquil, calm nights anchored in beautiful places. This boat promised adventure. She was a bank foreclosure and available for, well, a song. I bought her and sold my catamaran.

From then on I spent every available minute with her, cleaning her up, repairing this, improving that, and learning how to sail this new kind of boat. I spent nights on her often. She became my second home on weekends. I just loved waking up on her, in her berth in the marina. Then, I'd drink my coffee in the morning sun and later take her out...

I occasionally stayed aboard on some weeknights, too, just because I could. I'd wake up in the morning, get ready, and then drive into snappy, business-chic Las Colinas for work. What should I name this boat? It couldn't be just any old name. *Sloop Du Jour* was clever, and *Endless Summer* had nice connotations. *Gulf Cloud* reminded me of my grandfather, but the name somehow seemed better suited for one of the old majestic clipper ships. I ultimately chose the name

Mañana. It had a nice feel to it. This name brought music and sailing together, for this was also the title of one of my favorite Jimmy Buffett songs. Furthermore, it was a name that would be easy to understand coming across a marine radio.

There followed many wonderful days of sailing, either charging through the waves with spray flying or gliding serenely upon calm waters, according to the caprice of the winds. There were many beautiful nights anchored out in some remote cove amid a gorgeous sunset with Jimmy Buffett music playing quietly in the background, or perhaps nothing at all but silence, with a couple of good steaks on the grill and a bottle of wine. How *romantical!*

I never once regretted my decision to get Mañana. As I became more comfortable with her, I began longing to expand my horizons to a place with more room where I could broaden my sailing skills. I wanted to get out of fresh water. I was becoming ready to make a move—the move to salt water.

Where to go? I still wanted to be reasonably near to family and that part of the country. I needed a place where business computer skills were in demand. This meant one of the larger cities. Strategically this looked like being somewhere along the Texas coast. Houston, Texas, seemed like a good place to start.

For several months I went job-hunting long distance in Houston. It eventually culminated in an offer that I could accept. Nothing left then but to do the *scary thing*: quit my secure job with a large company in Dallas and move to Houston. At long last, I was going to get to live by salt water!

In the course of living between college and moving to the Houston area, I did, as a matter of fact, meet that special girl and get married. Like me, she enjoyed music and played piano as well. She had not done much sailing before we met, but she soon became a fan. She came with two children, and I identified as part of my parental responsibilities the job of showing them how to have fun with boats and water.

When the offer for the job in Houston came, it was still a few weeks before the end of the spring school semester. Since I needed to start in my new position before then, it made perfect sense to me to move the boat to Houston and live on it. The rest of the family would follow when school was out.

It was an exciting day when Mañana was pulled out of the water by crane and trucked from Dallas to Houston, with me following behind like a proud new father. Our destination was Kemah, a quaint, little community located on the Texas Gulf coast, where Clear Lake empties into Galveston Bay. It is a mecca for all types of water sports and is home to several large marinas.

To my landlubber's eyes, this area was very scenic. There were boats and water everywhere. There were palm trees and seagulls. Kemah was close enough to Houston to commute, if one must. Always before, I had made the decision to live near where I worked, not near where I played. That was backwards! This time, I made the decision to live close to where I would play, not where I would work. Commute I must and I was even happy about it. Well, almost.

It was there that we splashed Mañana, for her first taste of salt water. When she was in the water and her mast was proudly flying once again, I started her up and motored out of the shipyard into a brave new world—and a salty one at that. We went to find her prearranged new berth at one of the nearby marinas.

Proud I was to spend my first night aboard in salt water. It wasn't the beautiful, crystal clear, turquoise water of Bermuda, but I didn't care. It was the ocean! Within a couple of weeks, wife, kids, dog, and household arrived. We moved into a house in nearby Seabrook. We weren't right on the water, but it was within walking distance and that was plenty good enough for me. As far as I was concerned, Galveston Bay was our new backyard.

During the first year in our new home, I never touched a piano. I never even told anyone about being a musician. I was too busy having fun and exploring my new world. I was making friends, meeting sailors, and sailing. I was absorbing—and enjoying—every minute of it. It felt like home immediately. I loved the salty surroundings. I even liked looking at old, rusty shrimpers! I would always love my first home, Arkansas, but living by the coast was where I wanted to be.

Eventually, I ran into a sailor who was a musician. It was only a matter of time before *that* happened! Gene was a colorful and affable local character. We became friends, and when I let it slip that I played piano, he lost no time in inviting me down to play with him at his regular Friday night *gig* (this is a technical musical expression, don't worry too much about its meaning). Gene sang and played guitar in a little place not far from the waterfront called the Hoagie Ranch.

At first I resisted. Prior to moving from Dallas, I had been working full-time as a programmer, plus playing piano four nights a week, leaving little time for sailing or other things. I was still a little burned out. Then, one day I decided to take Gene up on his offer. The next Friday night I drove to the Hoagie Ranch with a keyboard. As I was getting it set up, people started arriving. Gene seemed to know everyone and introduced me around.

We played the first song and got a standing ovation right off the bat. Everyone wanted to meet me, and most wanted to buy me a beer. Many songs and several beers later, I felt quite at home and comfortable at the Hoagie Ranch. I could *do* this! I still wasn't much interested in playing music seriously, but this was different. It was a laid-back, unstructured setting where we could play fun music for local sailors. It sounded like great fun to me! Before long, Gene and I were playing there every Friday night for sandwiches and beer.

We played lots of tropical music, including songs by Jimmy Buffet. These songs are all about sailing, water, sand and sea, rum drinks, and the laid-back lifestyle. This kind of music, of course, goes very well with the waterfront. Soon, a good, local drummer, Gary, heard about all of the fun and asked if he could join our ranks. Fine with us. We welcomed him into the fold, and gave him the nickname "Boom-Boom," and then we were three.

Word of this "band" spread among the local sailing community, and soon there was a crowd at the Hoagie Ranch on Friday nights. It was funny because the tourists would flood into the waterfront for the weekend and go to the more visible places, but all the sailors would fog into the little Hoagie Ranch. We became sort of an irreverent and erstwhile institution. Our name? *The Kemah Bums.*

The Hoagie Ranch was a small, unpretentious family-owned place. It had a warm, inviting atmosphere. It had a bar, but it was by no means a dive. The sailing community around Clear Lake consisted of engineers, accountants, doctors, lawyers, pirates, ex-hippies, rocket scientists, and the occasional astronaut from nearby NASA. Some people were liveaboards. All came together in cutoffs and flip flops every Friday night to drink beer out of glass mugs shaped like boots, catch up on all of the goings on around the lake, and hear the Kemah Bums.

There were also the transient sailors who occasionally blew into Kemah with the wind one day, on their sailboats—true vagabonds of the world. They would anchor out in little backwaters for free for a few days or weeks. They would meet the local sailors—who were always happy to lend a hand or a tool, or give a ride to the grocery store. They always seemed to find out about the Hoagie Ranch as well. We got to know several nice and interesting people this way. One day they'd be gone again, riding the wind to some other port.

I mentioned pirates. There was one real pirate that I knew about and there were probably several more that I didn't. Tim was the pirate who I am referring to. He didn't look like a pirate—not that I was expecting skull and crossbones, eye patches, hooks, and a golden earring. One day Tim told me an amazing story. After hearing it, I realized that I had indeed met my first real-life, modern-day pirate.

One thing made this idyllic existence a bit less idyllic: our marriage didn't survive. It unraveled, the way things sometimes do in life. Affairs of the heart are never straightforward, and I may never understand why things like this happen the way they do. "The road to hell is paved with good intentions," my grandmother used to say. I never intended for the marriage to end any way other than naturally.

Its ending made me sad and left me with the desire to simplify my life. Divest of what had become a large and unmanageable accumulation of…stuff. My life had become cluttered up with *things*. I was beginning to feel that I didn't own these things—they owned me. I needed to downsize, re-group. Newly single, it wasn't much of a decision for me to move aboard Mañana to live full-time.

A liveaboard—now there would be no yards to mow. No gardens to water. No housework! By the way, vacuuming takes about ten minutes on a boat with a hand vacuum, and that's if you stretch it. I now would have more time to do what I wanted to do. Of course, there are always chores that clamor for attention, but when you live on a boat as opposed to a house, they seem fewer.

I loved living by, read that *on*, the water. I was saving money right and left because my expenses were low. My life was simple. I felt like I was living a life from right out of a Jimmy Buffett song. I was living "the dream." I was living *my* dream!

Living on a Boat

"To be happy for a night, get drunk.
To be happy for a month, get married.
To be happy for life, get a sailboat."

—*An old sailor's saying*

People who live on boats are there because they want to be there; they are happy being there. Living in a marina, you almost always run into friends on the dock, either coming or going. You meet your neighbors in a way that's different than when you live in apartments or neighborhoods. Friendships spring up effortlessly. People who live on boats automatically have a lot in common. Everybody has interesting stories of how they came to be there. Everyone watches out for everybody else's boats, retying loose dock lines and buttoning up other loose odds and ends.

Boaters are fun, close-knit people. There are lots of both married and singles. Some of the docks are real party docks with lots of colorful characters around. There, parties can just spring up for no reason as if by spontaneous combustion. Other docks are very quiet. If the place where your vessel is moored does not suit you, no worries—just move your boat.

At our marina, there seemed to always be something interesting or funny afoot. One time when I came home from work, I saw a small group of people on one of the docks pointing to something in the water, and walked over to investigate.

"There's an alligator over there," a girl said, throwing a bread slice over to where she had indicated. There had been a big rain recently and sometimes alligators are washed out of the creeks and bayous by them, and they end up in Clear Lake.

"Alligators don't eat bread!" I exclaimed.

"I know that," she replied. "But the ducks do."

As the implications of this remark sank in, I couldn't help but grin. A few ducks had swum over to get some bread, and while we watched, there was a ripple in the water, followed by a splash. The ducks were lucky this time, and the alligator, only a small one, missed his meal. While I liked the ducks in our marina, I knew that I was simply observing life in the food chain.

I particularly enjoyed this part: the marina where Mañana was moored was near the busy channel between Clear Lake and Galveston Bay. Clear Lake has a large boating community, and all boats must pass through this channel to get out into the bigger waters of the bay. Along this channel is a boardwalk with several restaurants, clubs with live music, shopping, and even an amusement park—all within walking distance of my boat. I liked living in a place where everyone else wanted to come to have fun. There was always something happening.

It was wonderful to be able to park my car Friday after work and not have to get into another car all weekend—just walk everywhere until Monday morning. It was a never-ending source of amusement to go sit at a pretty outdoor table along the boardwalk and watch the boats go in and out through the channel while enjoying a restorative. The boat traffic turned into a steady parade on most nice Saturdays and Sundays. The prettier the weather, the more boats that went by.

There was no telling what you'd see from day to day—everything from the biggest and most beautiful yachts to canoes. There were families out fishing, bronze-bodied weight lifters on sleek speed-boats, big shots wearing lots of gold on large expensive yachts, and bearded sailors on modest boats. Sometimes there would be a hot go-fast boat crewed by scantily-clad college girls. Occasionally there would be some unexpected excitement, such as a minor collision, accompanied by yelling and arm waving. If for some reason you couldn't take your own boat out on a pretty day, watching this show was the next best thing.

Sailing in and out of this channel was quite fun. I have an old, decrepit, beat-up baritone horn that I'd bought at a junk store for five dollars when I was in college. I would take it on the sailboat with me and serenade the crowd on the boardwalk as we went down the channel. I'd get up on top of the boat, rear back, and play *When the Saints Go Marching In*, *The Eyes of Texas*, and other offerings.

My horn can be quite loud, and I played these songs with vigor, not in a shy way. When I began playing, there would, at first, be startled silence, and then cheering. I wasn't the best of baritone players, but that just made it all the funnier.

More About Life on a Boat

"This next song is not a show stopper, but it does slow it down quite a bit"

—Gene Rutt

Mañana was a bit small for living aboard full-time, but not excruciatingly so. She was tied up at a marina, along with a few hundred other boats. I like to make the distinction to non-boating friends that my boat is a sailboat and not a yacht, and she stays at a marina, not a yacht club. Some of the people at the marina were liveaboards like me, although most lived elsewhere. Small communities of liveaboards make for a fun environment.

As a liveaboard, I'd begin my day as many do, with an alarm clock, and then rise to make a cup of espresso. Just one of those would catapult me all the way into mid-morning. Larger sailboats have bathrooms that are usable, but the "head" on Mañana was about the size of a telephone booth and that, by the way, included a toilet, shower, and sink.

There was no hot water heater on my boat or a place to put one. Therefore, I would grab my towel and shaving kit and head to the showers at the marina, which were clean, spacious, and had unlimited hot water. After showering, I'd go back to the boat and dress for work. Once I got the hang of this routine, I could get ready in the morning easily and quickly—even if it meant wearing a coat and tie, which I often did. With nary a wrinkle! I'd drive to work like everyone else, work, and then drive home.

I always looked forward to coming home to my boat. It was very comfortable. With her small air conditioner, she was cool in the summertime. With her little ceramic space heater she was warm and cozy in the wintertime. I had my little TV and DVD player, plus a small stereo. I had a tiny galley with a dorm-sized refrigerator and cooked most of my meals aboard. See? All the comforts of home.

When you live on a boat, where do you keep your musical instruments and other possessions that you don't have room for, but don't want to get rid of? A climate controlled, secure storage area was the answer, for me. I had some family keepsakes, books, an LP collection (that's *records*, youngsters), furniture, photographs, and other flotsam and jetsam that I wanted to keep. It all waited for me in the storage area until such time that I might again have room for them. With low expenses,

I could afford to pay for a storage area for a long period of time, if need be. I regarded this as a necessary expense of living the lifestyle.

In the evenings I'd visit with my neighbors, go to the marina hot tub and pool, or wash clothes at the little launderette. Or, I might run errands, meet friends for happy hour, go for walks, ride bikes, or many other enjoyable things. Sometimes on nice evenings we'd sail after work. On weekends I'd fish, take the boat out, fix things, upgrade this or that, and the like. Clean house. Bathe the parrot that lived on the boat with me. Oh, yes, and play gigs.

Some of my favorite times on the boat were cold, rainy winter nights. I'd crank the heater up, pull out the extra blanket, light a candle, make some herbal tea, and read while the rain fell softly on the cabin top.

"Storms?" you say. "What about storms?"

The boat was stable and secure, tied in her slip. Even in strong storms, she would not pitch and yaw. She would merely rock gently in a manner that was neither uncomfortable nor scary. Many a night I would be rocked right to sleep. Living on the boat was a nice life.

Want to know more about what it's like to live on a boat? If you are curious, the following may be for you:

Exercise One: Could You Live on a Boat?

1. Sleep on a shelf in the closet.

2. Replace the closet door with a curtain.

3. Have your mate periodically whip open the curtain, dash a glass of water in your face, shine a flashlight in your eyes, and yell, "Your watch!"

4. Wall off half of your bathtub and move the showerhead down to waist level.

5. When showering, shut off the water while soaping each time to conserve water. This is easy to remember if your boat doesn't have a hot water heater.

6. Cut the bottom out of the carton your new hot water heater came in. Draw a door on it in crayon. Cut this out as well. Place the box over your toilet. On an inside wall, mount a placard that reads: "In These Isles of Sun and Fun, We Never Flush for Number One." Live this. On the doorknob you drew with your crayon, tape a small sign that reads: "Out of Order." Even if it's not now, it soon will be. And while on the subject of heads, flush yours repeatedly until it backs up.

7. Put a pan of lube oil on your humidifier instead of water and set it to high. Savor this fascinating aroma. Work a little diesel fuel into the carpet as well.

8. Once a month, pick out a major appliance. Take it completely apart and put it back together again.

9. Put a dim fluorescent light under the coffee table, lie down there, and read a book.

10. If the wind outside is howling in the middle of the night, get up and race around the house in your nightie like an idiot. Tie stout lines to the four corners of your house, if they're not present already. Check them for tension and chafe, lest they break, allowing your house to pitch and yaw up against your neighbor's house.

    Then, undress and attempt to climb over your mate into your corner of the bed without awakening her. You accidentally bring your exposed posterior within range of your parrot that will take advantage of such an easy target and inflict an injury that causes you to bellow in pain. This startles your sleeping mate who sits bolt upright in bed, unaware you were at that point balanced over her. Her head collides with your jaw, causing you both to collapse in a tangle of arms and legs, along with the parrot, still attached to your derriere. Your momentum carries you both beyond the other edge of the bunk and you all crash to the floor in a crescendo of cursing, shrieking, and squawking.

11. In the morning, bump your head twice; pinch your index finger once, hard; stub your toe; and rap smartly on your thumb with a hammer. Perform this ritual daily.

12. If you really want to get the feel for living aboard, strip and don an already wet raincoat and soaked sweatpants. Pour a cup of water into each of your new deck shoes and put them on as well. Then, stand in a cold shower with an insulated cup of cold coffee in one hand and flush hundred dollar bills down your toilet.

13. The next time you need to vacuum your house, no sweat—just drag the garden hose into the house and get into your bathing suit. Open a beer. Put Jimmy Buffett on the stereo. Liberally spray the floors in every room with the hose. Use the sharp stream setting for stubborn dirt. Hey, relax—it'll all run down into the bilge!

For these next two boat bonding experiences, you are going to have to use your imagination. Those of you who have lived aboard can help those who haven't.

14. If upon arising in the morning, your foot splashes when it hits the floor, don't panic. Just flip the bilge pump switch on. If nothing happens, turn on the battery charger to recharge the dead battery and get a bucket to begin bailing. At this point, you may want to taste the water lapping over the floorboards. If it's salty, this will give you some idea of the magnitude of your problem. Accidentally maneuver too close to your parrot, which will nip you playfully. Apply a Band-Aid with dinosaurs on it to the small wound where the blood has started. A dab of toilet paper works here also.

15. If you turn on the faucet to draw water for your first cup of coffee and nothing happens, flip the fresh water pump switch on. If nothing happens again, turn on the battery charger to recharge the dead battery like you should have done in the pre-

vious step. If the faucet splutters, farts rudely, and suddenly spurts cold water all over your Donald Duck boxer shorts, turn the above switches off in reverse order. Draw a cup of water from the gallon milk jug of water under the stairs that you had placed there for emergencies.

If the water has all leaked out through the pinhole it developed from the time you kicked it over in the middle the night on your way to the head, go outside and fill the fresh water tanks from the hose. Dress first. Again, accidentally brush too close to your parrot. The parrot is growing weary of these continuing intrusions and wishes to get your attention. He delivers a well-placed attack to the closest appendage.

At this point, you may elect to just give up and opt to drive to the Parkit Market for the coffee, stopping at the marina showers on the way.

Chapter 3
Mañana's Epic Voyage of Discovery

I had plenty of fun living on the boat. I also had some grand adventures during that time. This is one of them.

When I moved from Dallas to the Texas Gulf Coast, I couldn't wait to explore Galveston Bay, my new backyard. I loved sailing and loved being on my sailboat, Mañana. I spent every minute I could out on the water. Sometimes I'd find excuses to just go and be on the boat, even when there wasn't enough time to go out. It was like my sailboat and I were in a *relationship*. We were, really.

I quickly learned how vast the bay was, and this inland sailor had to get used to the happy concept that you could sail all day or more and not see it all. It thrilled me that the waters caressing the hull of Mañana in her slip were the same waters that lap the shores of faraway places: the Caribbean, Italy, Japan. And you could get to all of those places by water—right from the very slip where Mañana was gently bobbing. People left Galveston Bay to embark on far-reaching voyages all the time. Maybe someday I'd get to voyage to some of those places too.

Before I could go anywhere, I had to learn how to do it safely and responsibly. I needed to learn more about basic seamanship, boat handling, and navigation. This I did by sailing as often as I could. Any time I could find two hours to rub together, I was "out there."

Many destinations around Galveston Bay were within an easy hour or two from my marina. Others were overnight trips. Beyond that was a whole world to explore. Sailing voyages were only limited by the constraints of time and money.

Still, when I moved to the Texas coast I just couldn't get around to all of the sailing destinations fast enough. I made it my business to sail everywhere it was possible to go by sailboat. I sailed to the closest places first and then gradually expanded my horizons. I ranged farther and farther away as I continued to build my confidence and skills. I was proud indeed the day I single-handedly sailed Mañana to the old seaport town of Galveston, a day's journey away.

Mañana was the perfect boat for this work. She was small enough to single-hand and big enough to take all but the worst weather Galveston Bay had to offer.

After two or three years of salt water sailing and living aboard, I felt that I was ready for a more far-reaching trip than just a weekend. Once this was established, getting the time and money together became a mere detail. The day I found out that my current work contract was wrapping up, I knew it was time for a voyage! I knew just where I would go, too: Port Aransas.

Why Port Aransas?

Port Aransas is a little fishing and beach town on the Texas Gulf coast that has played a role off and on throughout my life. My family took driving vacations from Arkansas to Port Aransas when I was small. It was later a place to go for spring break when I was in college, and it has been an occasional destination for driving vacations ever since. It is near and dear to my heart. Not only that, Port Aransas seemed like it was just the right distance away for the length of the voyage I was contemplating. I began making plans to sail to Port Aransas. There was a lot to learn! I bought the nautical charts for the area and started studying. I also talked to several people who had made the voyage.

Although I could have invited someone to go along, I elected to single-hand. I am an outgoing and people-loving creature, but I wanted to get a feel for sailing solo. Plus, I wanted to build my confidence by having only myself to rely on if I got into a jam. I thought I could learn the lessons such a trip had to teach, more fully, if I was alone.

Port Aransas is 215 miles south of Kemah by road. It is located on Mustang Island, a barrier island on the Texas coast located just north of Corpus Christi. There are two water routes I could take to get there: offshore, or via the Intracoastal Waterway (ICW), a canal that runs along the coast of the eastern and southern United States.

To go offshore means going out of Galveston Bay into the big, open waters of the Gulf of Mexico and then sailing nonstop to Port Aransas. This voyage would have to wait until I was more seasoned. I wasn't ready for offshore sailing yet. The ICW route, however, was within my reach. The ICW, called the "Ditch" by local sailors, is mostly protected waters and safer in several ways, although it has its own inherent dangers.

The ICW is a commercial route primarily used by barges, although pleasure craft may use it also. Barges could run around the clock, but they had experience and radar. I didn't yet have experience or radar, so traveling at night would not be safe for me. That meant stopping each night. This, of course, made for a much longer trip.

The ICW is largely landlocked and, therefore, protected from the wind and waves of the open Gulf. However, there are points where it is possible to get from the ICW to the Gulf, two to be exact. I could conceivably start out in the ICW and, depending on the weather and my courage, go offshore for certain stints.

The ICW traverses land that is mostly uninhabited. There are long stretches where there is nothing but swampy coastal prairie. Some find this boring, but I found it interesting and pretty. I would not be able to stop just anywhere along the route. I would need to be safely anchored or tied up in a marina each night, away from barge traffic.

Given Mañana's average speed without pushing too hard and the array of available stopping points, I determined that I would be stopping to spend the night four times. I should arrive at Port Aransas around noon on the fifth day. My first long trip—wow! And that was pretty close to how it went. A luxurious four and a half days to get there, a couple of days on the island, and four and a half days to return.

In the midst of this planning, a fortuitous event occurred: the Kemah Bums got a booking to play—where else? Port Aransas! A sign from above. Now I even had a *reason* for the trip—as if I needed one. I could arrive by boat; meet the band, who would be driving down, play the party, and then sail home. Ain't life grand?

I finished making my plans. I studied the charts until I felt comfortable with the route. I checked over Mañana from stem to stern and pronounced her fit for the sea. I stocked up on provisions, and then I was ready to go.

And go, I did. The following excerpts are from the Ship's Log.

• • •

We left Kemah one Sunday in August, after delaying the departure by one day for rain. We set out into headwinds and overcast skies, which quickly degenerated into torrential rain. We, being myself and Patches, Parrot of the Sea (and woe to the hapless sinner who would trifle with him).

Patches was great company and the best crew I ever had. Patches was named so because he looked like he was made out of spare parts. He was a colorful little parrot with a brilliant orange head, green wings with blue tipped feathers, red breast, and a blue tail. He made the trip in his small cage that was secured to a little platform right in front of the steering pedestal under the shade of the bimini, where he could see everything and help me keep an eye out for trouble.

From there, he could talk to me, and I could solicit his opinion on this or that nautical point of interest. As I talked to passing barges on the radio, Patches hailed all the passing seabirds.

This day, Patches was below. The rain persisted almost all the way to Galveston, our first stop, where we arrived wet and cross. We anchored outside of the Galveston Yacht Basin for one of the most dreadful nights I have ever known. It was very hot and there were billions of mosquitoes. Swells from passing ships and crew boats jostled us all night. I arose the next morning, still cross. Almost bit the parrot. There was another bad forecast and there were black clouds overhead. This trip wasn't going the way I wanted it to!

I decided to lay out a day, and attempted to get the anchor up. This took some doing because the line had become wrapped around and around the keel sometime during the night. When it was finally disengaged, I motored into the Galveston Yacht Basin to find a slip. This afforded a calmer place to stay and allowed me to use the air conditioner, which could only be run using shore power. Texas weather in August will make a tough man crumble.

I was tired after my sleepless night and almost decided to scrub the mission. This would have been a grievous mistake. However, after taking a nap I felt better, and after reviewing the charts my enthusiasm for the voyage returned. A good meal ashore and a glass of wine restored my "sunny disposish." Life wasn't so bad after all, and I decided to press on. I'm glad I did.

Bright and early the next morning, I was up in order to get under way in time to clear the Pelican Island Bridge, a draw bridge, before they closed for rush hour. I just made it. On to Freeport, thirty-two miles away. A couple of hours later I was motor sailing in calm weather and making good time when my keel dug into the bottom. I had strayed out of the channel. Almost knocked Patches right off his perch! Running aground in Galveston Bay is usually more inconvenient than it is dangerous and it was this day as well. Twenty minutes of maneuvering and a little cursing got me back into deeper water and we resumed course.

I cleared the Galveston Causeway Bridge and entered the ICW without further incident. The ICW in this stretch was tricky. There was shoaling and lots of barge traffic to make it a white-knuckled day, although the last stretch into Freeport was placid and deserted.

I arrived at Freeport hot and tired. I didn't care; I had survived my first day and would live to tell about it. There was a marina there with a ship's store, a restaurant, and a pool with a swim-up bar. I got a slip, tied up, and made the boat ship shape. Then I headed for the pool, leaving Patches on watch.

Observation: when single-handing in the ICW,

There're not enough hands to:	Not enough eyes to:
• get lunch and drinks	• watch the chart
• handle sails	• watch my heading
• talk to barges on the radio	• spot channel markers
• update the log	• keep an eye on the water depth
• fix problems	• watch other traffic
• investigate strange noises	• read cruising notes
• play upon my horn	• keep up with the GPS

…all at the same time!

The next day I would travel from Freeport to Matagorda, thirty-nine miles away. This was a much better day. I was off shortly before seven o'clock. We got to the Brazos River floodgates around mid-morning. There, we danced around with a barge and a workboat while we all attempted to get through them. There were lots of logs coming downriver from recent rains. Patches didn't have any breakfast. He was either trying to watch his weight or perhaps he had a touch of the *Mal de mer.* Maybe his crop wasn't well suited for the sea.

My new GPS told me exactly where I was at all times. It was magic. The ICW was in much better shape in this stretch—wider and deeper—than it had been. There was not much traffic either. I found a way to raise and douse the jib sail without having to leave the wheel. At mile marker 410 I nosed Mañana gently aground in a muddy bank where she stayed placidly while I treated myself to a luxurious swim. At lunchtime, my can of chili that had been left in the sun all morning was hot and ready. Ahhh, "Chili Del Sol," followed by a can of pickled quail eggs for dessert— I'm something of a gourmand—yum! The pretty little fishing town of Sergeant slipped by.

After lunch I noted that I had only eleven miles to go to Matagorda Marina, my next stop. I had lots of time so I put up sails and killed the motor. To pass the time, I decided to do some fishing. I broke out my rod and rigged it up but caught nary a fish. A funny fishing yarn came to mind:

One morning, a Cajun man named, ah, Boudreaux, went fishing. After only a short time ran out of worms. Just as he was beginning to pack up and go home, he saw a cottonmouth water moccasin with a frog in its mouth. Frogs are good bass bait. Boudreaux knew the snake couldn't bite him with the frog in its mouth. He reached down in the water and grabbed the snake right behind the head. He took the frog and put it in his bait bucket.

Now, he had a problem: how to release the snake without getting bitten. Boudreaux grabbed his bottle of Jack Daniels and poured a little whiskey in its mouth. The snake's eyes rolled back and he went limp. Boudreaux tossed him into the bayou and went on fishing using the frog. A little while later, he felt a nudge on his foot.

He looked down and there was that same snake—with *two* frogs in its mouth!

• • •

I arrived in Matagorda after an easy day and cleaned up Mañana. I had a refreshing hose shower and Patches enjoyed a gentle squirt. This he dearly loved, fluffing, dancing around, and squawking. His appetite had returned, and he was evidently enjoying the trip. Again, I left Patches in charge and went for a walkabout.

I encountered a deckhand from a dredge in the little store. We began chatting and I learned how dredges work. Very interesting! Wouldn't it be fun to go out on a dredge for a day to watch them work? It would be even more fun to set up a lawn chair at the end of the discharge pipe and see what all got sucked up off of the sea floor. Nice shells and interesting rocks? Fish, crabs, and oysters? Gold, rubies, and priceless porcelains? An ancient tablet that deciphers the Rosetta Stone? After our conversation, I went to the Harbormaster's cottage to check in. A hand-painted sign on the little porch read:

An old fisherman lives here with the best catch of his life

Down the ICW a little ways beyond the marina where I was tied up were the Colorado River and the Colorado River locks. The locks are there to help control water levels between the ICW and the river, whose level rises and falls. I needed to contact the Colorado River Authority to make sure that the locks would be open for my transit the next morning. It's a good thing I did. The locks were being worked on and would be closed all the next day. If I wanted through at all, it had to be before seven o'clock the next morning.

It was pitch dark the next morning as I untied the boat and headed for the locks. I got a little too close to a barge coming through in the dark. It was hard to see it because its lights were superimposed against the bright lights of the locks behind it. In fact, I *didn't* see it until the last minute. A little up-close illustration of the dangers of traveling in the ICW at night. I made it through the locks without mishap, and would live to play another day. I enjoyed an inspirational sunrise.

Some might say that the trip from Kemah to Port Aransas is no big deal, but to me, it was a great adventure. This was the logical next step in my development as a sailor. Someday there would be other sailing trips that were farther, longer, and more exciting. Making this trip was the way to make those dreams come true. Port Aransas was my Cape Horn, and the Colorado River locks were my Panama Canal.

I felt my grandfather's spirit riding with me. The parrot and I enjoyed a Pop-Tart, which he followed with his morning bath. Around nine o'clock that morning we entered Matagorda Bay. I decided to try my fishing luck. I was following the channel markers and about to doze off when the fishing reel went—

Zzzing—something hit my bait!

I leapt up, spluttering, hands and feet all going in different directions, grabbed the rod, and…and…*and…*

Almost instantly, the line broke. Swivel, leader, shrimp, hook, everything—gone. Great Zeus, what kind of monster could have broken the stout line so easily? Shark? Devil ray? Giant octopus? I'll never know. Fishing is a kind of torture…

I transited the bay, arriving at Port O'Connor in the early afternoon where I would stay that evening. This was a short day because of the manner in which the overnight stops along the route fell. I got a slip, plugged into shore power, and turned on the air conditioner. After cleaning up the boat, I walked into town to find a big lunch, returning with a hush puppy for Patches. Lunch was followed by a long, cool siesta in the air conditioning. I was beginning to get into the cruising lifestyle. I liked it, too!

There were only fifty miles to go to Port Aransas. The next day would be the longest of the trip, but I would be there that night! I pushed off from the dock the next morning at first light. There was only a light breeze, so I went with motor on and sails up. *Charge*! Around noon as I was passing through the Aransas Pass Wildlife Refuge, the wind died altogether. The boat became a sweat bath that soon had me reexamining my decision to undertake a boat trip in August. Lest I succumb to heat stroke and my friends find my bones later in the half-submerged wreck of Mañana, I went over the side for a swim. That partially restored me. Presently, the wind returned and I was soon flying down Aransas Bay.

I love Port Aransas. I was excited and proud to be arriving by water. As I got closer, I raised St. Joseph's Lighthouse. Just beyond it I entered the Lydia Ann Channel, rounded a bend, and…I was there!

I felt Grandpa's presence, almost as palpable as the sunlight as I pulled into the harbor on this joyous day. Six dolphins swam beside me in radiant attendance. I'll never forget that long moment of supreme happiness. I had made the fifty miles in eleven hours. This had been the longest day of my trip.

If fifty miles in eleven hours is a little underwhelming, remember that sailing vessels were once a major mode of transportation for the whole world. Back when there weren't any faster choices.

Today, there are of course many faster choices. Yet, there is something about sailing that resonates with me through and through. When I'm on my sailboat with wind filling my sails and silence all around, sailing slowly to no place in particular, I am at my happiest.

I arrived at the city marina at five o'clock. There happened to be some people I knew from Kemah there, and they came over to catch my dock lines. I made it, Grandpa!

I spent the rest of the day taking the pulse of the town. Port Aransas is a good place to bicycle and I was glad I'd brought mine. I rode it to the beach. I rode it to the jetties to go fishing. I crawled through a couple of tacky shell shops. I had a wonderful dinner and then went on a pub crawl. That didn't take very long in a little place like Port Aransas!

The next day found me similarly engaged in pursuits of happiness. The rest of the Kemah Bums were driving down to Port Aransas that day. When it was time, I tore myself away from the life of the itinerant sailor and got a ride to Island Moorings so I could live the life of the itinerant musician. I was there to welcome Gene and Boom-Boom, and we set up the band in a pretty courtyard outside by the pool next to a seafood buffet. This party was going to be great fun.

Ahhh, the life of the itinerant sailor and musician!

We got the party started and a large crowd gathered. In attendance were residents and guests of the marina, plus several fans and friends who had driven down from Kemah. There then ensued the usual riotous Kemah Bums debacle. Everyone kicked off their shoes and danced by the pool. It was a beautiful, mild evening with a gentle breeze blowing. The rum flowed freely, and a glorious time was had by all.

Back on the boat that evening I noted that a tropical depression had moved into the Gulf. Uh-oh. Those who dance must pay the piper. Later that night it started raining. I didn't want to think about having to leave the next morning to go back. I had been thinking about going offshore for much of the return trip, however, the depression caused a contrary wind to blow, and I elected to return home via the Intracoastal Waterway. I set out the next morning. I made it to Galveston without mishap. The next morning I set sail for Kemah. What a great trip it had been! I had learned more about boat handling, seamanship, sailing, and myself. I was a little better mariner and a little wiser. I was proud to have completed the voyage. By doing it alone, I had greatly increased my confidence. It was good to be home.

And, as I am fond of saying at the conclusion of any great adventure, "I had cheated death once again!"

Chapter 4
He Did What?

Not all of my adventures were on a sailboat. I had bought a Jet Ski, which I used for fishing and exploring all of the places that were too shallow for a sailboat's keel to go. One day I had an idea. What if I were to take a long trip on the Jet Ski?

It so happened that the sailing club of which I was a member was planning a trip from Kemah to Lake Charles, Louisiana for a festival called Contraband Days.

Why not ride my Jet Ski to Lake Charles?

The Jet Ski is named the Scalded Hog. This is because when you give her the gas she runs like …well, you get it. The more I thought about riding it to Lake Charles, the more excited I got. I couldn't think of a single reason why *not* to.

I started planning. The sailing club included both sailboats and powerboats. Of course, neither are as fast as a Jet Ski, so they would be leaving for Lake Charles before I would. The trip would be made in the ICW.

My girlfriend, Georgia, aka. "Excitable Crew," was usually up for any zany adventure I came up with. For this one, she volunteered to be my "shore support" crew.

Here is the story. We begin on the morning the adventure was to commence:

The time was one hour prior to the set alarm time. I didn't want to wait for it, I was fully charged. My eyes flew open. I sprang out of bed straight up, changing into bathing suit and reef runners in mid-air, and landed on the deck dressed. The Scalded Hog was already trailered up and ready for the road. She was running good. Like me, she was up for the adventure.

Excitable Crew was something less than excitable at five o'clock in the morning. She stirred and attempted to come to life. She knew the drill. To resist wouldn't do any good.

After a good breakfast, we drove to Galveston. I wanted to begin the trip there. This would cut the twenty miles of rough, open bay water from Kemah to Galveston from the trip.

Uh oh, trouble. I discovered during a gas stop that my duffel bag of supplies was missing. I couldn't make the trip without it! After much self-recrimination I realized that we would have to drive back to Kemah to get it and then return to Galveston. This we did with much gnashing of teeth, arriving back in Galveston around nine o'clock. We were still okay, time wise.

More trouble: the Galveston Yacht Basin, where I had wanted to begin the voyage, didn't allow Jet Skis. This annoyed me mightily. I was having a hard time getting this voyage underway!

Excitable Crew has an idea. "Why not take the ferry across to Bolivar Peninsula and find a pubic boat ramp there?"

I couldn't think of any better ideas, so we headed to the ferry. On the other side, we came across Shirley's Bait Camp, right on the ICW. We put the Jet Ski in the water, and I got ready to put to sea. When all was ready, I hit the start button and the Scalded Hog roared to life.

I revved her up a couple of times until it was perfectly audible to the people in the next county. Then, with cries of "Aargh!," "Boats away!," and "Shiver me timbers!" I roared off for Lake Charles and Contraband Days. Excitable Crew would drive to Lake Charles later, pulling the Jet Ski trailer.

The ICW here was familiar waters to me. It was calm and flat. I set a comfortable, if not quick pace, and soon the Scalded Hog and I were loping along at a nice clip. It was a beautiful morning, calm and mild. I was already having fun.

The Stingaree, Steve's Landing, Rollover Pass, and other "crime scenes" of yore whizzed by. I spent a very happy hour, totally in the moment. The High Island Bridge is a long day's trip from Kemah in my sailboat. I made it there in an hour and a half. Under the bridge were some people fishing. I slowed to idle so as not to disturb their fishing, and when I got within earshot, I asked "Excuse me, which way is New Orleans from here?"

Confused glances this way and that, and then they pointed east, the correct way.

"Thank you," I called cheerily and again roared off, under their puzzled stares!

I didn't stop again until I got close to Port Arthur. I did lazy S-curves, flat out speed bursts, and slowed down to prowl for 'gators. What a glorious ride! No other pleasure craft were in the ICW that day. Sun out. Wind nil. Water flat. I opened 'er up.

The trip was approximately 130 statute miles. There was only one place on the way to buy fuel, but it was located three quarters of the way there. I would run out of gas before I got there. Not only that but the industrial area of Port Arthur ran for several miles prior to the stopping place. There would be lots of ship traffic in that stretch, and no safe place for a Jet Ski to stop. Not a good place to be testing the limits of my fuel supply! To remedy these problems, I carried two plastic gas cans strapped to the little deck.

Around eleven o'clock, I was nearing Port Arthur. I found a little dock and stopped to top off the Jet Ski's fuel tank from the extra cans. This allowed me to cruise through Port Arthur without fear. And not at a slow speed, either.

The fuel stop was just on the other side of Port Arthur. It was a small bait stand located a little ways up the Neches River. When I got to the Neches River I turned upstream. There it was, right where it was supposed to be, underneath the Rainbow Bridge. I pulled up, dismounted stiffly, and lollygagged for a few minutes in the shade.

After a brief rest, I topped off the gas in the Jet Ski and the two spare cans. I re-checked my charts, climbed back aboard the Scalded Hog, pressed the starter, and roared off to continue the adventure. Back down the Neches River. Hard left into the Intracoastal Waterway. Skirt Sabine Lake and Tally Ho!

Just ahead was Adam's Bayou. I wanted to visit the two sunken yachts I had discovered there on a previous trip. I turned up the bayou and went to the defunct marina that had been their final anchorage. I found the motor-sailor first. She was worse off than before. I coasted up to her, tied the Jet Ski off to a stanchion, and invited myself aboard for a look around. She was about forty-five feet long and had once been a fabulous and expensive yacht. The pilothouse and mast were about the only things still above water. Her sails were still on the spars and hanging in ghostly tatters. What a sad sight.

The other boat was the kind you would see in pictures of fine sailing yachts of old: long, graceful, and sleek, with gleaming teak decks and flying crisp, white sails as she rounded Nantucket Lighthouse. She was sunk into the mud of the bank. She had at one time been a ravishing beauty but would never sail again.

I left these two vessels to rest in peace and got back onto the Scalded Hog. I left the little marina and prowled into the swamps, enjoying their beauty and looking for alligators. I saw nary a 'gator, but knew they saw me, and were probably licking their chops. Turtles, waterfowl, and big gar abounded. I spent an hour exploring and then headed back to the ICW to continue my adventure.

Back on my way. I flew out of Adams Bayou and into the Intracoastal Waterway heading east. Soon I was passing barges like they were standing still. Like Commander Cody sings in the song *"Hot Rod Lincoln": "...Them telephone poles look like a picket fence ... and the lines on the road just look like dots ..."*

I crossed the state line into Louisiana. I could just imagine those Cajun skippers of the towboats, talking about me on the radio:

"Hey Boudreaux! Ay, look beehin' yo'self. Eet look lik we hab a leetle *mos-ki-TOE* over our shoulder!"

A little later I was cruising along, amusing myself by doing lazy S-curves. It was hot. I was getting drowsy and was wondering how I was going to work in my three o'clock nap when a large cigarette boat suddenly roared past. Sweet mother of God—I hadn't been able to hear its approach over the noise of the Scalded Hog. Cigarettes are loud, and it startled me so much I almost jumped overboard in a panic. It was followed by ten others in hot pursuit. They made quite a sight. The roar from their performance engines was deafening. It rattled the very gates of hell! They were on their way to Lake Charles for Contraband Days. Suddenly wide-awake, I decided I had lollygagged enough and gave the Scalded Hog the spurs.

Shortly, I came to the Ellender Bridge. The entrance to the Calcasieu River was just beyond the bridge and Lake Charles was just twelve miles up the river. I was sorry the journey was about to end. I was enjoying myself immensely and wasn't ready to get out of the water. I would happily have kept going all the way to New Orleans!

Lake Charles is actually a natural bight, or elbow, in the Calcasieu River. I went through the narrow cut at the lower end of the lake and could see the big casino at the far end, my destination. There were the boats from the sailing club, already tied up there. I glanced at my watch. It was almost time for "docktails." I was just in time.

I was preparing to give the throttle all hell, so as to arrive in style when I just happened to look back over my shoulder. To my surprise, I was being hotly pursued by the United States Coast Guard—with lights flashing, no less.

Uh-oh. Trouble. Had I violated a "no wake" zone? I cut power and waited for them to come alongside. They were merely performing safety checks. It would be a busy holiday weekend with lots of pleasure boats and I was glad that the Coast Guard was there. I passed the safety inspection and they waved and sped away. On to the casino.

I arrived to a hero's welcome from the sailing club. They were expecting me. Well, some of the nay-sayers weren't! Everyone was assembled aboard the vessel *Shorty* and happy hour was already underway. *Let the good times roll!*

Contraband Days is a celebration held by the city of Lake Charles every year to celebrate the history of the area. This includes the daring and sometimes bloodthirsty rampages of pirates such as the notorious Jean Lafitte, who once marauded the Texas coast. One event in particular that supposedly transpired is re-created and commemorated.

According to local folklore, the town of Lake Charles was over-run one day with pirates who pillaged, plundered, availed themselves of the ladies, and generally behaved badly. During the ensuing mayhem, they captured the mayor and pitched him right into the water.

Lake Charles stages a reenactment of this each year. As part of the enactment, a pirate ship sails up. Rakish, swashbuckling pirates (and some awfully cute swashbuckling piratesses) in full pirate regalia swarm out and terrorize the town. Lake Charles adds to this show the modern accoutrements of live bands, power boat races, a midway, food booths, bathtub races, etc.

All of this silliness was just the flimsy excuse we were looking for to bring our boats over to Lake Charles to have a good time.

Excitable Crew arrived and met us on *Shorty*, and we walked over to enjoy the festivities. Contraband Days was just getting started. I had just gotten a temporary pirate tattoo when all of a sudden there was a tremendous *Ka-Boom* to end all Satan. I looked out to sea—or lake—and saw a real pirate ship. We were under attack by pirates! High excitement!

The local militia quickly mustered up eight cannons along the shore to protect the citizenry. The cannons fired thunderous black powder charges to repel the invaders. The marauding pirates made pass after pass, brandishing their cutlasses, ogling the women, hanging precariously from the yardarms, and taunting the local officials.

Valiantly, the ragtag militia held them off with wave after wave of cannon barrages, but the pirates landed anyway and promptly captured the mayor. There was a hastily arranged mock trial with the mayor as the defendant.

"He who would defend this coward step forward," thundered Lafitte, the pirate.

No one did.

"I hereby pronounce you guilty," he declared, and there commenced a great unholy caterwauling among the rabble on the pirate ship.

Now to determine his punishment. A five-year-old girl was appointed out of the crowd of onlookers to do the job. When asked what was to be the mayor's penance, she demurred, "Dunk him!"

The crowd took up the chant: "Dunk him! Dunk him! Dunk him!"

The mayor's fate was sealed, and he was surreptitiously led aboard the pirate ship. There were more jeers and taunts on the part of the pirates, amid pleas for clemency from the mayor. The pirate wenches yelled lustily.

Alas, there was no help for it. The mayor was doomed. At the insistent prodding to his stern quarters from a long cutlass, he was compelled to walk the plank, with a doubloon clenched in his teeth. When he hit the water, a great cheer went up from the crowd and the Cajun band ashore struck up the first dance. Contraband Days was underway!

After this fun, all hands went back to the casino to gamble. Excitable Crew bought into a roulette game with twenty dollars and walked away with two hundred. I, on the other hand, lost every nickel I wagered. I did find one machine over in the corner that worked for me. You put a dollar bill in and it returned four quarters *every time!*

The next morning, the Scalded Hog was still in the water and needed a proper put-away, but first to explore. I had a nice ride around the lake. It was great fun to cruise amidst the festivities and see all of the hoopla. The lake was full of boats of all sizes, shapes, and descriptions. Many were decorated and everyone was in a festive mood. BBQ grills were going and the air was filled with delicious aromas. Everywhere people on the boats were listening to music, laughing, talking, swimming, and floating on air mattresses. Others on the shore strolled around visiting the food booths and riding the rides in the midway.

I left the lake and rode over to explore nearby Contraband Bayou, a pretty little watercourse leading back into the swamp. It was fun, cruising sedately underneath the cypress trees. There were beautiful natural scenes of lush Louisiana swamp draped with Spanish moss, punctuated here and there with shady landscaped yards stretching expansively up to the patios of gracious Southern homes. After this mini-tour, I returned to the casino whereupon the Scalded Hog got trailered up and washed down.

Back at the Lake Charles Civic Center, a Fais do-do was in full progress. This is an old-time Louisiana party, complete with a real Cajun band. It had started at eight o'clock that morning and would go all day long and into the night. It was crowded with tourists and locals alike, dancing as if there was no tomorrow (this is what Cajuns do). We walked over to listen. I had some fantastic smoked boudin, a Cajun dish resembling sausage that I dearly love, which is made with pork, rice, and seasonings.

We spent all day enjoying the Contraband festivities. We rendezvoused that evening with friends for dinner where yarns were swapped, lies were born, and others embellished. We capped a perfect day off with several hands of blackjack that stretched long into the night, and then off to bed.

Sunday was the leaving day and we all dispersed to the four winds. All boats went back down the Calcasieu River to head west for home, except for *Shorty* who continued east to New Orleans, and us to the highway home, the Scalded Hog in tow on her little trailer.

Any thoughts I had about riding the Jet Ski back home again evaporated when I attempted to get out of bed that morning. Everything hurt! It was three days before I could walk completely upright again. It was all worth it. It had been a great adventure. I made it home alive. And, as I am wont to say, "We cheated death once again!"

Chapter 5

It All Began

"I'd rather be in my boat with a drink on the rocks than in the drink with my boat on the rocks."

My idyllic existence of living aboard a boat lasted for about five years. Fun though it was, I began to wish for a little more room toward the end of this time. I began to get restless. What next? A bigger boat? A place to live ashore? What?

Maybe I should get some land. Land? Where did *that* notion come from? Land could serve as an investment, if prudently bought, even if nothing else ever came of it. Or, it could have a small shop/ storage place built on it. Or I could have a small cottage to weekend in. A place for band practices, a place to store and use tools, a place to put a desk and computer, a place where I could take all of my books out of their boxes, a garden out back...

These thoughts had merit! Nothing here suggested I had to move ashore; nothing said I had to get rid of the boat or give up sailing. I began to muse over plans for a simple little cottage. I got a sheet of notebook paper and drew a simple rectangle for a house. I selected a back corner and drew a bathroom, and in another, a kitchen. How much space should each one of these take? I needed some graph paper so I could dimension some things out. I got the graph paper and started over.

This time I added a porch. I gave more than passing thought to this porch because I knew I would want to be out on it a lot. On this porch would be two comfortable rocking chairs. From this porch on this little cottage, tucked away in a tropical enclave, I would sit and watch the world hurry by. The porch could also serve as a dining room in nice weather. It would need some ceiling fans. Better start a list of amenities.

I might be able to build an aviary on one end. I then shared my boat with a Paco, the parrot I got after Patches. Paco was a striking Mexican Red Head[1]. I would love to build an outdoor walk-in aviary at the little cottage for Paco, plus any other parrots that might happen to come my way.

As I was considering all the ways that porches could be enjoyed, it struck me that the porch could even double as a stage. I could have parties—with bands. Wow! Better remember to have enough electrical outlets. I could make the end of the porch by the driveway very easy for unloading instruments—an integral loading dock.

Back to my drawing, I dimensioned out a bathroom and kitchen that I hoped would be large enough to operate in and a bar by the kitchen for quick meals. I drew in a long, narrow closet along one end of the house for clothes and storage, and I planned a place for a washer, dryer, and hot water heater. Uh-oh. By the time I got all of these things added in, it was time to expand the dimensions of the house. Start over again.

Here is what I envisioned: the house would have just one large room that would serve as living area/bedroom/dining room/kitchen, with an enclosed bathroom. Except for the bathroom, there wouldn't be any other interior walls. You would walk into the house through a

---

1 Up to that point my only experience with Mexican Redheads was in one of the border towns over Spring Break when I was in college, but then that's another story.

pair of attractive paned French doors. In the left back corner would be the bathroom. In the right back corner would be the kitchen and bar. Right in front of you would be a little sitting area with island-style wicker couch, chairs, and a coffee table. Behind that would be the pretty antique bed I rescued from my grandmother, who was about to send it to the Salvation Army one day when I happened to be there, visiting. To the immediate right would be a dining room table, near the kitchen. To the left would be a little study.

Frankly, I might have been tempted to not have any walls at all and just enclose the bathroom with curtains. "Feminine influences" in my life soon dashed those notions. It wasn't just her—in her voice I heard the voices of all women everywhere. Really, what woman could ever take seriously a man who had a bathroom with no walls? Fine, the bathroom would be enclosed. I'm not really all *that* unconventional!

By then, I was getting a pretty good idea of what I'd like the little cottage to look like. With each iteration the design became more refined and detailed. This was getting exciting!

I started another piece of graph paper on which I situated the cottage on some land. I attempted to figure out how much room I would need for driveways, the front yard, and the backyard. This process also required several iterations. The project grew into a bigger lot with the cottage, and even another house on it as well, should I ever want to expand. I could put the two houses in sort of an "L" configuration, sharing the same backyard. Wow, *two* houses. Think of that. Wouldn't it be grand?

I'd build the little cottage first and see how it went. If I survived this experience, then I'd build the second house as phase two. The cottage would be built on short pilings with a floor about waist high. The second house would be somewhat bigger, but not much—maybe medium sized. It would be more conventional, with regular walls and rooms. I would build it up, around ten feet high, on pilings, in the Texas coastal beach house style that I love, with parking underneath. Every available inch of un-built yard would be thickly planted with palm trees and other tropical foliage, like in Bermuda.

Bermuda

When I was in college, I was lucky enough to get to go to the island of Bermuda and house-sit while the owners, Americans, came back to the States for vacation. Bermuda. What an exotic sounding place! I knew nothing about Bermuda, but the name conjured up beautiful beaches for sunning and walking, sparkling turquoise water for snorkeling and sailing, and palm trees.

I got this wondrous chance through Aunt Earlene who lived in New York. Her longtime neighbors there had moved to Bermuda to live. When they took vacations, they invited Aunt Earlene to stay at their house. She extended the invitation to anyone in our collective families who were able to go. I wasn't *about* to pass this opportunity up. All I had to come up with was airfare and a little expense money while there. I could stay free. *Woo-hoo!*

I scraped together the money for airfare. I would get to stay for a luxurious two weeks. I found out that to get around on the island we would be renting scooters. This was sounding better and better! I asked my aunt where in Bermuda the cottage was located.

"Oh," she said. "That's easy. When you land, get a cab, and tell him you need to go to Southline Road in Padget Parish. The cottage is named the "Gables", and it's on the left, right next to the banana patch."

"What's the address?" I asked.

"There's not one. Bermuda is so small that they don't need street addresses."

That was all she said.

About two weeks before I was supposed to leave, I got a phone call from a promoter, who I worked with occasionally on various musical projects.

"Andy, are you open to play Saturday, July 23?"

I glanced at my calendar and noticed that was the evening before I left for Bermuda. It was an early flight the next day, too.

"Thanks, Bob. I'd like to, but I don't think so this time." And I told him about the trip.

"I don't think you want to let this one go by," Bob replied. "It's to play piano with Chuck Berry."

"*The* Chuck Berry?" I spluttered.

"Yes…"

"I'll do it!" I yelled.

It was all set up. I'd play with Chuck Berry on Saturday night and get up early for my flight the next morning. How exciting! Who needs sleep?

Saturday finally arrived and I couldn't sit still. I had been packed for two weeks for Bermuda and was ready to go. I would have taken off *walking* if I could have gotten there any faster. The day dragged by. At last, it was time to go to the large venue where the concert was being held. I entered the backstage entrance and found the musical director, and the rest of the band. We walked out onto the spacious stage. On it was a concert grand piano and a Hammond organ set up to my specifications, ready to go.

The band did a sound check and we ran through the intros and outros of some of the songs. The musical director coached me on a few specifics for the show.

The star, Chuck Berry, was not yet there, but he arrived by limo right after we were through with the sound check. He was wearing canary yellow pants. We met backstage, relaxed, and visited until it was time to go. Chuck Berry was generally acclaimed to be the father of rock and roll, and a huge crowd had amassed to hear him. I had cut my teeth playing his songs. What an honor to get to actually play with him!

When it was time to play, the band went out onto the stage first. This was the largest crowd I had ever played for, and our appearance brought immediate cheering. This continued as the drummer counted off the first song, *Sweet Little Sixteen*, and we started playing. The cheering changed to a loud roar when Chuck Berry walked out on stage a minute later. I had never before gotten stage fright, but just at that moment, I definitely did. But just for an instant. I had a job to do. Couldn't let several thousand music lovers distract me!

The band started rocking and sounded great. Chuck Berry was obviously right at home, and took his time as he put on his guitar and went up to the microphone. When he did, the crowd was instantly on its feet, arms in the air. My stage fright was gone, evaporated after only two measures.

Playing the show that night was glorious. I had the time of my life! I loved the energy, the crowd, the band, and all of the excitement. The stage setup and sound system were large, state-of-the-art, and run by experts. I could hear and see everything perfectly.

We played all of Chuck Berry's hits, song after song. I felt right at home playing the classic rock'n'roll piano parts. I patiently waited for my chance to shine, and it came soon. Chuck nodded at me to take a piano solo. I was ready, like a tightly wound spring— that uncoiled! Playing with this legend was a defining moment in my life. I didn't want it to ever end…

The show was over with all too soon. The crowd wasn't ready to leave, and we took three encores. When we finished the last one, we all went back to the dressing room where we found lots of good things to eat and drink, and fresh towels, for we were all wet from the exertion. Refreshed and relaxed, we visited all around. I shared the name of my favorite Texas barbecue restaurant, the best-kept secret in town.

What I wouldn't give to play with Chuck Berry full-time… Yee-ha! Since I was only substituting with the band, a full-time position wasn't available. Ah, them's the breaks. I did, however, press my card into the hand of the father of rock and roll when I thanked him and we said our good-byes.

After the show, I still had a lot of energy so I met some friends for a night out on the town, finishing off the evening with breakfast in the wee hours. Since I had to catch a ride to the airport at five o'clock that morning, I never even went to bed.

I made it to the airport in plenty of time to catch my flight. Bermuda, here I come! I was still too excited about the last few hours and the next several days to get any sleep. In Atlanta, I changed planes and was joined by my sister and her husband. Off we roared for Bermuda. Wonder of wonders—that flight had complimentary champagne. Now *that's* how to get a trip to Bermuda started off on the right foot!

Finally, we approached the island. The rich indigo of deep sea turned into the lighter azure of shallow water and we began to see little reefs and small islands. Soon we could see tempting beaches and the little sugar-white roofs of cottages painted in assorted pastel hues set in the palm trees. I could see immediately that I was going to like Bermuda. I couldn't wait to go exploring. We landed at the little airport, collected our bags, and flagged down a cab. I was skeptical about Aunt Earlene's instructions on getting to our cottage, but I gave them to the cab driver. "Oh yes. Know right where it is," he exclaimed. We climbed into the cab and started what became a stellarly beautiful ride. Every single foot of the way was filled with views of quaint cottages, beautiful gardens, craggy rocks, and sweeping vistas of a gorgeous sea in uncountable shades of blue. There was riotous tropical growth everywhere. I was thoroughly in love with Bermuda long before we got to our destination.

We were joyfully met at the cottage by Aunt Earlene, who had flown in the day before. Bermuda was old hat to her. She lost no time in giving us the lay of the land as we listened excitedly. Our first order of business was to rent our scooters. Leaving the luggage at the cottage, we cabbed off to the cycle livery, returning on bright red scooters. The next thing to do was go to the tiny grocery store to lay in some supplies. Aunt Earlene climbed on her scooter and led us single file like a mother duck and her ducklings to the store where we bought such staples as wine, cheese, and cereal for breakfast the next morning.

We finished these orders of business in time for the *Afternoon Swim*, so we changed into our bathing suits and took off for Elbow Beach. The water was beautiful and refreshing. I knew I was going to love each and every minute in Bermuda.

I would happily have stayed in the water until bedtime, but Aunt Earlene had other plans. We had reservations at a restaurant on a hill overlooking the sea, and she took us there for a triumphant welcome to Bermuda dinner. There, we exchanged many toasts and filled the air with laughter.

Back at the Gables, we took a candle and some wine out onto the porch to continue our visit, accompanied by the soft, musical piping of the tree frogs in the banana patch. Aunt Earlene had to hear all about playing with Chuck Berry, a tale that I enthusiastically related. Had that only been twenty-four hours ago? It seemed like a dream. I truly wanted to squeeze every last ounce I could out of this memorable day, but alas, I could hold my eyes open no longer. Off I went to bed, well and truly smitten.

Mom and Dad flew in the next day. For the next two weeks, we owned that island! On my scooter I found out all of the best snorkeling spots and where the local fishermen gathered to sell their catch. I would often ride down there and return with fresh wahoo or whatever had been caught that day to grill up for supper.

I discovered the best nightspots and made the rounds every few nights. I will treasure always my memories of the Swizzle Inn (and swagger out), the Lobster Pot, and the Hog Penny. I'll never forget flying along on my scooter down the wildly beautiful South Shore Road, with its steep cliffs that drop off dramatically into hidden coves with tiny beaches and crashing waves.

In Bermuda we went everywhere by scooter. When shopping or going to the grocery store you had to be careful how much you bought because you still had to get it all home. I became an expert in transporting such unwieldy items as cases of beer and large, frozen pizzas. Everything had to go either in the small basket, or hanging in bags from the handlebars, or held between my knees. I always managed to get scooter, groceries, and me home without mishap.

We discovered quaint little waterside cafes where you could get fish chowder with sherry peppers and a shot of black rum, an island specialty that I came to adore. Sometimes we'd go out for dinner in beautiful settings, perched on the rocks overlooking the sea. Or we'd roar off to any number of pretty pink beaches, snorkel gear flung in our baskets. Other times we'd jump on our scooters and go around the island, just for the ride. Occasionally, we'd go into Hamilton, the capital, for shopping on the days that the cruise ships were absent.

We took very good care of the cottage. We watered the house-plants, walked the puppies, cared for the yard, and lived in it like it was our own—gypsies in the palace. We must have done a good job because after that year, we were invited back to house-sit several additional summers. Each year, upon hearing that we could go back, I hoarded every available cent to be able to go. I loved those idyllic, carefree days. Merely not having to get into a car at all for two weeks was a nice vacation in and of itself. How I would love to live in a place where you could go everywhere you needed by scooter. This wasn't practical and probably not safe in the places I've lived. Even so, a bright red scooter with a step-through frame and running boards was in the parking lot of the marina, for rides around the little streets of Kemah. It would be fine, also, parked beside a small cabana—one that I wanted now, more than anything else, to build.

Navigating Uncharted Waters

"Obstacles are things we see when we take our eyes off the goal"

—*Farmers' Almanac*

How do you start building a house? Where to begin? I looked dubiously at my frayed and smudged notes and drawings. How much for building materials? How much to get utilities? I had not the faintest idea about how to get from Point A to Point B. I needed a sage.

Remember the Hoagie Ranch? The friends I had made there were from all walks of life. JJ was one of them. He was a character and had a predisposition for mischief and fun. JJ had a friend named Bob who had been involved in construction for many years and was a construction guru. He was familiar with all aspects of house building, general contracting, and financing. JJ hooked me up, and a meeting with Bob convinced me that he truly was a knower of many things. I could benefit greatly from his knowledge and experience. He agreed to become a de-facto consultant. I had my sage!

"How do you plan to finance your project?" Bob inquired, early on. "Might you need to get a construction loan?"

In other parts of the world like Jamaica, people don't need construction loans. They build houses the old fashioned way: pay as you go. There, you work and earn some money, which you use to buy a batch of building materials, like cement and cinder blocks. A cement slab is poured and a row of cinder blocks is mortared in around its perimeter, which defines the walls of the house. Rows of cinder blocks are added, and the walls rise off of the slab. Building continues until you run out of blocks. Work halts until there is enough money to buy more blocks. The building is all done in stages, based on the available money.

Eventually, the walls, roof, doors, windows, utilities, and interior are all completed. The finished house is painted in gay colors, and one day it is ready to move into. On that day, the house is completely paid for. Who needed a construction loan?

As appealing as that sounded, it didn't sound feasible to me. I could maybe afford to buy land or build a house, but I couldn't do both at the same time. Where was I going to come up with the money?

"Get a construction loan," soothed my sage. "You can use it to pay for materials, labor, anything you need for your project."

This sounded practical. Problem solved. Or was it? Where to get a construction loan? How big of a loan would I need? And the even bigger, more obvious question: how much money was it going to cost me to build a house? Could I even qualify for a loan? I was unable to answer these questions that swirled around in my head and kept me awake at night.

I was starting to feel overwhelmed, until I remembered some timely, Zen-like advice given to me once:

Question: how do you eat an elephant?

Answer: one bite at a time.

Break a job up into steps and then do the steps one at a time. I have come to believe that it's a luxury if a project can be handled this way. This isn't necessarily a "given."

In any case, I was going to need some land. If I could find some property that fit my criteria and that I could afford, I wouldn't need a loan to pay for it. Very well, I would begin my search for land, and give this project my undivided attention. I would tackle the construction loan afterward. That night I slept soundly.

Land Ho!

"Better done than said when it's all said and done."

Off I went to find land. A place upon which to stage the great adventure. I had already decided that it was going to be staged right here on the Gulf Coast of Texas. Why here? The area was vulnerable to hurricanes, there were mosquitoes, the humidity was high, and the water was brown.

The truth is, I was already attached to this area. It felt like home. Here, I could sail any time I wanted, year round even. There were lots of live music venues. The climate was fairly tropical. *Really* tropical if you were from up north. It was within a day's drive back to family in Arkansas. Besides, real estate prices were lower on the Texas coast than places like southern California or Florida. The water was murky, but the standing joke was, if the water were much prettier, nobody could afford to live there. Hurricanes and mosquitoes? Well, no place is perfect.

I already had some ideas of where to look in the Clear Lake area. Most of the waterfront land was expensive. Imagine that! However, there was a little community called San Leon that was a few miles south of Kemah, down the coast and right on the water. I decided to begin my search there.

San Leon occupied a peninsula that jutted out into Galveston Bay. It was sometimes referred to variously as the "Redneck Riviera" and "Brown Water Barbados." San Leon was very eclectic. There, you could find shrimp boats; charming little weekend cottages; dilapidated shacks; , roomy waterfront homes, and house trailers— all thrown in together, cheek and jowl. The streets were small. It was quiet, pastoral, and bucolic.

The scenery around the shore of the peninsula was pretty. It had the coastal look that I was looking for. If you wanted to take a leisurely drive on a Sunday afternoon, San Leon was the place to go. The interior of San Leon was—well, it was "emerging." There were a couple of fun little seafood places in San Leon right on the water, and a sprinkling of old honkytonks.

The people of San Leon were a diverse lot. Doctors, retirees, and fishermen rubbed shoulders with shrimpers, oystermen, fishing guides, and carpenters. There were others who were nefariously employed, unemployed, or whose employment I would be reticent to inquire about. There was the occasional (perceived) alcoholic or drug user. All manner of people from all walks of life. I wouldn't have been surprised to discover someone who was in the Witness Protection Program living there. All of the above called San Leon their home. People there pretty much left each other alone and got along fine.

Some residents evidently saw San Leon for what it was, not what it was not. They were moving into the area, buying land, building homes, and cleaning up the place. People who cared what their yards looked like. Perhaps I would be one of those people.

In San Leon, golf carts shared the road with Mercedes and rusted out pickup trucks, some of which were missing fundamental body parts. One morning you might see a stretch limousine driving down your street and a loose donkey running full-tilt down it the next (this really happened). Cell phone service there was sketchy. I think the good people of San Leon liked it that way.

There is some interesting history to San Leon and its surroundings—complete with Indians and pirates. I was thrilled to learn that a skeleton was once discovered at Eagle Point, along with old, Spanish coins around it. There are probably many interesting, fascinating, and mysterious secrets of San Leon. I'll bet the best ones never made it into any book!

I got a map of the area and started studying. I wanted to find some land that wasn't right on the water, but wasn't very far away from it, either. I considered waterfront property too expensive. Besides, I wasn't keen to own land that was exposed to the full fury of Galveston Bay with her relentless tempests that blew in regularly every winter, plus the occasional hurricane. Let Mother Nature chew on someone else's real estate. I was okay with not having a waterfront view. It was enough just knowing that the water was right "over there." I confined my search for properties to a zone that was between one and three blocks away from the water—all the way around the peninsula.

I spent the next several weeks driving around San Leon with a notebook and a printout of real estate listings. I jotted down phone numbers and addresses and researched appealing properties at the courthouse. Many interesting parcels of land I came across weren't even in the real estate listings. Good, that was where the deals could be made. I sought out properties that appeared to be neglected. I was looking to luck into a deal.

I became an expert in San Leon real estate and a regular at the Topwater Grill, a little place on the water where I could stop in for a sandwich and regroup from time to time. I soon found out that they made the best fish tacos around.

I found several attractive lots in San Leon that fit my criteria. I narrowed them down to ten properties, then five, then three. One of the properties was very enticing, but it had a tear-down house on it that would have to be removed. No problem—some friends, guitars, beer, lighter fluid, matches, marshmallows, and a balmy summer evening could fix that little detail! Alas, this property had a high asking price.

One lesson that I learned early on is this: just when I think I've found the deal of a lifetime, a deal too good to be true, something so wonderful that it compels me to drop everything and grab it, lest the opportunity be lost…chances are likely that another deal just as good or even better will come along right behind it. The deal turns out not to be as rare as it first seemed.

I have had this happen to me several times in life. Whether I went for it or not. And sometimes that something comes along surprisingly soon. This lesson helps me keep my head when the object of my desire is something I want badly. True, there are once-in-a-lifetime deals, but they are much less common than I once presumed. This hard-won wisdom served me well again, and I abandoned the lot with the tear-down house and continued my search.

One evening after work, I was once again driving around San Leon. I happened to be going down a street that I had been on several times before. As I glanced to my right, I saw a piece of property I had somehow never noticed before. It was wild and apparently had never been cleared. It was upholstered with lots of oleander bushes. The bay was dead ahead only a block and a half. I headed for the courthouse the next day to do some research.

The property turned out to be several lots together—room to spare for me. It also happened that there was a freshly installed storm sewer manhole right across the street, indicating that utilities were close at hand. I had already learned that vacant lots too far away from utilities could be a deal breaker.

Later I went back to the lot to look around. Much of it you couldn't walk through. It was choked with trees, shrubs, vines, thorns, and poison ivy. There was discarded trash and junk every-where. The mosquitoes were fierce and standing in one place for more than a few seconds alerted the fire ants. That was the day I first saw the Black Hole of Calcutta, the wrecked ski boat, and old boat dock sections.

This lot was attractive to me because of its location so close to the water. It was about a half of an acre in size, plenty large enough to build on and then have some yard left over for planting palm trees. Best of all, this land looked like it had been neglected for years. This could be used as a bargaining point.

With mounting excitement, I contacted the owner. Yes, they would consider selling it. The price? One I could afford and very attractive, below current land values. A good deal! I made a low offer at the risk of being perceived as insulting. Business is business. If a low offer is rejected, you can always come up, but once the offer is made, you can never lower it.

A day or two went by, and the phone call came. The owner accepted my offer. "*Woo-hoo!*" I hollered aloud to no one in par-ticular, in my best Homer Simpson voice. I found a title company to conduct the purchase transaction, which included a land survey and title search. I wanted this transaction to be executed properly. I've heard stories of "rightful owners" popping up out of the wood-work with some sort of claim to a property that had been in their family long ago. If that happened, could the claimant evict the cur-rent occupant and assume possession of the property, even though in the meantime someone else had bought it, built a house, and raised a family there? In San Leon, there's no telling. I don't imagine every single land transaction was executed perfectly, with every "T" crossed and "I" dotted.

When a clear title to the property was ascertained and the sur-vey was completed, we set a date for the closing. The closing went smoothly. I was a landowner. How exciting! When it was over, I drove back to look at the lot again, through the eyes of its new owner.

I got out of the car, but I couldn't really walk around much, because it was overgrown and muddy and I was in nice clothes. It was *mine*. My trees. My thorns. My fire ants. I returned to the car and sat for a long time, gazing at this wild place until it was too dark to see.

Picking Up Steam

When I wasn't driving around San Leon purveying real estate like some big shot, I started investigating construction loans. The same old tiresome questions came back to haunt me: how much money would I need? That depends, of course, on how big a house it was and what it was made of. How much do building materials cost? What about labor costs? I felt ridiculously naïve.

I needed my sage. We arranged a meeting. I arrived early, and when he got there, I jumped up and unleashed a barrage of pent-up questions.

"Hey, wait a minute—hold it, *breathe!*" he said, jokingly. "Do you have a drawing I could look at?"

I produced the latest iteration of the cottage I had drawn and fidgeted while he studied it. He scrutinized it for several moments, asking questions here and there. He had a calming demeanor that disarmed my fears.

Presently, he said, "Okay, I think I have a grasp of what you would like to do. You're concerned about costs and need to come up with a figure to base a loan on. Because my company builds lots of houses with different constructions, we are in touch with current labor and materials costs. For each construction method, we have a pretty good idea what the total cost to build is, calculated on a square foot basis. Tell me what type of construction you want, and I'll give you the figures you need for your planning." Well hell, why couldn't I have thought of that? Cost to build on a square foot basis. Suddenly I felt dumb—and then immediately much smarter.

"I can give you both low and high square-foot construction figures, depending on how fancy you want your house to be. You already know the total square footage of the cottage from your draw-ing. Multiply that by the cost to build per square foot amount. Of course, there are still lots of variables involved, but this is how you can arrive at a useful figure to take to a loan company."

I got out my calculator. All of my questions were about to be answered. The total amount I arrived at both startled and amazed me. It startled me because of how much it was liable to cost to build just a simple wood-frame house but at the same time, I was sur-prised that it wouldn't cost more. The cottage was only going to be a small one; 924 square feet, excluding the largish porch. However, as long as I was building little, I wanted it to be a *nice* little cot-tage. I didn't want the finished house to look cheap, but I didn't want it to appear ostentatious, either. I wanted to use lots of natu-ral products. For example, I wanted real wood floors, no veneers or "manufactured" items. Real, stone countertops in the kitchen and bathroom—not man-made. And real, knotty pine walls—not man-ufactured paneling.

I arbitrarily picked a figure about three quarters of the way up between Bob's low and high costs to build per square foot and rounded it up a little for safety's sake to arrive at the dollar amount of the loan I would ask for. I didn't want to run out of money before I was through building.

All of the cost questions that had been keeping me awake were suddenly answered. After talking to my sage, I felt relieved. I could go loan shopping. It was time to get this show on the road! I was tired of my mind running endlessly in circles—it not having all the data required to move forward.

The process of procuring a loan to build went something like this:

> Banker One: "Good morning. How can I help you today, Mr., uh, Upchurch?"
>
> Mr. Upchurch (that's me): "Yes, good morning, thanks. I'd like a loan to build a house."

Banker One: "Are you a general contractor?"

Mr. Upchurch: "Well, no."

Banker One: "Have you ever built a house?"

Mr. Upchurch: "Actually, no."

Banker One: "Do you have any house-building skills?"

Mr. Upchurch (slightly nervous about the way the conversation is going): "No, but I intend to learn as I go, and I will seek the expertise of professionals along the way to help me build a house that is built correctly, built well, will last a long time, and be a good investment."

Banker One (setting down his pen, leaning back in his chair, and cracking his knuckles): "Mr. Upchurch, I'm afraid we can't help you."

I was crestfallen but undaunted. It's not enough to ask the right questions. Sometimes you have to keep asking, until you find the person who will give you the right answers.

The Second Attempt:

Banker Two: "Ah, good morning, Mr., er, Upchurch, is it? Yes, well is there something we can help you with today?"

Mr. Upchurch (effusively): "Yes, good morning. I'm looking for a construction loan."

Banker Two: "Are you a general contractor?"

Mr. Upchurch: "No."

Banker Two: "Have you ever built a house?"

Mr. Upchurch: "No."

Banker Two: "What makes you think you can build one?"

Mr. Upchurch (with distinct feelings of déjà vu, I took a slightly different approach): "I enjoy working with tools. I've always got some project of one type or another going. It is gratifying to me to undertake a job and get it done. And not just done haphazardly, done the right way. I am prepared to do all of the research to learn how to build a house correctly. I plan to use part of the loan to hire professionals with the expertise I need to come out and help me." I leaned forward, warming to my subject. "Besides, I have a lot of energy, and I make it a point to see a task through to the very end. I also have a lot of patience (this last remark was a bald-faced lie)."

Banker Two (plays with his pencil and exhales slowly): "Mr. Upchurch, I'm very sorry, but we can't grant loans to people for house construction unless they're a general contractor."

I was beginning to feel a little put out with bankers. Maybe what I had heard about bankers is true: bankers are people who will loan you an umbrella when the sun is shining and ask for it back when it starts to rain!

I was, by then, thoroughly psyched into thinking I too could really build a house, but I couldn't even get out of the starting gate.

Attempt Three:

I parked my car in a place that was visible and hope it didn't become a crime statistic. I pressed the button on the heavy glass and aluminum door. A buzzer sounded, allowing me ingress. Slimy is the word I would use to describe the little man with darting eyes who appraised me as I strode into the room. He sat at a small, cluttered desk at the rear of the room that was dimly illuminated by a flickering fluorescent light. His hair was slick, and his shirt was loud.

Banker (using the term loosely) Three: "Have a seat. What can I do for you?"

I wanted coffee, but changed my mind when I saw the pot sitting amid a collection of dirty cups. The well-worn chair protested as I sank carefully into it; the carpet beneath the chair was worn down to its backing. I tried not to touch anything and ignored the dead cockroach, capsized on top of the credenza.

Mr. Upchurch (tentatively): "Good morning. I'm a friend of JJ's—"

Banker Three (cutting me off): "JJ—that old bottom-feeder? Boy, we've been through some times together! How is he?" He smiled broadly and then his eyes suddenly narrowed. "He hasn't come to any harm, has he?"

Mr. Upchurch: "Oh no, JJ is fine. I'm just looking for a construction loan."

Banker Three: "Um. I figured that you must be needing some kind of money." He lit a cigarette and leaned back in his chair. "We loan money to all kinds of people, even if they have been turned down by other institutions who considered them to be high risk."

(This sounded good to me so far).

"We ask no questions. We don't even want to know what it's for. We don't do background checks, either. The money is good, and it can be in your hands tomorrow. Of course, this convenience costs a little more…" And the man with the weasel face nudged a piece of paper toward me.

I began to read the document in front of me. It was a contract, and I couldn't conceal a slight gasp as I got to the terms. I began to experience a breach of confidence in this particular "financial institution" and tried to think of ways to extricate myself.

Mr. Upchurch: "Uh, let me think it over. Can I take this with me?" I picked up the contract and got out of the chair.

"Hey, relax—where are you going?" he asked, but I was already halfway to the door.

He shrugged and got up also. "Okay. Just give me a ring if you need me. I'll still be here."

Secretly doubting this, I thanked him politely. I bumped my nose on the glass, the buzzer sounded, and I opened the door to freedom.

"Tell JJ that Guido said hello," Weasel-Face called out after me from beneath the bail bonds sign.

I knew there had to be a way to make this construction loan happen. I was the eternal optimist. Besides, I was fueled by a strong belief in what I was doing.

The next morning, I went to the bank where I did business. I had on business attire. Miss Oglethorpe—a thin, bird-like creature of thirty-something with big glasses—showed me into the expansive office of the senior loan officer, Dave Bloom, who greeted me warmly.

He reminded me of a television evangelist. He wore a perpetual, toothy smile that made me nervous. His hair was…perfect. After some brief courtesies, I told him my story. I was logical, business-like, and to the point. As I spoke, Dave listened thoughtfully. If he formed some initial reservations about my scheme, he kept them to himself. When I had finished speaking, Dave remained silent. At least he had not nixed the deal right off the bat as the others had done. He was contemplating my proposal. I felt a glimmer of hope.

Dave continued to stare thoughtfully. At length, he spoke. "Let me present this to our committee. It's a little unusual, but it is a prac-tice of this bank to foster growth and development for small busi-nesses and individuals in our area. We like to try and help out the little guy, and we sometimes grant loans that might be considered a little unorthodox. We put faith in our customers and, as long as their requests aren't too far-fetched, they most often turn out to be good experiences for the bank." He paused for a moment and then continued. "You have been a customer for a few years. If you have a good credit history, we just might be able to help you."

Pregnant words—would they result in a delivery?

"Thank you very much, Mr. Bloom," I said gratefully. "I hope you can help me. And if not, thank you very much for your time."

"Well, I hope we can as well," he said, rising. "You've got a lot more guts (not the actual anatomical word used) than I do."

I stood to go, smiled, and shook his hand. Leaving the bank, I was a bit humbled. I had the promise of an answer by the end of the week. I took this meeting as a sign of encouragement.

The following Friday, Miss Oglethorpe called—my loan was approved. The stars must be in alignment. Things were starting to go my way!

I sat in the lobby of the bank, ready to set up the construction loan. My starched shirt did not reveal the fact that I lived on a boat. My tie was snappy but all business. My shoes were shined. Miss Abigail Oglethorpe walked briskly out into the lobby through a doorway to receive me, and extended a scrawny hand. I returned her handshake and smiled gamely at her. Abigail Oglethorpe reminded me of Henrietta, the chicken on the old Warner Brothers cartoons[2]. Her ridiculously large glasses made her eyes appear twice their normal size, and I had a hard time concentrating when they were fixed on me.

She showed me in to Mr. Bloom's office and took a perch next to him. The closing began and soon it was raining paper. I signed this, initialed that, and did my best to follow the proceedings. An inch-thick pile of documents was generated that went into my briefcase. I wondered if the Louisiana Purchase had generated that much paperwork.

The construction loan had a time frame of one year. It was mid-February. Anything I was to do had to get done by then. I took a deep breath. It was showtime.

Abigail Oglethorpe showed me back to the lobby. She offered what I took as a smile, but it actually looked more like a grimace. I strode out of the bank with a new confidence. I was a house builder!

I felt real big as I walked down the stairs to the sidewalk and got in my car. House builder—now what was the first thing the house builder was supposed to do? I needed my sage. I couldn't wait to tell him the news!

Bob listened to my breathless account of getting a construction loan. When I was done, he nodded.

"It sounds like you are ready for an architect. I happen to know a couple. I'll give you their numbers so you can talk to them."

---

2 The scrawny hen that Foghorn Leghorn, the loud-mouthed rooster, kept trying to court.

This sounded logical. I wanted to do the building, but I needed it to be done right. I needed an expert to tell me how pier and beam foundations are built to make the house strong and secure. An architect could tell me about things like floor joists and stud spacing and what size lumber should be used. He would help me end up with a house that was nice looking and well built.

Richard, the architect I ended up using, was a seasoned vet. I met him at his home and was pleased to note his house was attractive, tasteful, and not the slightest bit ostentatious. Richard was sharp, competent, and pleasant. We started working on the plans.

I knew nothing about roof pitches, subflooring, and a hundred other building considerations, but that was all right—Richard did. I peppered him liberally with questions, and he did his best to keep up. He knew just what questions to ask me as well and in a short amount of time was able to turn my piece of graph paper into buildable blueprints. The plans contained all of the features I wanted, including a wide, covered front porch.

I was beginning to see the complexity of a house, even a simple one like this. I pored over the blueprints, trying to learn all I could from them. I also began to have reservations about whether I could actually do this myself. Oh no, mustn't think about that now.

Another of life's lessons came into play here: when the way before you becomes cloudy, filling you with doubt, fret not. It is unrealistic to think that you can have all of the answers immediately. You don't have to solve all of the problems at the same time. Try to concentrate on just the *next best step*. Some lessons I just can't seem to learn once and "get" it. I have to keep learning them over and over again. This is one of them.

Remember the elephant…

In the meantime, there was something to do that was crystal clear. It was something I *did* know about, by God—clearing land. Here was some real work to do, and a lot of it. I would worry about the rest later.

Chapter 6

Crop Circles

"Yesterday is history. Tomorrow is a mystery. Today is the present, so open the gift."

They came from a distant planet. They infiltrated our galaxy. They monitored the earth and recorded their findings. Some say they spirited away small children, the elderly, the psychic, and the accused witch. Occasionally they mutilated our livestock, presumably as part of their scientific surveys. They left strange, geometric designs etched before recorded time in the mountains, deserts, and plains of the world. And, in later times, the farmers' fields in Old England, and in more recent times, still, Iowa corn fields.

• • •

Back to clearing land. It was a new day. I put on my cleanest dirty pants and shirt and drove to San Leon. There I took my twenty-five-dollar lawn mower (the one with the heart of an adventurer, remember?) and got started. I headed into the rugged underbrush to create…crop circles. At least, that's what it must have looked like from the air. A curious passer-by stopped to view my progress. We chatted amiably for a moment, and I told him about the crop circles.

He allowed that perhaps I should mow the word "HELP" into the lot. Okay, very funny.

I enlarged the old paths and started new ones. There was the path to the marina, the path to the Black Hole of Calcutta, and the path to St. Louis. The paths skirted the prevalent stands of oleanders, which I spared. The more I thought about it, the more fitting the name Oleanders became for my new oasis. I preserved a blackberry copse or two. I mowed circles around a few stunted trees. I'd need those trees soon, for they would hold the wrecking lights.

Wrecking lights are lanterns that are lit at dusk. From out at sea they would resemble the lights of a safe harbor, replete with taverns, willing young lasses, hot baths, and big meals. Lured in by the lights, ships would attempt to land and meet misery upon the rocks of San Leon. Then, my band and I would steal forth in our dories to do our dirty work. The whole night through we'd toil, stripping the wretched hulks of treasure, cargo, and anything of value—and be gone ere first light.

By the time the sun had risen to its zenith, the spoils would have been sold, and the only traces remaining of the previous evening's plunder would be a few burned strakes bobbing along the shore. By then I would be sound asleep in my hammock with my fat purse tucked safely underneath me, catching forty winks, which would serve me in good stead when the next dusk fell.

The wreckers of yore in places like Key West also affixed lights to donkeys that, from a distance, might look like townspeople walking to and fro, furthering the illusion of a settlement. Maybe I should get a goat. It could walk around at night, lit up like a Christmas tree. It could help with the mowing as well—kill two birds with one stone!

I was getting more and more excited about beginning construction on the little cottage, but I couldn't start building anything until I finished clearing the lot. Patiently I toiled. I mowed. I whacked. I slashed.

Wrecking Lights

My lawn mower, heart of an adventurer or not, broke down about once an hour and had to be fixed. But I prevailed. The jungle was receding, succumbing to mower and machete. Already I had established Base Camp; K1; under a tree. This would be the command center for the foreseeable future. K1 consisted of a locked box of tools and some lawn mower gas cans. I added a couple of dilapidated chairs and a table I found. From this modest outpost I launched sorties into the bush.

All was well, until I entered the PI Zone—the corner with poison ivy. At first, I worked around it. But on second thought, I decided to go ahead and whack while it was not actively growing. I mowed bravely into a large snarl of poison ivy, ever mindful not to touch it. I took gleeful satisfaction in watching the lawn mower reduce it to mulch. All was well again. Or so I thought. At the end of the day, I went home to take a shower. That very evening I started to itch.

The next day it was worse, despite an all-out Calamine lotion blitz. I soon had a rash all over both arms. This puzzled me, until I remembered it had been windy, and the wind had blown a shower of clippings across my bare arms. Oh, man! By the next day the itching was unbearable, and I was thinking amputation. I refrained from scratching and tried to tough it out over the next several days, but it just kept spreading, due, I suppose, to systemic circulation. I finally had to go to the doctor and get a shot to bring it under control.

I was well and truly miserable. Why did I keep forgetting how it was growing up in Arkansas, which surely must be the Poison Ivy Capital of the world? Finally, after a horrible bout that I'll not soon forget, it subsided.

The crop circles grew larger. The lawn mower kept breaking, and I put out the call for lawn mowers, free or cheap. I got one of each. The stable now contained three. The original one, the "Alpha" mower, had two sisters to help shoulder the load. Perhaps they too would contain the hearts of adventurers. Between them, I should be ready when it came time for the archaeological survey. Maybe I could bolt them all together into a "V" formation. Think of it—the Flying Wedge. *Then* we'll see who could cut some grass.

Or open a lawn mower shop: Honest Andy's Lawnmower Emporium. To be incorporated and publicly listed as HALE on the SLSE (San Leon Stock Exchange).

By then, many paths had been mown into the landscape. This one would keep the extra terrestrials in deep space puzzling for years. Most of the paths led nowhere. Apian Way, the original path, was wide enough to allow the passage of two TV championship wrestlers. On the corner of Heartache and Pain I stomped on a rusty nail. Right through my deck shoe it went. I treated it with hydrogen peroxide, antibiotic ointment, and a Flintstones Band aid. All was well until a friend related to me *his* rusty nail experience, which touched on red streaks running up his leg, blood poisoning, and a hospital stay.

This talk about blood poisoning made me nervous. Maybe a tetanus shot would be wise. Going to the clinic for one turned out to be such an aggravation (I have a low tolerance for needlessly complicated procedures and paperwork) that I just gave up and asked the nurse what the symptoms of tetanus fever were: lockjaw. Relating this tale later to some friends caused some laugher, and one of them asked if he could bring me some more rusty nails!

I found more than rusty nails. One day while I was whacking away, something caught my eye. It was partially obscured by brush, but it didn't look like it belonged there. When I looked closer, my heart skipped a beat. It was a gun—a handgun! I froze and then looked around to see if I was being observed. I wasn't. What should I do? Leave it there and call the sheriff? Run away and hide under the bed? Continue working and pretend it wasn't there?

I gingerly picked it up and started back to the car. I bet it was a murder weapon. It looked like it had been there for a long time. Wow, big excitement, right here in San Leon. Perhaps an unsolved murder would be laid to rest, all because of my sharp eyes. Maybe a drug deal had gone bad or there had been a long-standing feud like the Hatfields and McCoys. Maybe I'd get into the newspaper!

Speculations came thick and fast as I made my way to the car. I was almost there when a neighbor ambled over, inquiring what I was holding. My first inclination was to conceal it and say nothing. However, he had seen something in my hand and was giving me a questioning look.

"What's that in your hand?" he asked.

I showed him the gun and began peppering him with my best speculations. I was still speculating away and working up to some ridiculous crescendo when he interrupted me to point out that the weapon was constructed mainly of light blue plastic and had what appeared to be an aperture on the top for adding water...

Boardwalk and Park Place

A few years prior to my coming to San Leon, there had been a sheriff's sale of land on which taxes had not been paid in several years. Sold 'em right on the courthouse steps they did. Several of the lots had been purchased by a small oil and gas company that was interested in the mineral rights. I heard through the grapevine that the company was selling the lots for what they paid for them—i.e., *dirt* cheap. The lots were sprinkled all over San Leon, and two of them happened to be adjacent to my land.

Here was a chance to expand my holdings. Let's see, in medieval England, what is the term that denotes a landowner? Squire? What would be the term to signify a squire with several holdings? Duke? How much land must one acquire in order to be king? (Answer: all of it.) How about Boardwalk and Park Place for the names? It was feasible to acquire these two lots at a good price, and they became part of the Oleanders. The empire was expanding.

I discovered a small book in a local bookstore that had written about the history of San Leon.[2] I bought a copy and read it in the evenings, between scratching the "seven year itch" and treating bites from those cute little pygmy rattlers who lived in the brush (just kidding, Mom). I didn't know that the original name of San Leon was North Galveston. I also didn't know that it used to be possible to walk, or wade, completely across Galveston Bay between Smith Point and Eagle Point. That's a long way! To the eye it just looks like a large expanse of water, but I read in my book that the early settlers even drove cattle across it once upon a time.

The book had many fascinating stores about the early history of San Leon. Among other things, I learned that San Leon had been completely wiped out in the great storm that decimated Galveston in the early 1900s. And, most fascinating of all —in 1921 the skeleton of a mammoth was discovered and excavated…right at the end of *my* street!

Poor Chris

Chris is a nice guy. He is liked by all. He is young, hard-working, honest, dependable, funny, and intelligent. The girls say he's good looking as well. Chris and I worked together. One Friday afternoon, Darwin, another co-worker, asked Chris what he was going to do over the weekend.

"I've got to replace the water pump in my car," Chris said with a long face. "It will probably take me all weekend."

I all but forgot about this until the following Monday morning. When I got to work, I asked Chris how his weekend was.

"I got my water pump replaced," he said, beaming.

Chris doesn't deserve friends like Darwin. When Chris wasn't looking, Darwin went out to the parking lot with a soft drink, knelt down, and carefully poured a small brown puddle on the ground underneath Chris's car, right under the water pump. Then he came back inside and said, "Chris, there's something leaking under your car. You'd better come take a look."

Chris got up and went out to his car, looking worried. He saw the puddle.

"Oh, no!"

He got down on his back and slid underneath to take a look. Darwin had followed him back outside and was standing nearby. He couldn't keep a straight face and started to snicker. In a moment, Chris slid back out and eyeballed Darwin suspiciously. Darwin started laughing, and after a few moments, he confessed to the prank. Chris, good sport that he was, eventually started laughing too.

When this story made it around the office, poor Chris had an afternoon of smart remarks and good-natured ribbing to deal with. I considered the prank pure genius on Darwin's part, and wished I'd thought of it first.

I tell that story to tell you this one. Chris doesn't deserve friends like me, either! I had been thinking about the old junked ski boat that was at the Oleanders. Surely there was a way to have some fun with it, but I couldn't quite think of how. Suddenly, I thought of the perfect way.

Chris liked the water and owned a fishing boat, but he always seemed to have trouble with it. He had mentioned it again, and that is what gave me my idea. The next Monday morning, I went over to Chris's desk, all full of excitement.

"Chris!" I exclaimed. "Have I got a deal for you!" My warped sense of humor works perfectly with my twisted mind.

Again, I said, "Chris!" I can generate excitement that is quite infectious when I put my mind to it.

"There's a lady in San Leon who is selling a ski boat. She saw her husband flirting with another woman, and now she wants to get even with him. She has always resented his boat, and she's going to sell it for *one hundred dollars* to the first person with the money who will come cart it off."

Chris's eyes got wide. I moved closer and continued, "I saw the boat myself this weekend, and it's beautiful. She let me start it up, and it runs fine. It has a trailer and everything!"

Chris went for the bait. "Hey," he exclaimed. "This sounds interesting."

I carefully added a little fuel. "You know this deal isn't going to be here long…"

Chris was getting caught in the trap. "When can we go over and look at it?"

"I'm busy tonight," I said. "Why don't we go over there during lunch today?" Now, in the meantime, I had driven around town until I located another boat, roughly similar to what I had just described to Chris. It was fairly new and looked nice. I had taken a picture or two of it, just for this occasion, which I handed to Chris for inspection. It did the job. His over-excited eyes drank it in, and he swallowed the bait.

"Okay. How does eleven forty-five sound to you?"

Lunchtime. Chris and I got in my car and we drove to San Leon. On the way, I fanned the flames by talking about things like swimming, fishing, and whether or not he could water ski. Presently, we arrived at the lot. By then, the brush had been cleared completely from around the boat so that when we walked down the path to it, it was plainly visible in all of its horrible glory. When we got close, I walked up ahead of Chris to the boat, turned around to face him, crossed my arms, and grinned expectantly.

Chris beheld the poor, decrepit derelict behind me with a mixed look of incomprehension and disappointment. He looked back at me, and then gaped again at the boat. Then he said, "*Is this it? You dragged me all the way out here for this?*"

I knew what Darwin must have felt like a couple of weeks ago. I started laughing. Chris just stared at me in bewilderment while I stood there, cackling like an idiot. Chris was initially mad, but soon he was laughing too. He couldn't help it. We both laughed for another minute, and I had to go sit down.

When I had regained my breath, I said, "Chris, you're a great sport. You don't deserve friends like me! Come on, I'll buy you lunch, at any place you want to go."

And I did, too.

We got back to work, late of course. Everyone there knew what had just happened thanks to my big mouth from before we had left for lunch, and Chris had some more ribbing to put up with.

Chris and I are still good friends to this day. The boat? It eventually got hauled to the dump. The last I saw of it, a Caterpillar tractor was about to run over it and send it to its eternal rest.

"Chris's New Boat"

The Amazing Oleander Puller

There were lots of oleander bushes to clear. I didn't want to get rid of all of them, for they were pretty when they bloomed. I left a border of them lining the perimeter of the yard, where their dense green foliage made for a fine sense of seclusion. Some of the bushes were perfectly fine specimens; they were just in inconvenient places. I opted to transplant some of them in order to fill in thin spots.

I invented a device to assist me with this task which I named the Oleander Puller. It consisted of a ten-foot-tall wooden tripod, with a hook at the top from which a come-along was suspended. The lines from the oleander puller instruction manual, if I had cared to write one, would have looked something like this:

• • •

Thank you for purchasing The Oleander Puller, part #1357924680TR/OP (MSRP $999.99).

Your Oleander Puller is constructed of the very finest materials available and is designed to give you years of happy, trouble-free operation.

Tripod Assembly

Attach 3 stout LEGS parts (A), (B), (C) to TRIPOD TOP (D) using BARN DOOR HINGES (E), (F), (G). Drill ½" hole in the center of TRIPOD TOP (D) and attach EYE BOLT (H) eye side down using 2 FLAT WASHERS, LOCK WASHER and NUT.

Operation

1. With spade or sharpshooter, cut a circular pattern around bush, severing lateral roots.

2. Position tripod up and center over hapless oleander.

3. Suspend upper hook of come-along from eyebolt (H) of tripod assembly.

4. Take three (3) wraps around crown of hapless oleander with a stout rope, securing with a slipknot. Tie a bowline at the bitter end of the rope and place loop into the lower hook of the come-along.

5. Take up slack on come-along. When rope becomes taut, operate come-along lever, applying upward torque to oleander.

6. Roots of oleander will start to give way. Continue applying pressure. As oleander comes out of ground, use the spade to cut remaining roots. Whack root ball with spade to loosen excess dirt.

7. Deftly swing oleander to the side. Release lever on come-along to play out cable, dropping oleander into waiting wheelbarrow.

8. Place oleander into new hole that has been prepared for it. Repeat for all other oleanders.

• • •

As you can see, the oleander puller can winch oleanders right out of the ground. Well, that was the theory, anyway. However, like most of my ideas, this one excelled in theory only. It didn't work, and I ultimately had to write it off as a complete waste of time.

A Wondrous Tale

One evening, at the end of a long and exhausting but satisfying day of working at the Oleanders, I was taking a little break. I had just enough energy and daylight left to dig up one more oleander bush that was in the way. I grabbed my shovel and got to work.

I bent to my task, digging and chopping. The resilient ground finally yielded the last root. I found a good bare spot to replant it in and started to dig. Again and again I swung the mattock, through the earth, roots, and rocks. It was hard digging, and I was just about played out. A child's ball emerged from the dirt and then a coat hanger.

Just a little deeper still, and then... *Whang*! Damn, a rock. Almost broke my mattock. Wouldn't you know it? Two feet to the right or left, and I would have missed it. I found the edge of the rock with my shovel and dug the hole beside it. Perfect. In went the bush. It would never know it had just been transplanted.

I raked dirt off the rock to pack in around the roots and noted that the rock was an almost perfect rectangle. Curious, I dug out around the other edges. When I had dug to where I could get a shovel blade underneath it, I pried it up. It was flat, like a stepping stone.

Something metal underneath it glinted weakly in the failing light. Somebody could have a great time with a metal detector around here. I stooped and brushed away the dirt and beheld a curious object.

It appeared to be made of rough wooden planks with iron braces around the edge, and they seemed very old. What in the world could this be? Forgetting all about how tired I was, I continued digging to expose more of it. It was a box of some kind.

My heart began to beat quicker. What had I found? By then it was almost completely dark, and I could no longer see to dig. My excitement told me to get my floodlight and keep digging. But what if this object turned out to be very old, or very valuable, or both? And, what if I was observed, digging feverishly after dark, with a light? No, couldn't do that—mustn't draw attention. What to do?

I decided to cover it up and leave it overnight. To the casual observer and the nosy neighbor alike, it would look like a bush had just been planted. Believe me, I didn't want to go back to the boat, but I tore myself away. I showered, ate supper, and went to bed. As I lay there, my thoughts were racing. My excitement was out of control. What if I had found treasure? What if I'd found Jean Lafitte's treasure? What if, if, if...

If, if, if...

My ears were being assaulted by a rude buzzing. My eyes flew open. I was on the boat and it was morning. The sun was streaming brightly through the window, filling it with golden cheer and hurting my eyes. Foggy from a deep sleep, I turned off the alarm.

What a great dream! Isn't it something, how vivid and life-like they can appear after you wake up? You know, I've been spending too much time reading that San Leon history book. With all of the things I've read about Jean Lafitte, treasure in San Leon is not really so far-fetched.

Lots of work to do today. Better get moving...

The Jungle Recedes

Clearing the lot and getting it ready to become a construction site was not a quick or easy process. My weekends and most evenings after work consisted of mowing brush, fixing the lawn mowers, piling up the trash, sawing trees, and fixing the lawn mowers again. The paths became wider and longer and then merged together. I could have paid to have the land cleared, but then how was I to discover its secrets? Anyway, it was also a great way to get some exercise. Then, one day I was finished. I went back to the boat that evening with a wonderful sense of accomplishment.

The next order of business was to burn the huge pile of brush that had accumulated. This took place over one very long day with occasional trips to the Quick Stop down the road for refreshment. The little store had everything you would ever need if you were passing through San Leon: ice, cigarettes, and fishing licenses. A sign in the window advertised: Guns, Wedding Gowns, & Cold Beer. Hmm!

"Quick Stop"

As I worked my way through the brush pile, I was very glad to not encounter any Mid-East camel spiders lurking there. I had seen some hideous images of them, sent back from people in our military who were stationed there. They were huge. I was happier still not to see any San Leon spiders either. They lived in the dense brush in webs at about eye level, waiting for some unlucky person to come tripping down the path. Several times when doing just that, I hauled up short, just in time, with one just inches away. Unnerving. I'll bet a San Leon spider could beat up a Mid-East camel spider with four of its arms tied behind its back!

The burning of the brush pile elicited pyrotechnical tendencies from deep within me, latent since I was about eight years old. It also presented a fairly provoking photo op, which I succumbed to. The photo of the large blackened spot where the fire had blazed begged a caption.

How about: "Errant SCUD missile from irate ex-wife, narrowly misses home in San Leon."

They Say Indians Once Lived Here

• • •

Location: San Leon town site
County: Galveston
Block: 172
Recorded: Plat Volume 254A, Page 32
Excavation: Grid
Collection Method: Surface collection, test pit

The archaeological survey commenced under the supervision of one J. Andrew Upchurch, the renowned para-archaeologist. The following is excerpted from his field notes:

We drove our vehicles to the area under study. We advanced into the territory that I would characterize as crudely cleared of vegetation. Our initial pass revealed that the site had been occupied at one time, possibly as a homestead, as evidenced by large numbers of mature oleanders on the property. However, no foundations or evidence of any permanent structure were found. The occupation was likely for periods of shorter duration by what appeared to be adolescent males, due to the preponderance of beer cans and cigarette butts scattered throughout the site.

A principal feature of the area was a pit at one end. A future excavation might reveal more clues as to its purpose. Already we know that the early inhabitants subsisted mainly on beer, tinned chili, frozen dinners, and chocolate bars. This lends support to the theory that these people camped where food was available nearby. In fact, a source of these food items still exists today in the form of a convenience store, located not far away.

A test pit two meters square was gridded and excavated to a depth of one meter. The contents were screened and foreign objects reserved and catalogued. The site yielded an abundance of midden, or household trash, which, when analyzed, will provide a good picture of what life was like for these primitive inhabitants.

The excavation, when completed, will be turned over to cultivation.

I say cultivation. This is where the tomato garden would go.

I have always been fascinated by archaeology. Another glance at my San Leon history book revealed that some plowed fields have indeed yielded Indian artifacts such as arrowheads and pottery shards. You don't know what this does for my imagination.

• • •

The Oleanders was cleared of brush and ready for construction. I was eager to get started, but first I was going to use a day to take care of something that had gone neglected for too long. I'm glad I did because, as it turned out, it was many a day before I was able to do it again.

I went fishing.

The Fishing Report

"He riseth up early in the morning and disturbeth the whole household. Mighty are his preparations. He goeth forth full of hope. When the day is far spent he returneth, smelling of strong drink, and the truth is not in him."

—My favorite fishing quote

Up I brought me early this day as well, for today I would fish! I fished on my Jet Ski, the "Scalded Hog."

Jet Skis aren't generally known as fishing vessels. They are more for charging at breakneck speed across the water. The thrill derived from this activity is considerable. I love mine. Jet Skis are feared and disliked—hated, even—by power boaters and sailors alike. They regard Jet Skis as noisy, annoying, and dangerous. Jet Skis are all of these things. I share these sentiments. Unless I'm the one on the Jet Ski.

Don't worry. With my sailing background, I can be counted on to ride with more than the usual amounts of safety and courtesy. Oh, sure, I do my share of childish cutting up: wild flat-out speed runs, swooshing, high speed S-turns, and tight donuts that send rooster tails of water that probably contain small fish and crustaceans high into the air. To indulge this immaturity I always go way "over there," far from other boats, the shore, etc.

Fishing on a Jet Ski is a great way to fish. You can get out to your fishing spot quickly, and you never have to get up or move around too much. You can't, you'll capsize. To be sure, there are things about the normal fishing drill that you have to change in order to make it work.

For one, I went down to the discount store and bought a child's "Snoopy" fishing rod. It was only about three feet long. I needed a short rod that would be easier to handle on my small craft. I removed the toy reel and replaced it with a better one that featured a good drag. I also attached a lanyard to the rod that I could clip onto my life vest, for such times when I needed the use of both hands. This little rod was the perfect setup for my diminutive vessel. I got funny looks from other fishermen whenever I brandished this weapon. Let them snicker; it catches fish. I named this rod the "Shark Slayer."

Then, also, these purchases: a small mushroom anchor that would be easy to deploy from the Jet Ski, and a minner (minnow) bucket. A big, ridiculous, floppy hat for sun protection. A small canvas tote bag for fishing tackle that I could wear on my shoulder. A small net. Last, but not least, a fish stringer, the old-fashioned kind.

Everything must be tied onto the Jet Ski. Well, not everything, just the things you want to keep.

On this particular morning, I assembled these items of fishery and approached the Scalded Hog, sleeping peacefully beside the sailboat on her little floating dock. Would she start? Would she run? I gave her an exploratory crank to which she snorted once and returned to her nap. She would have stayed there had I not been prepared with a can of starting fluid. With no intended irreverence, may I humbly submit that starting fluid is the absolute *Blood of Christ* to all small gasoline engines. One squirt of this magical elixir into her craw, another crank, and she roared into life, before she even knew what was happening.

I leapt aboard, shoved her down the ways, and was off before the whole marina came down on me with torches and pitchforks, as it was still early. Jet Skis don't have running lights and it's illegal to add them, too. Damned glad I am of this. They are dangerous enough in broad daylight. I shudder to think about inebriated drivers roaring blindly around the waterfront at night. For me though, this meant waiting until dawn before I set off. At least, morning was trying to dawn as I ran out of patience and stole down the channel a little early to see Stephanie.

Stephanie is the young Asian girl whose family has a shrimp boat and a bait stand across the channel from the Kemah Boardwalk. They opened at six o'clock in the morning for fishermen. She smiled when she saw me coming, with my too-big floppy hat and my too-small fishing rod. She filled my minnow bucket with live shrimp. Live bait evens up the playing field. In no time I was off to the killing fields. I wish the saying were true: "Women love me, fish fear me!"

The morning was a dawnin' for sure by the time I had gotten my bait and motored out of the channel. There are several spots I like to fish. One of them is the place where the Kemah channel empties into Galveston Bay. The Kemah Boardwalk is located right on the corner. The bank is a bulkhead there. Tides swirl around this corner, and it is a good fishing spot. I'd anchor a little ways away and cast toward the Boardwalk. I referred to it as fishing "The Wall." However, I opted to pass up The Wall that day and keep going around to another favorite spot of mine, in the flats. I shall politely, but firmly, decline to elaborate further on this location.

When I got to my spot, I heaved my anchor over the side and rigged up. I consider it good luck to kiss each shrimp before it is hooked. I let the first shrimp fly and before long I had a customer. He nibbled and I waited. The classic definition of fishing is "a little jerk on one end and a big jerk on the other!" Suddenly, he bought. Fish on! A scrappy fight ensued. Trout? Redfish? Flounder? Drum? How to prepare? Grilled, broiled, fish tacos?

I played it up to the boat. The fish was not at all happy about having its freedom curtailed, either. It was a redfish. Redfish are good eating! An illegal red, smaller than the legal limit. I returned it to the bay to play another day and grow into a monster for some other lucky angler to catch.

By, then, other fishermen were arriving. I baited up, kissed my surprised shrimp, and committed him to the deep. This time I hauled in my anchor so as to drift across the flats and cover more ground. The sun, which had been truculent at first, was making an appearance in earnest. It was a beautiful morning—mild, calm, and serene. The cloud art was superb. I can conjure up a nude out of any cloud.

Suddenly, the line went taut. The drag on the reel sang—hookup! My mind snapped from the erotic sky back to the present and I started reeling. The fish was game and so was I. I got it all the way to the Jet Ski and beheld: a big, fat trout. Onto the stringer. When fishing on a Jet Ski I have learned to put the fish on the stringer *before* removing the hook. I learned this the hard way by losing more than one nice prize.

Dinner was assured. I glanced around and half a dozen other fishermen took a sudden interest in their lines. After only a few minutes more, *Bam,* I had another fish on! It was another nice trout, caught right under the jealous noses of the other fishermen. I kept it as well and decided to head back in, as the sun was growing hot.

I stowed my gear and liberated the rest of my grateful bait. Mumbling something about going in to buy a fishing license, I decamped. Not bad for a morning on the water. Those fresh broiled trout would go well with some parsley new potatoes, a sexy salad, and some jazz!

• • •

And with that, I vowed to return the very next day to house construction in earnest and must now close this chapter. Oh yes, I almost forgot: HALE is up an eighth. I must remember to feed Bones when I get back to the Oleanders…

Chapter 7

The Project Revealed

"If you can only go left or right, and you know that left isn't right, then right must be right because it's the only way left."

This is how the real estate ad in the realtor's MLS will read:

STUNNING HOME NOT FAR FROM THE WATER. A SPACIOUS TWO-HOUSE PROPERTY ON LARGE CORNER LOT. MAIN HOUSE IN FRONT ON PIERS WITH PARKING UNDERNEATH. DECK ON ALL FOUR SIDES, TWO STORIES, THREE BEDROOMS, SEPARATE CABANA IN THE BACK, BUILT LOW ON PIERS. BOTH HOUSES FACE ONTO LAVISHLY PLANTED COURTYARD WITH HOT TUB, FISH POND, AND SUBDUED OUTDOOR LIGHTING IN A TROPICAL MOTIF. CABANA FEATURES ITS OWN WIDE PORCH THAT FACES COURTYARD AND THE LARGER HOUSE WALK-IN AVIARY CABANA FEATURES MANY ACCENTS SUCH AS KNOTTY PINE WALLS, WOOD FLOORS, AND DRAMATIC VAULTED WOOD CEILING. KITCHEN FEATURES MARBLE COUNTERTOPS AND STONE FLOORS. MUST SEE TO APPRECIATE!

Construction was about to begin at the Oleanders. The cabana would be built first. As advertised, it would be a smallish house with one big room, save an enclosed bathroom in one corner. I imagined it would take some getting used to, no longer having to hunt down the bucket in the middle of the night when the head was not working. *ARRRRRRR, Them's what happens when the sailor moves ashore.*

As originally planned, it would have a Pullman kitchen in the other back corner with U-shaped countertops. The kitchen would have a bar facing out into the room where I could sit and drink my morning coffee. There would be real marble countertops and real stone floors in the kitchen and bathroom. The dining area, living area, and bedroom area would all share one big space. There would be vaulted ceilings to give it an open, airy look. I wanted the cabana to remind you of the little fishing cottage your father used to take you to when you were nine years old.

I envisioned lots of real wood. The vaulted ceiling would be of an attractive, light-colored wood and have a couple of large, exposed beams. For the walls I favored wide, knotty pine boards set vertically, if I could still find knotty pine. My grandmother's parlor had been that way when I was growing up, and it was a very warm and inviting room. Real wood for the floor as well—nothing else would do.

I liked the idea of double, multi-paned French doors for the front door. They'd open out onto the generous front porch that would have two big, white Adirondack rocking chairs for sitting and contemplating the day. There would be lots of big paned windows around the house to let in the light.

In front of the porch I could have a shady, lattice-covered, brick patio. Off to the side of the patio, nestled among the flora and fauna, would be a good place for a hot tub and gazebo where I could enjoy a restorative and soak away the cares of the world. Tucked in a back corner of the yard would be a small shop/storage building (to be named the "Oar House"?), where I could work on small building projects and conduct my evil experiments.

I thought about someday having summer parties, with a band playing on the porch and everybody sitting on lawn chairs and blankets in the yard, among the tropical foliage. What a happy picture! That day however seemed very far away.

The second house would be built at some point in the future. It would be built on stilts with room underneath to develop as outdoor living space as well, such as a comfortable seating area with tables and chairs, flanked by an outdoor kitchen.

The second house would be bigger than the cabana but still not large. It would be more conventionally built than the cabana, with regular rooms and walls. It would have a wraparound porch on all four sides and may also have a water view from the side, facing the bay, if one could see over the small houses at the water's edge. It would take a fire truck with a tall ladder to climb up and find out.

Other than these general thoughts, I had no preconceived notions for the main house. It could be two stories. I might add a widow's walk, a small, rooftop balcony where in the olden days ship captains' wives would go to watch for their husbands' ships returning from the sea. I would cross this bridge when I got to it. Speaking of bridges, the high porch of the main house could be connected to the low porch of the cabana with a series of small, multilevel decks and stairs. Wouldn't that be wonderful? Kind of like a tree house.

Somewhere near the house could be the aviary. I have always had an affinity for parrots. I love their beautiful colors, their comical ways, their interesting vocalizations, and their intelligence. My parrot, Paco is a much-loved pet. He is a handsome parrot—brilliant green with a bright red head. His black, beady eyes and menacing, curved beak inspire respect. He was twenty-one years old when this story began. He had had an accident a couple of years earlier that left him permanently crippled. He had flown off of my shoulder and hit a stone floor—hard. It fractured his spine. My veterinarian, an avian specialist, agreed to take Paco on as a mercy case. Under her expert care, Paco eventually recovered, although at one point he stopped eating and a feeding tube had to be inserted. Today, Paco is, from all outward signs, a happy, healthy, and pain-free parrot. He lives in a specially modified cage where he is comfortable and can move around without much trouble. He wants and needs my attention. He is a "lap parrot" and likes to be petted as I watch TV or read.

An aviary would be wonderful for Paco. The aviary could have lots of live plants with fluorescent plant lights to keep them healthy. It could have a small outdoor table and chairs where I could sit and commune with the parrots. The ground of the aviary would be covered with pea-sized gravel that can be hosed and raked. I might even put a natural rock fountain with running water there, as well, to be the parrot's water supply.

Serving both houses from the street would be a circular drive of oyster shell, like the little roads in the quaint seaside village of Port Aransas. The back porch of the larger house and the front porch of the cabana would look out onto a shared courtyard. This would be thickly planted with palms, bananas, ginger, and hibiscus.

Into the cabana I shall move, once it is completed. Though small, I imagine it would feel like the Taj Mahal after living on a twenty-seven-foot sailboat. If and when I was able to build the second, larger house, the cabana would presumably become a guest house/rehearsal room/office.

Building a house would be a great adventure of the first order and the highest magnitude! I had already decided to do as much of the building as I could myself. A goal. Something to conquer. An intriguing project. An epic journey! Did I know anything about framing? No. How about foundations? Or roofing, flooring, plumbing, electrical, heating, and air conditioning? Of course not! But I would learn.

Living along the Texas Gulf Coast has some inherent dangers, namely hurricanes. They can, and do, strike the Texas coast, although, thankfully, not very often. I found myself beginning to fixate on them and soon it was driving me in a fair way nutty. The threat was there, but there was no sense in blowing it all out of perspective. I decided that maybe the best way to proceed would be to take all of the reasonable precautions I could, get adequate insurance, and let come what may. If you're going to choose to live by a vast, capricious entity like Galveston Bay, you may someday have to live with the consequences. Anyway, the time to worry about hurricanes is *before* you buy the land, not after.

So, what could I do construction wise to help my house better withstand a hurricane? Build the house higher? No, I wanted it fairly low; I'd take my chances. Besides, a house can be damaged in a hurricane by more than rising water. Some houses survive the floodwaters only to be torn apart by wind. I pondered this dilemma as I got ready for bed that night. I was almost asleep when the solution planted itself into my brain. Boat docks have flotation built under them, which allows them to float. They are anchored to stationary pilings and rise up and down with the tides.

That's it! I'd drive four twenty-four-foot pilings into the ground, at the corners of the house. Then, I'd attach the house to them with some large rings that slide up and down. Lastly, I'd place large Styrofoam blocks under the house. Then, if it flooded, I'd simply rise above it!

Before I could build anything, I needed to arrange for electricity. I might as well investigate water and sewer services while I was at it. Also, I would need a culvert so that supply trucks could get across the ditch. It became apparent how many things in life I take for granted. I realized that any and all of those things, if they were going to happen at all, were only going to if I caused them to happen. Things like electricity, water, sewer, and a culvert.

The need for a culvert bubbled up to the top of the list. It was possible to drive onto the lot if you had a vehicle with high clearance. You had to get a running start and charge through the ditch Kamikaze style, along with a blood-curdling scream. Applying any brakes during this operation was discouraged. If you were successful you came to rest on dry ground.

During this phase, I managed to get stuck in the mud on account of several inches of rain that had fallen over the preceding two weeks. Patience is not my strong suit, and as it rained on and on, I became indignant. I *deserved* to drive onto the lot. *My* lot. And there was work to do. With a bad case of cabin fever, I barely gave the rain a chance to stop. I drove back over to the Oleanders to resume work.

The ground there was still much too wet, a fact I chose to ignore, yet my car plunged through the ditch and slid to a halt without mishap. Things were ok until I attempted to back into the place where I wanted to work. I became immediately stuck. Fine, just fine! You know, some people just don't like to be told they can't do something. Could I be one of them?

I worked for an hour trying to get the car free, thoroughly covering it and me in mud. *My* mud. My car was a gnarly SUV-type vehicle, but, despite its rangy good looks, it was not any better than a street car when you got it off the pavement. *Hmph.* A city slicker's car, for sure.

At length, a neighbor in a passing pickup truck stopped to help. This Good Samaritan immediately became stuck also, and there we both were. We didn't get either car out until the neighbor called a friend with a four-wheel-drive Jeep who came over and pulled us both out. The big brown blotches of mud made my white car look like a cow. A humbling experience to say the least. Guess I forgot, again, what it was like growing up in Arkansas, which could arguably be the Mud Capital of the world as well.

After this learning experience, I arranged to get a culvert put into the ditch. This meant having to know precisely where the driveway was going to be located. That meant having to have a pretty good idea of where the house was going to be. My God, did *everything* have to be so intertwined?

A little more work with the graph paper with both houses on it helped me sort this out. Even this seemingly clear-cut task took me longer than it should have. I got it all drawn out to scale and then went out to the ditch and marked the place where the culvert should go with stakes. I found a place where I could buy culverts. The price included delivery and placing them into position. A day or two later, a truck arrived. They placed the culvert sections into the ditch and smoothed a load of gravel over them. That was all well and good, but I wasn't done. The culverts merely enabled you to drive ten feet into the property…and *then* get stuck. The ground was still soggy. How to fix?

The next day, when a neighbor came to view the results of my labor, I mentioned my mud problem. This elicited a "Hell, you won't be able to get a car in yonder until mid-July!" from him, a statement that caused the color to drain from my face and my knees to clatter. Now what? I had just closed a construction loan with an end date I was expected to meet. How to get the driveway area dried out *now*, enough to allow heavy trucks in, regardless of the weather?

Maybe ditches on either side of the driveway? How to do this? Rent a ditch digger? No, it was too wet. By then I had enough experience with San Leon mud to know that it was nothing to trifle with. I was afraid a ditch digger would become bogged down and not be able to work. Wait for dry weather and then rent a ditch digger? I didn't have time. I opted to dig the ditches by hand.

It had been raining cats and dogs again (I almost stepped in a *poodle*) turning my patch of San Leon into a bog. Honest to Pete, I could have started a catfish farm.

The classic song "Sixteen Tons" began running through my mind the morning I drove to the Oleanders to begin digging the ditches:

"…I was born one mornin' when the sun didn't shine, I picked up my shovel and I walked to the mine,

I loaded sixteen tons of number nine coal, the straw boss said, 'Well bless my soul …"[3]

I took up shovel and mattock and attacked the ground with enthusiasm. It was slow going. Stumbling around drunkenly (I have had some experience with this) I flailed at roots and brushed away leeches, real or imagined, in the ankle-deep water and mud. I toiled long into the wee hours of the afternoon. While I dug, I was reminded of a funny incident, which I shall relate here:

. . .

Not so many years ago, Kemah had been a sleepy little town of fishing and sailboats. It was a pretty place, right on Galveston Bay. There were a few little shacks where you could get oysters and beer. This area caught the attention of a prominent developer. He began buying the little waterside joints, quietly at first, and then much of the rest of Kemah. Presently, word got around that there were plans in place to build a multi-gazillion-dollar dining and entertainment complex. The dozers came in and razed the oyster shacks. Then the cement trucks came. Kemah staggered and then disappeared under three feet of concrete. Out of the chaos arose—the Kemah Boardwalk.

Needing parking space for the legions of customers, the developer was still acquiring land. Property values skyrocketed. Longtime residents were selling and profiting handsomely. There is a favorite saying of mine:

> You have to take advantage of the opportunity of a lifetime during the lifetime of the opportunity.

People were definitely taking advantage. Little old ladies and the Vietnamese fishermen who had been living in small, dilapidated houses for years profited thus. I heard that many sold their modest homes and were living in swank walk-ups in tony Houston neighborhoods.

Soon, it was learned by those of us who lived in the adjacent marina that the marina itself had been purchased by the developer. You should have heard the uproar *that* caused! Speculation ran rampant and rumors were born daily. Would the marina be closed? Would we all have to move? Would the marina be filled in with dirt to create parking? A few people actually began moving out on the strength of the rumors alone, even though nothing had happened.

During the height of this frenzy, I got this little idea. It was a very bad idea, as most of my good ideas are. The very next Sunday morning was warm and beautiful. The marina was full of people, there to enjoy the pretty weekend. Early, early, I snuck out to the front gate and affixed a sign to it. The sign read:

FILL DIRT WANTED
INQUIRE WITHIN

I then left for San Leon for a day of work. I'm sure the reactions were many and varied. I heard later that the sign disappeared, but not before it had done its worst. It had only fanned the fire, and I'm sure it made trouble for the marina staff. The manager of the office? Gene. Kemah Bums Gene—who knew only too well who had done it. He happened to spot me as I was returning to the marina that evening and came out of the office to confront me. There was much laughter, and while he couldn't condone my juvenile stunt, he did concede that it had been one of my "better ones."

• • •

Back at the dig site the next day, I was very glad to not be digging ditches for a living. I worked until my pathetic, quivering body could take no more. I stopped, straightened, and turned to survey my work. Behold, stretching into the distance lay twenty feet of ditch. I felt like I had just dug the Panama Canal.

I crept back to the marina where I knew I could find a hot shower and a soft bed aboard the sailboat. My hulking, muddy, tattered form, lurching across the parking lot, must have appeared menacing, although it was honestly more of a painful progression. Nonetheless, mothers held their babies close as I passed.

I dug every evening after work, rain or shine, until I had two sixty-foot ditches running back to the house site. The ground started to dry up. The ditches had water in them. They were working! For good measure, I got a load of gravel delivered to put in the driveway to make a "work track" with a solid surface for driving on. Later, I would cover this with oyster shells to help give the Oleanders the look of the little oyster shell drives in Port Aransas. I called a friend I'd made, Mike, who had a tractor with an attachment for spreading dirt and gravel. He spread the gravel, and the mud problem was finally solved for good.

The next step was to put pilings in the ground on which the house would be built. Alas, I had to abandon my great idea of a floating house! I have always liked the look of a house sitting on short pilings, just a couple of feet off the ground, with ferns planted around the porch. I wanted the cabana to have this look, but I had to learn what the codes concerning building heights were. I also had to find out which governing entity I had to answer to for these regulations. It turned out to be the county[3]. I found that building low would be permissible, so long as the house was above flood level. The guidelines for building heights were a little confusing, as guidelines from governing entities are wont to be. The following discussion will attempt to cover the high points of how this works:

> Years ago, the land was systematically surveyed to create geographic contour maps. The maps were divided into zones of elevation, which tell the general land elevations. This information was combined with historical flooding data, and from this association; a building height guideline was established. This height is called "Base Flood Elevation." All of this collected data suggests that struc-

---

3 In conjunction with the Federal Emergency Management Association (FEMA). Insurance companies have an interest in this as well.

tures whose first floors are above this elevation are reasonably safe from the threat of coastal flooding. Not completely safe. Reasonably safe.

In this county, some zones are above the base flood elevation and some are below. If you are going to build a house within the county, you must obtain an elevation certificate, which gives the zone your property is located in, the base flood elevation for that zone, and the elevation of the soil at your address. If your property is above base flood elevation, the county does not care. You may build the house right on the ground. If your property is below base flood elevation like mine, you must make up the difference. That is, you must build your house higher so that it is above base flood elevation.

All new buildings must adhere to base flood elevation. If you build a structure that is below it, the county has several unpalatable recourses: they can fine you, or they can force you to bring your house into compliance. I shudder to think of what kind of effort that could take for a freshly built house. Not only that, you will be unable to obtain flood insurance. Finally, the county can prevent stubborn violators from establishing electrical service. Ouch!

I had heard of people building houses that did not adhere to the elevation guidelines. Their houses failed the inspection and had to be either brought into compliance or torn down. I could see how important it was for me to be correct. This is not a bad thing. These measures are obviously there to protect people like me from making big mistakes.

Base flood elevation is measured off the sea level of Galveston Bay, with a calculation to allow for the wave surge of a hurricane. Base flood elevation has nothing to do with the surface of the soil. According to my elevation certificate, the base flood elevation in my zone was eleven feet. The elevation of the ground at my property was eight feet four inches. The difference was two feet six inches. I had to build the house up off of the ground by that amount.

But, ground is uneven, you say. You are correct. What you must do is this: around the county in various published locations are elevation reference markers. They are made of bronze and permanently mounted in some structure, such as the base of a bridge. You can look up one closest to your property and use it to find the exact elevation of your ground.

How is this done? I will hereby supply the answer, at the risk of becoming tiresome:

> You will need a pretty, young assistant and a surveyor's laser light. You use the laser to walk the elevation to your property. You do this by going to the marker and setting up the laser to project a laser beam, at the exact height of base flood elevation. You then adjust the beam to be level using the level that is built into the top of the laser. Then you direct it toward some distant structure which is in the direction of your property. Telephone poles work well for this. While your pretty, young assistant minds the laser, you walk to the pole and drive a nail into it at the exact point where the laser beam strikes it. Your pretty, young assistant then brings the laser over and sets it up by the pole and adjusts it to the height of the nail you just drove. You beam the laser toward another pole, and repeat the process over again.
>
> Pole by pole you go, all the way to your property.

Are you keeping up?

I called the county and found out where the nearest marker was. I drove to the spot and found a small concrete bridge there. Sure enough, imbedded in its base was a round bronze marker. I elected to forgo the pretty young assistant in favor of an experienced surveyor. I didn't need any mistakes here! The surveyor and I began the marking process, and marked telephone poles for the six or seven blocks, around corners too, all the way to the Oleanders.

When we got to the Oleanders, I dug a hole and planted a stout wooden stake at the edge of the yard. We beamed the laser on this stake, and I drove the last nail in it to use as a reference. This mark showed the base flood elevation on my property. Pretty neat!

That was the level my floor had to be built up to. After the pilings were in, I could again use a laser to project this line onto each piling. Then, the pilings could all be cut off level, regardless of the surface of the ground at each piling. A little knowledge is a dangerous thing!

The actual cut line on the pilings would be lower than the floor height line to allow for the beams and joists beneath the floor. After making this adjustment, I added a few inches to the height as a margin of safety, just to make sure the floor would be above base flood elevation when all was said and done.

Enlightened about building heights, I could make informed decisions about the foundation pilings. I could move forward. My house plans told me how many pilings I would need, as well as their pattern and spacing on the ground. They also told me what size lumber to use. I now knew also how tall they had to be. I took string and stakes and marked the footprint of the house, ensuring that it was square with the property lines.

I had had quite enough of shovels after digging my ditches, thanks, and was in no mood to dig the holes for thirty-something pilings by hand. As it turned out, I didn't have to. A little investigating *unearthed* a company that set pilings for new buildings. I called to inquire. I was in luck. They would come out, mark the building site into a grid pattern, dig the holes, and place the pilings. The pilings would be guaranteed to be square, accurately positioned, and straight. We struck a fair price, and I engaged their services. I also called the lumber company and placed my first order: thirty-two, eight-inch by eight-inch by eight-foot pilings, pressure treated to prevent decay.

The lumber company I selected to supply all of my wood was a small, family-run business that had been around for years. I favor using establishments like this whenever I can. As it turned out, all of the home-building establishments large and small in our area got a good piece of business from me over the next year. This lumber company delivered for free, too. One fine day, their truck backed down my driveway without sinking up to its axles, thanks to my heroic efforts with the ditches, and off-loaded my pilings—the first of many loads of materials over the next year.

The pile-setting crew arrived right after that with a miniature ditch digger on a trailer. I was already there waiting for them and, arising, I slipped/slid through the remains of my mud to meet them. The digger was a tiny thing. It sat upon two small tracks like an army tank and had a miniature hydraulic arm with an auger that looked like a large drill bit. It resembled an overgrown riding lawn mower that had been exposed to harmful radiation one day and featured an extra appendage, not unlike the frog that was discovered in Missouri a few years back with an extra leg. I tittered at first, but laughed no more when it navigated effortlessly through the mud, churning it into a very fine creamy consistency as it went.

Steve, the company's owner, put me at ease immediately. He had been setting pilings for years in the area and was very comfortable with it. The first thing he did was string out the house footprint in a grid pattern, checking it several times for straight and true. Then, he drove the miniature digger over to the location of the first piling and started drilling. I stood by and greedily watched for gold and rubies in the tailings. Alas, no gold. No silver. No bones, even. What did come up, however, were some interesting rocks that resemble geodes.

What? You don't know what a geode is?

Think back to when you were young, and you and your family were taking a driving vacation through the sticks to visit your cousins who lived several boring states away. Along the side of the road there would be the occasional rock shop with tables under the trees of brightly colored gems and minerals.

You and your sisters clamored in such a shrill manner that your defeated father pulled over. You all got out to behold the wonderful natural treasures: beautiful crystals, smooth river rocks, stalactites, copper ore, fool's gold, petrified wood, and fossils. There would be lots of garishly colored pieces of what looked like glass, but was actually slag, a byproduct of the iron ore smelting process.

In a box in the corner were a bunch of curiously round rocks that were fairly unremarkable on the surface. Some of them had been sawed in half, revealing beautiful, delicate, naturally occurring, crystal formations within. These are *geodes*. We called them "Arkansas baseballs."

The rocks that came up in San Leon resembled geodes, although they were smaller and egg-shaped. They were surely fossilized something. What could they be? What if they were dinosaur eggs? Could I get my picture in the paper? Would the Smithsonian Institution send out a team of geologists to excavate what would later prove to be the greatest fossil discovery of recent times? Could I become famous and be asked to go on a lecture tour as Mark Twain did in the late 1800s, as chronicled in the book *Following the Equator*?

Whether they actually were dinosaur eggs or not, maybe I could market and sell these curious rocks as such. I could make a fortune! I'm not sure my brain works like everyone else's. It certainly takes me down some bizarre paths!

• • •

Steve dug holes for pilings with the auger at each string intersection of the grid pattern. Each piling went into the ground four feet and protruded up in the air four feet. We straightened up each piling, using a level, and backfilled the holes with cement. In our area, you can just pour dry cement into a hole around a piling and go away. There is enough moisture in the ground to cause the cement to harden. No additional water need be added. Interesting!

And thus the pilings were all set very straight, square, and true. I thanked Steve & Co. and they left at day's end. I went back to the K1, Base Camp, to sit in my dilapidated chair at my warped table underneath my scrawny tree. I was all alone. I was tired and muddy. I looked around me at the mud and piles of brush and trash. I was happy, sitting amid all of this squalor. I saw not piles of trash and mud, but beauty. I turned my gaze to the field of new pilings and was pleased. I gathered up my tools, got in the car, and headed home to the boat where Paco would be yelling for his dinner.

"Pilings"

Chapter 8
Onward Through the Fog

"Be like two fried eggs and keep your sunny side up."

The next morning I was up early, having coffee on the boat and making lists. I realized it was time to think about electricity, for I would be needing to run power tools in the near future. I contacted the electric company and arranged for a pole to be installed.

I also needed a legitimate street address. I couldn't very well just call the lumber company and say, "Deliver it to the Oleanders in San Leon, please." I didn't know what authority supplied street numbers to new buildings: i.e., county, city, someone else. The answer was, at least in this area, the electric company. They set me up for electrical service and assigned the address. This I painted on a piece of wood and nailed it to a tree. Yes, a real class operation.

The electric company came and installed a T-pole, or temporary pole, and ran electric wires to it, which connected me to the grid. It was fitted with a meter and would supply me power during the construction process. Later on, this would be converted over to permanent electrical service.

The next thing I needed to do was to rig some electrical outlets on the pole. They would be mounted in a box containing a circuit breaker and a main switch for safety. This dangerous job called for an electrician. One of my boat neighbors, Wayne, was an electrical engineer so I called him for help. Money and beer changed hands, and soon I had my outlets. Why couldn't everything be this simple? From the pole would run a network of extension cords that I could use to power fans, lights, tools, hair dryers, makeup mirrors, espresso machines, blenders, George Foreman Grills, waffle makers, and the like.

At the same time, I figured I'd better see what official paperwork needed to be filed, and with whom, lest I commit some unknown bureaucratic building infraction and have to go to jail. This paperwork turned out to be a building permit. Back to my sage.

"Sage," I began. "You are a knower of many things. How/what/where/when do I get a building permit?"

Bob frowned at me. "You were supposed to have that before you started building," he replied.

Great.

"You take a copy of your house plans to the county. They review your plans and issue you a building permit. This allows construction to be in progress should anyone from the county drive by to check. No building permit, no building. If someone drives by and you're building without a building permit posted, you're in trouble."

He continued, " I'm going to the Galveston County offices this Thursday. Give me a copy of your plans, and I'll file for a building permit for you."

I took my sage up on this offer. Bob, in turn, honored his offer, and you guessed it, alcohol changed hands. It was a done deal, and I didn't have to go to jail. I received the permit, which was nailed to the temporary electrical pole for all to see.

Before I got much further, I realized I'd better start thinking about water and sewer. Like everything else, I had lots of questions about this process, but a call to San Leon Municipal Utilities District got answers. It was easy. Sign up for water and sewer service, and they do the rest. Oh yes, pay first. All I had to do was to put identifying stakes by the street as markers for where the water meter and the sewer line should be placed. The county would provide the utilities to the edge of my property; it was up to me to get them to the house.

I elected to run the sewer line down one side of the drive and the water line down the other. I put my stakes out, and in a day or two a backhoe arrived from the county. They had consulted the county maps beforehand and knew where the nearest water and sewer lines were located to tap off of. It wasn't far away, just to the corner. The backhoe made quick work of digging the ditch from the corner to my stakes.

The new water and sewer line spurs were constructed of PVC. Their installation went quickly and included a water meter, which was placed by the street.

Something told me that it would be a good idea to run these lines to the house site before building anything else. Still sore from digging the drainage ditches, I opted to let the construction loan pay for some labor to help me with this.

There was a little convenience store I knew of not far away called the Quik Pak where men looking for work congregated. The next morning I was there at six thirty to find someone to help me. There was a group of maybe twenty people who came over and surrounded my car, clamoring for me to choose them. Definitely a buyer's market. Most were of other ethnicities and I must say, honestly, that I felt a trace of fear for a moment—human nature being what it is.

This almost instinctive reaction was unfounded and uncalled for, and afterward I felt ashamed. Looking back, I imagine that the instant of fear I experienced, when extrapolated to cover an entire race or nationality, has something to do with how wars get started. I was reminded of some valuable life lessons I had learned from playing music long ago, in South Dallas.

South Dallas

During the time I attended music school I was steeped in a rich broth of esoteric music. The music curriculum included theory, composition, arranging, and history, in addition to piano lessons taught by some of the most proficient faculty in the country.

No rock music here. Not much country and western or pop music, either. We're talking classical and jazz. I have always liked a wide array of music: rock, pop, blues, swing, and country. In music school, the music I gravitated toward was *jazz/funk/fusion,* a blending of genres that is often shortened to just *funk.*

Funk is characterized by cutting edge jazz. In it is much opportunity for improvisation, which good musicians creatively supply. A high level of technical musical knowledge and proficiency on the instrument are required to play it. It is interesting, melodically and rhythmically. It is also very lively and infectious.

Perhaps the best thing about funk is the soul element, which is both strong and ubiquitous. That is what initially attracted me to it. The songs weren't merely performed; they were *delivered,* with great expression and feeling. This music was *real!* I began seeking out like-minded musicians to play funk. This continued after graduation as well. My quest led me to South Dallas.

South Dallas was a rough part of town. It seemed to be in the news more than other parts of town in various, unflattering ways that involved prostitution stings or foiled drug deals. The economy there was depressed and the population was predominantly black. There had been black families where I grew up in Arkansas, and Fayetteville was supposedly integrated. Still, the white and black communities there coexisted in parallel universes in many ways.

This was little understood by me in grade school. Prejudice and segregation were not taught to me at school or at home, but those elements did exist to a lesser or greater extent. I'm not proud of this heritage.

This was also true for Dallas. There, several of the so-called "black communities" were seen as crowded, dirty, run-down, and dangerous. South Dallas was definitely less desirable real estate. The perception was that if you were white, South Dallas wasn't a place to go after dark if you wanted to stay healthy.

I got a tip from a musician friend of mine about a club in this part of town where an extremely good band played funk. This warranted investigation! They were playing the next Friday night, and my friend and I decided to go check it out. The fact that this friend was white gave me a sense of security. We found the club, which was seedy and run down. We parked and went in, feeling conspicuous. Me and my friend, and maybe one or two others, were the only white people in the whole place, which was crowded.

The band was already playing. They were good, and I liked them immediately. Every song they played was extremely funky. It was soul with a capital "S." And it was so … well, *ethnic*. I loved it!

The musicians were wonderful, but I knew they were not privy to the music education I had just completed. They had learned to play in the school of hard knocks. It doesn't matter how or where one learns to play. Many of the very best names in music never went to music school. The players I heard that night had learned to play somewhere, and they played well. The music was honest, gritty and soulful. I hung on every note.

I was content to sit and just listen, but when I was asked to sit in, I jumped at the chance. I sat down behind the keyboard and waited to find out what the first song would be. It was *Mister Magic*, a funk standard that I was well familiar with. My fingers knew what to do, and I found plenty to contribute. I felt right at home. I played three or four songs with the band, enjoying every minute. I stayed at the club until the end and wasn't ready to leave when it was over.

The next few days I couldn't stop thinking about my wonderful discovery. What a treasure! I had never suspected Dallas concealed such a rich and vibrant musical vein and that I had known nothing about it. I felt lucky to have found it. I began going there whenever I could.

One day I heard that there was another club in the same neighborhood called the Golden Slipper that also had a band that played funk. Lo and behold, they were looking for a keyboard player. I went there to listen and perhaps sit in. They were even better than the first band!

Fronting the band was a pretty, petite singer named Cynthia. Her brother Tommy played drums. Rounding out the band was Benois on guitar, Ricky on bass and Richard on saxophone. Tommy's drumming was complex, with interwoven jazz rhythms thrown in everywhere. Benois had evidently played jazz before and a lot of it. His playing was legendary.

Ricky was just about as funky as you could get. Richard was a large and imposing figure. Intimidating, even. If I was alone on some dark street in South Dallas and ran into Richard and didn't know him, I would have started running. Every single note that came out of his horn was passionate and full of feeling. His tough persona belied his gentle nature. I felt very lucky when I was asked to play piano with this group, and we all soon became great friends. The band was called *Just Us*.

Just Us played three nights a week at the Golden Slipper. Despite its run down appearance, it turned out to be a fun place to play and a great gathering spot. Its owner was a high school principal named Ernest. The people that went there were diverse. There were no hookers, felons, or drug dealers, at least as far as I could tell. There were lawyers, schoolteachers, and accountants. Respectable people from all walks of life…just not the *white* walks of life!

The ages of the people ranged from twenty-something to sixty-something. Some there really were the black counterparts of my own parents. Everyone was warm and friendly. Each evening, we laughed and talked together, and I made some great friends. Whether or not I realized it on the first night, I had nothing to fear by being there. Gradually, I lost my uneasiness about being in South Dallas. The first few times I went to the Golden Slipper, I removed everything from my car I didn't need, and I took all but a few bills out of my wallet. This precaution was needless. As Richard told me after I had been in the band for several months, "Nobody was going to mess with you. No one in the band or in the audience was going to *let* anyone else mess with you."

In fact, there was no trouble there at all. I never saw so much as one person raise an angry voice or shove anyone in the entire year that I played there. Yet, I occasionally played in nicer parts of town where brawls and other unseemly behavior would occur.

I started talking about South Dallas with my other white musician friends. Like me, nobody had ever heard of the band or the club. Word spread, and soon, the best musicians in town were standing in line to sit in with us! They were getting the same excitement as I was out of it.

Even in music, a field you would think was color-blind, I found segregation and unequal opportunity. The reality was that the musicians of South Dallas didn't have the same opportunities available to them that I enjoyed. They seldom got called to play the better jobs in the nicer parts of town, but I did. It was unfair. I resolved to make a difference whenever I could. Every time I saw an opportunity to help my deserving friends out with a lucrative engagement or a quality reference, I took it.

Any reservations I had about people with different colored skin than me was thoroughly scotched by South Dallas. Because of this experience, there is not a prejudiced bone in my body. Even if South Dallas *was* crowded, dirty, run-down and dangerous, it wasn't a skin color issue. I suspected political and economic factors that were unkind, unfair, unfortunate and undeserved.

I spent a wonderful year playing with *Just Us* at the Golden Slipper. We remained friends for long after. I wouldn't trade that experience for anything. It was invaluable to my playing. I learned the notes in music school, but I learned how to play with *feeling* in South Dallas. This is something that can't be learned from any book. The lessons I learned there went with me from then on. They are still with me. Today, I still listen to a wide array of musical styles. I love classical music. I love straight ahead jazz and be-bop. I love old Beatles songs and early 70s rock and roll. I love Jimmy Buffett and tropical music. I like country and western music, too. But funk remains my favorite.

. . .

Just like in South Dallas, I realized that day at the Quik Pak that I had nothing to fear. The people there were human beings, just like me. They had wants and needs just like me. They wanted only jobs. They were willing to work hard and only asked a fair wage in return.

I selected two energetic guys. We negotiated a fair hourly rate and off we went to San Leon. Jose spoke a little broken English; Hernando spoke not one word of English. I spoke only very crude, broken Spanish, probably about at the preschool level. This made for an interesting day of it, but despite the language barrier, we got along very well.

We drove to the Oleanders. I showed Jose and Hernando the string I had placed to mark where the ditches for the water and sewer were to run. We got three shovels and went immediately to work. Jose and Hernando were hard workers and pleasant company. Just ordinary guys. Here and there, we found a little common ground we could use to cross the language barrier. I learned the Spanish words for work, ants, and mosquitoes. Jose and Hernando learned English names for T-bone steak and a little English slang for beautiful women. It was when I put a Santana CD in the CD player that our friendship was cemented forever.

We worked hard. I shared my Pop-Tarts for our breakfast, and we took frequent water breaks. At noon we went to the Parkit Markit to get food for lunch. We dug so fast that we were finished with the ditches by mid-afternoon. I drove them back home and we parted friends. From that day forward, any time I needed a little extra help for this or that job, I had no problems with going back to the Quik-Pak. I never had a bad experience with it.

After saying good-bye to Jose and Hernando, I still had some time left, so I went to the local do-it-yourself store, whose floor was so large it needed it's own zip code, to look at plumbing supplies. I had been talking to people to find out about plumbing. What type of pipe to use, what the considerations were when routing pipe, and, well, everything.

Chris (you will remember Chris, the callow youth who I played the cheap boat trick on) had a friend who was a journeyman plumber, Justin. Justin was in some ways similar to Chris—twenty-something, enthusiastic, and instantly likeable. He had a young family to support and needed some money. I was more than happy to help him out.

Justin became my plumbing consultant. We met at the Oleanders one evening and he spent an hour and a half teaching me all about plumbing. I left there with a shopping list of pipes, connectors, and other things I'd need. There was much discussion on what kind of pipes to use. Like many things in life, there were several choices and each had its advantages and disadvantages. After weighing the evidence, I decided upon PVC.

PVC was something I had experience with. For it was out of PVC that the biggest and most beautiful decorations in the entire Clear Lake Boat Parade were made.

Boat Parades

Sometime after moving to Clear Lake from Dallas, I found out that there was a big Christmas boat parade every year. *Boat Parade?* The notion sounded like so much fun that I signed up for it immediately, and waited impatiently for December. I asked some of my Dallas friends to come help decorate the boat and be the crew, an offer that was enthusiastically accepted. December arrived and the Dallas crew came down. To decorate the boat, we strung some lights up to the masthead on Mañana and brought them down and attached them to the lifelines all around the boat, to resemble a lit Christmas tree. We used a small generator to power it. When the decorating was finished, we could hardly wait for the sun to go down. When it did, we powered the lights up. Mañana never looked more beautiful!

We motored to the starting point, all full of joy and expectation. There were good friends, good food, and strong drink aboard. Alas, when we got there and the other boats fired up *their* decorations, I have to tell you that we were sadly out-gunned! Many of the other boats had obviously been in the parade before. This wasn't their first rodeo! The big and beautiful creations that people had fabricated were astonishing. We gasped at the magnificent displays of Christmas beauty, but we were not the least bit ashamed of our own valiant effort.

There were all kinds of boats, large and small, sail and power. When the parade set off across the lake, it was a beautiful sight to behold. This boat parade was one of the largest in the country. There were hundreds of spectator boats anchored in Clear Lake to watch it. I'll never forget the sight of all of those sailboat masts, with their masthead lights on. In the darkness, it looked, for all the world like a Mediterranean village all built up on a hillside, with the lights of houses twinkling—absolutely beautiful. The aroma of people cooking out and the sounds of Christmas merriment were in the air. It was one of the most "Christmas-y" things I've ever done.

Even if our decorations couldn't compete in this league, we had a secret weapon that nobody else had: me, dressed in an angel get-up, complete with wings and a halo, out on the front of Mañana with my trusty five-dollar baritone, playing Christmas carols.

There were not hundreds, but *thousands* of people lining the parade route on the shores of the lake. When we'd get to a large crowd, I'd rear back and blast *Joy to the World*, and let me tell you, it was every bit joyous!

We didn't win any prizes that first year, but I assure you that *nobody* had more fun that night than we did. I got what I wanted. Just being in it was all that I desired. Now I was educated about Christmas Boat Parades.

The following year I was ready. We made a giant Christmas tree in my driveway and hung a huge assortment of illuminated

Christmas decorations in it to make a very beautiful and impressive decoration for the boat. We did much better in the parade, getting a first place in our sailboat size range, but I wanted more. I wanted to work with a bigger boat and create even bigger decorations. Mañana was too small.

I had just joined a large local boating club. One day I approached the club's governing committee and offered my services to spearhead an entry for the club in the next Christmas boat parade. If the owner of one of the larger boats in the club would volunteer his craft, and if the club would provide a budget and manpower, I would be the organizer. The club thought this was a wonderful idea. A boat was quickly volunteered (or perhaps commandeered, I don't remember) and over the next few weeks I started investigating designs and building methods. All of those fantastic creations we had seen were made of just ordinary materials like chicken wire, nylon, cable ties… and PVC.

That next parade, we came up with a great design: a thirty-foot-tall angel, lit with many, many lights. The angel featured a PVC frame. That decoration was very beautiful, and we did in fact get the award for the "Most Beautiful" boat in the parade.

We went on to be in the Christmas boat parades for the next several years. Each time we completely changed our decorations and refined our building methods. We got better and better, and our decorations put us in the winner's circle several times.

Some of our designs were very ambitions. One year we designed a Mississippi River paddleboat, complete with smokestacks belching red and green smoke; giant, turning, sixteen-foot, PVC paddle wheels on each side; and a live Dixieland band on the front. Another year, we designed a working Ferris wheel, my personal favorite. Each year I got what I wanted. Award or no award, I got to help create some of the biggest and most beautifully decorated boats in the parade.

• • •

Who would have thought that being in Christmas boat parades would help me build a house? PVC pipe is PVC pipe, whether you're using it to put up thirty-foot Christmas decorations or routing water through it. I had become a PVC expert.

I began my plumbing project with the sewer line. First, I laid the PVC pipe sections down in the ditch that we had dug. I used PVC cement to glue the pipes together and used my new carpenter's level to achieve a good, even, downward slope from the house to the street. I installed a clean-out cap, and stopped. One step closer to a bathroom! This would be a celebrated amenity. St. Louis, the field latrine, remained as a clearing within the last remaining stand of thick brush I had thoughtfully left growing around it. It was within this leafy glen that one went to "ponder." It was becoming odiferous!

The PVC water line was even easier to install. It was smaller pipe, and there was no incline to worry about. Its ditch did not have to be as deep, either. I installed two hose taps only—one by the street for watering gardens and one by the house to use for cleanup. I completed my connections and turned on the taps for the first time. I felt a great sense of accomplishment to see water gushing out of them. Another major thing off the list, another creature comfort added. Again I was struck by some of the really big things we take for granted. That is, take for granted…unless the thing is missing.

Gardens, you say? Yes, and I was going to start one right away, since I had a way to water it. As far as I am concerned, homegrown tomatoes are a rare and coveted commodity. I have been known to pay large sums for them. I wasn't about to miss a season for planting some; just because I was too busy building a house. However, I didn't spend a lot of time on it. I nailed together four boards to resemble a ten-foot square sandbox and filled it with dirt. This was planted with tomatoes. Did you know that it's almost impossible to think bad thoughts while eating a homegrown tomato?

It was late spring by then. I was feeling good about the house being underway at last. All I was doing these days was going to work and then spending every spare minute with building-related matters. Oh, all right, the tomato patch was not building related, but I was still plenty busy researching building materials and techniques, and asking questions. Right then, out of the blue, I got laid off from my job. Along with Chris and Darwin. Not for being bad boys, although we probably deserved it. The real reason was a "business cycle contraction." At first, I felt insecure. However, after the initial shock wore off, I began to see this event as not devastating at all. I was, in fact, lucky that it happened that way. I had been able to show employment during the loan approval process. What would have happened if I had gotten laid off before I had my construction loan?

Prior to the layoff, I had been planning to work on the house on weekends, weeknights, and days off until it was done. In hindsight, that was unrealistic. Even without working a regular job, the house ended up taking over a year to build, and it was not even a very big house.

There are many ways to build a house: quick ways, easy ways, cheap ways, expensive ways, prudent ways, imprudent ways. Right ways and wrong ways. I wanted the house to turn out well, and that meant spending a lot of time to find out how to do things the right way. I also found that, when I got into the actual building process, it took me much longer to do things than it would an experienced carpenter. It turned out to be a good thing that I wasn't working. I decided not to worry about my next job...until later.

Chapter 9
Oleander Construction, LLP

Oleander Zen: "Never run through a screen door. You might strain yourself."

It is a new day. The pilings are in place. There is a gravel driveway to allow trucks in. There is electricity, sewer, and water. Now, I can run power tools and water my tomatoes. Dinosaur egg sales are down, I'm sorry to report. As we saw in the preceding chapter, the archaeological survey failed to turn up any evidence of Indians.

To revisit a subject I'm sure you wish I'd left behind, I love archaeology. I was an avid arrowhead collector as a boy. In fact, I found the most perfect little bird point I have ever found—not quite an inch long—right in our front yard. Growing up in the Ozark Mountains, you could find arrowheads in any direction you cared to go outside of town. The hunting was particularly good in the spring after the farmers plowed their fields and right after a rain.

Across the street from our house in Arkansas was a spring, complete with a little stone springhouse. Grandmother had told us stories of how gypsies used to camp around it in the olden days. It was easy to imagine that. It was also easy to imagine that the whole area, including our yard, being the site of an Indian village before that.

There was a low mound in one corner of our yard, just across the street from the spring. It was evenly round, about ten feet in diameter, and rose up about two feet from the surrounding ground. It caught my eye because it didn't look like it belonged there. I thought there was a good chance that it was an Indian mound, maybe even a burial site. One day, I decided to find out. I was walking toward it with a shovel when my mother happened to glance out the window. Fearful for the yard, she came outside to ask me what I was doing. When I told her, she exclaimed, "That's no Indian mound! That was your great-grandmother's rose garden."

Ha! Mother was relieved that she had intercepted me before I dug up the yard, and I was disappointed that it had not been something more exciting. At least I had not done a lot of digging for nothing.

One other afternoon when I was around twelve, I was chasing my cousin Clayton with a stick around his yard when I happened to look down. There, staring right up at me…was an arrowhead. I stopped dead in my tracks and picked it up. Immediately underneath was another one…and then another, and another. The chase was forgotten. We got some shovels and started to dig. The arrowheads just kept appearing! Never had I seen a cache like this. Why were they there? How long had they been there? My cousins lived just one block away from us. This part of town wasn't exactly rural; I would characterize it as older residential. Why hadn't these arrowheads been discovered before then? We dug until dark. We recovered maybe a couple of hundred arrowheads, mostly broken. Could we have found an old Indian trash heap? I was so excited I couldn't sleep that night. What a great mystery! Finding an occasional arrowhead was plenty exciting enough, but to find so many of them, right together? How could we find out how they got there? Would we ever be able to learn the real story?

My mother knew the chairman of the archaeology department at the University of Arkansas Museum. She gave him a call and told him about our discovery. Dr. McGimsey was very interested and asked to see me. Here was somebody who could help. A few days later, I walked to the university after school to meet him. He recorded all of the details of our find, and registered it as a newly-discovered archaeological site with the museum's archaeological department. Clayton and I kept digging and kept finding arrowheads, but then the concentration of arrowheads suddenly and mysteriously played out. Beyond a certain area we found no more. This puzzled us. We enlarged the hole, and the yard began to take on the appearance of a construction site. Nary another arrowhead did we find, until…a few yards away, we again hit pay dirt. It was another cache of arrowheads. This gave us renewed energy. Like the first batch, they were mostly broken as well. We recovered another couple of hundred arrowheads, and then this cache also ended abruptly. The mystery was compounded.

By then, Aunt Patsy had several sizable foxholes in her yard. If she was upset about this, she kept quiet, surrendering it over to the exuberance of youth.

My mother contacted the local paper, the *Northwest Arkansas Times*. They wanted to send a reporter out to write an article. I was quite certain we were making history. In the meantime, Dr. McGimsey called back. He had done some research and was able to tell from the shapes and styles of the arrowheads the time period they were apt to have come from: around 2,000 BC.

This was so amazing to me; it still is:

I see an arrowhead on the ground. It was made by a human being just like me, but long ago. It was probably part of an arrow that was used against game, a dangerous wild animal, or another human being. Maybe it missed its target and became lost in the brush.

There it lay, year after year. The shaft rotted away soon afterward, but the stone point lay there in the same spot, for hundreds or *thousands* of years—until I, a young boy, happen to come along and find it. I am likely the first human being to gaze upon it in all that time.

I pick it up and hold it. It is back in the hand of a human being for the first time since it was made, so long ago.

That has deep meaning to me. It is the closing of a great circle. It happened right there in front of me. It is almost spiritual, this remarkable chain of events, this link to the past. The arrowheads that I have found among the hills and streams of Arkansas are among my most prized possessions.

What happened next unraveled the mystery of these new arrowheads and vaporized all of my expectations, all in one fell swoop. Aunt Patsy had contacted the previous owner of their house and told him what we had found. He became amused and informed her that *he* had buried the arrowheads there himself. Also a collector, he had found the arrowheads in and around the valleys of the White River. He had culled the broken pieces out of his collection and buried them in his yard several years prior so that some young boy might experience the thrill of discovery some day. *Oh no!*

When I heard this devastating news, I was completely shattered. Some great archaeological treasure indeed. I was thoroughly crushed. The arrowheads were indeed authentic, but that didn't do much to make me feel better.

The newspaper reporter was scheduled to come out the next day. Great. The reporter knocked on our door after I had come home from school, and my mother let him in. I was so embarrassed I barely said hello and then slunk away, leaving the job of explaining to my mother. The reporter, upon finding out that there was no story after all, and no doubt needing material for the next issue, took some photos of my sisters catching snowflakes in the yard with their tongues, which ran in the next day's paper. I even missed that. Oh, the unfairness of it all!

It was over. No glory. No fame. Only humiliation. It had all been much flap about nothing. Aunt Patsy made our excavation into a flowerbed; I carefully boxed my arrowheads and added them to my collection in the basement, and things got back to normal.

Another aunt, who lived in New York where you can find anything you want, located a company there that would make up faux newspapers with any story you wanted, printed on the front page. Except for the headlines that you supplied, they looked just like real, ordinary newspapers. Aunt Earlene had some printed up with two-inch tall headlines that screamed:

Schoolboy Discovers Arrowheads from 2000 BC

She sent them to me. Everyone else thought this was hilarious, but I was still disgusted from the way it had all ended up and couldn't appreciate the humor in the situation…until much later.

Oleander Enterprises

Back to business. The company is named *Oleander Construction, LLP.* Under this umbrella falls an array of wholly owned subsidiaries with the following DBAs:

- Oleander Plumbing

- Oleander Landscaping

- Oleander Roofing

- Oleander Framing

- Oleander Electrical

The company was formed for the sole purpose of building up to, but not to exceed, two houses. Upon completion, the company will then, more than likely, be dissolved, followed by the retirement of the head of the company, which happens to be me, the Managing Operator of Operations Management.

The next order of business for Oleander Construction was to cut off all of the pilings level, in preparation for bolting on the sills, or floor beams. My friend Darwin came out with his laser sight. We set it up at the post where I had marked the elevation. We beamed the laser onto each piling and made a line. After all of the pilings were cut off at this line, they would be exactly the same height.

For this, I purchased a chainsaw. Piano players have no business operating power saws of any kind, particularly chainsaws. When you press the trigger on a chainsaw, it saws, and it doesn't care what's in its path, be it a tree limb, an eight-inch piling, or your leg. With much fear and trepidation, I progressed through the field of pilings, chainsaw snarling, and cut them all off. When I was through, thirty-two midget pilings stood at attention. All digits and appendages were intact. I soon learned that my accuracy with a chainsaw left something to be desired. That was okay; the cut tops didn't have to be all that straight, as nothing would be resting on them. Luckily. Rather, the floor beams would rest in notches I would have to cut into the sides of each piling.

I used a skill saw to notch the pilings, or, in my hands, perhaps, an "unskilled" saw. These cuts did have to be straight, but alas, some of them were not very. Darwin was out helping me again, and I fretted aloud about the cuts.

"Relax," said Darwin. "We'll fix the crooked ones with shims."

A venerable and ubiquitous part of any construction site is the shim. I'll bet even the Sistine Chapel was built with them. They would save my house too, lest it resemble the Leaning Tower of Pisa. Shims placed in the bottoms of the notches that were crooked would restore my foundation to level. I would once again be able to hold my head high among carpenters. We cut several wedges out of scrap wood to be used for shims.

We began attaching the sills, which were two-inch by twelve-inch by twelve-foot boards. They rested on their edges in the notches I had cut into the pilings. We shimmed as necessary as we went, to ensure a level foundation.

I had never paid much attention to the concept of level, but now I was becoming obsessed with it. How embarrassing would it be for some friend, a pretty girl even, to walk into my finished house and step upon a floor that sloped drastically toward one corner? The pretty girl would most likely laugh at me and go away, still laughing. I hate it when that happens!

With this fear goading me on, I checked the sills often for level. I used a string level, which works like a normal level in that it has a liquid-filled tube containing a bubble. It is smaller than a normal level and designed to be hung on a string. To use one, you stretch a string tightly between two points you want to check for level, say, two floor sills. Then, hang your string level on the string. Hold your breath and check to see if the bubble is centered. Is it? Sweet! No? Shim the low side up until it is.

I attached the sills on the two long sides of the house and checked for level. Then I attached the inner rows of sills and checked for level again. I began using my string level incessantly. Along the length and width, diagonally, along each row of sills, everywhere I could think of. Wherever I found low spots, I corrected with shims. I spent a ridiculously long time with this. I can get so hung up on details that I get sidetracked. You have to keep your eyes on the prize.

I attached the sills with big nails at first, and when I was finally happy with the level, I went back and through-bolted them in place with big galvanized nuts, bolts, and washers. The tool that was the best suited for tightening the big bolts was the oldest, most worn tool in my toolbox. It had been my grandfather's.

Grandpa's Hands

Grandpa had everything in his basement. If there wasn't one of what you needed there, you probably didn't need it after all. Grandpa and Grandma lived next door to us when I was young and they were in their autumn years. They were loving grandparents, but they were not afraid to administer a little tough love when the need arose.

Under their gentle guidance, we kids were the better off. Grandpa loved boats and water and would regale us for hours with stories of his many adventures. With his wooden leg and gruff, gravelly voice, he was every inch the pirate in my six-year-old eyes.

Grandpa's basement was an endlessly fascinating place. It was full of hiding places, treasures, and mysteries. It was a scary place if you were very young and there at night. Grandpa always had something interesting going on in the basement. I liked to go over and sit and watch him work at his workbench. This was likely the very first inspiration that led to me building a house.

After Grandpa and Grandma were gone, we kids went through the house to get whatever keepsakes we wanted to remind us of them. I wound up with Grandpa's handmade wooden toolbox and old-fashioned tools. One tool in particular was a heavy pipe wrench with a wooden handle; worn shiny from years of use. Building the house, this tool had an uncanny way of being exactly the right tool for the job in many instances, starting with the floor sills on which I was then working. I named this wrench "Grandpa."

When newer and more expensive tools were the wrong size, or when they broke the very first time I tried to use them, I'd go get Grandpa, usually the tool I should have started out with in the first place. This tool was indestructible. It not only survived the entire building process, it is still in my toolbox, waiting for the next chance to be of service. It makes me think of Grandpa every time I use it. Thanks, Grandpa!

• • •

Once the sills were all in place and bolted, it was time for the floor joists. These were the boards that rest on top of the sills and support the actual floor. The next morning, I was greeted by a pile of lumber that had arrived for that purpose. Alas, the boards were not all milled to the exact dimensions. This threatened the level of my floor again. What could fix this?

"Ah," you say, "Shims?"

You are quite correct. The obsession was back. I had a fear that when the house was finished, someone would come to visit and maliciously drop a marble onto my floor and laugh cruelly as it rolled downhill toward the nearest wall. Snippets of the old nursery rhyme tormented me:

"There was once a little man in a crooked little house ..."

I forcibly ejected this fear from my mind, and started grabbing boards and nailing them. Soon, there was a song in my heart. While I banged floor joists together, the wild parrots flew back and forth overhead, screeching, on their way to some important parrot business.

Yes, wild parrots live in the area—just another tropical serendipity to complete the picture. They are beautiful and I am glad to have them. Their happy racket comforts me. Perhaps later I could build them a nesting platform, but what could I do to get them to stop sooner? *Aha*, a bird feeder. I would have to pick one up.

And this thought crossed my mind again as I slid gratefully into bed that night after a long, hot day of work. Time to close my eyes and donate the day to history.

"Wild Parrots on Bird Feeder"

A Small Mind at Large

I was starting to amass a respectable collection of tools. Among them was my hammer. Recall from your world history class that the hammer was originally employed as a weapon of war. I used it for the destruction of what had once been expensive building materials.

Hark: right next to it was my carpenter's knife. I used this tool every day. It was good for opening and slicing through the contents of cardboard cartons that came in the mail, particularly the one my new leather jacket had just arrived in.

Then there were my screwdrivers. The straight one was for opening paint cans. As the name implies, the Phillips screwdriver was for stripping out the heads of Phillips screws.

There was also my electric hand drill. I had used it for so many jobs I was surprised it still worked. I bought a wire wheel attachment for it. One of its many capabilities was removing hard-earned guitar calluses.

I had several types of pliers by that time. The vice grips were my favorites. They crushed anything they came in contact with.

Hanging on a nail above the toolbox was my hacksaw. Hacksaws transform human energy into a crooked, unpredictable motion. The more you attempt to influence its course, the more dismal it becomes. Another handy tool was my hose cutter. I used it for making hoses too short.

• • •

One Sunday night, a friend came over for dinner. I knew for a fact that she loved boats and water, and I also knew that she hadn't been on a boat at all in over a year. I had been so occupied with house building that I was ashamed how long it had been since Mañana had been out of her berth. I decided right then that dinner that evening would be "out there."

We cast off the dock lines and made our way out into the bay. It was a balmy Saturday evening. It was neither hot nor cold, and a welcome, gentle breeze made the sailing serene and delightful. We dropped anchor away from boat traffic and lit up the grill. I charcoaled thick, juicy, pork chops as the sun set. Hours later, as we were reluctantly returning after a perfect evening, I found myself thinking, *Now exactly why again was I building a house?*

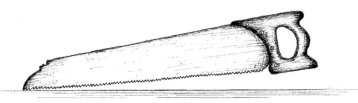

Chapter 10
Off and Running

"A pessimist sees the difficulty in every opportunity; an optimist sees the opportunity in every difficulty."

—*Winston Churchill*

Back at the Oleander Construction Zone, it was hot. Even the robins had to use potholders to get worms out of the ground! I carefully re-checked my floor joists for level. I found that the trueness of a particular joist depended on what was running through my mind at the time I was mounting it. These threads were often musical. Influencing factors included marveling at the impossible speed with which Oscar Peterson played *Autumn Leaves*, or the simple beauty of the Allman Brothers Band's song *Whippin' Post*. Extenuating circumstances affecting building quality included how tired I was, and whether I had just hit my thumb with the hammer.

As I stood there in the hot sun in my torn jeans with my tool belt around my waist and my sweaty T-shirt and dirty baseball cap, I paused for a moment. What a different life I now had! Just a few short years ago I had been on the road, playing with an Elvis Presley impersonator. Man, if I had been able to look into the future and see myself now.

Life with Elvis

When I graduated from college, I looked at several musical opportunities that came my way. One was a position with an Elvis Presley
impersonator as the musical director/arranger/ keyboardist. I decided to
audition for it. I accepted the position when it was offered to me, even
though I didn't know much about the Elvis repertoire. Rehearsals were
in progress to develop and polish a first-class show. Plans included tour-
ing the United States and Canada, with stints in Las Vegas. It sounded
great to this starry-eyed, restless kid, fresh out of college.

Boy was I in for a surprise. Elvis Presley had been deceased a
couple of years by this time, but he left an enormous legacy of music.
There were still a large number of fans who had by no means been
satiated before his untimely death, as I was to find out when we
started performing.

The Elvis repertoire was fun to play on the piano. Directing the
excellent band was even more fun, and the arranging I did of the
Elvis repertoire was challenging. I possess a natural musical gift
called perfect pitch, which allowed me to be a fast and accurate
musical arranger.

Elvis fans were not like any other group of people I had ever
encountered. About Elvis they were loyal, passionate, and reverent.
They were kind, good people, with big hearts, and knowledgeable
about anything having to do with Elvis Presley. When we performed, some of this devotion was transferred to our band. Elvis
fans came to our shows in force to hear us.

Our Elvis impersonator, Bobby, came across from the stage as he
was in real life: warm, sincere, friendly, funny, and compassionate.
He was always quick to emphasize that he was not trying to *be* Elvis
Presley, and meant in no way to be degrading or irreverent. Instead,
he made it clear that we were performing a respectful tribute to
Elvis. This made it easier for those who might have been offended
by the whole idea to enjoy us.

Bobby had a great voice. With a full band playing faithful rendi-tions of all of the favorite songs, he was wonderful. Although he didn't really look much like Elvis in real life, he was handsome. However, makeup, hair styling, wardrobe, and stage lighting all contributed to make for a realistic Elvis-like tribute. In full swing, the band deliv-ered electrifying performances that would have made Elvis proud. Playing from the stage, we saw firsthand the joy, laughter, and tears in multitudes of people that were reserved for the memory of Elvis Presley, but evoked, at least for the moment, by us.

Life on the road with this entourage was plenty of fun. There was a fan club for our band, and fans from home followed us all around the United States and Canada. Everywhere we went we made new fans and friends. It was a large, exciting, and close-knit camaraderie.

At one performance in Canada, some people heard us and fell in love with the band. They decided to do something to make us feel special— these poor, misplaced Texans, so far away from "home on the range." They invited the whole band over the next day for a chili dinner. What do you suppose these Canadians put in their chili? Besides the normal things, like beef and chili seasoning, it contained such ingredients as green peppers and mushrooms. It was thick and hearty and reminded me of spaghetti sauce. It was good, but it wasn't chili! Still, we appreciated the kindness that was shown us and ate every last bite. We smiled about Canadian chili for a long time afterward.

Later, when some of these same fans followed us back to Texas, we treated them to a dinner out at an old and venerable Mexican restaurant in the Fort Worth Stockyards where they prepare *right-eous* Mexican food. Our Canadian friends thought they had died and gone to heaven, and ate all they could hold.

Back on the road, security was necessary at some of the larger venues where we appeared. There were all sorts of shenanigans, such as girls claiming to be in our entourage or other deceptions to get the room number that "Elvis" was in. In some places we were on the local evening news when we hit town. I loved all of this hoopla. I had not been a particular Elvis fan when I hired on with the band, but at the end of a year I was, and still am. I had seen the magic, and knew what Elvis music could do for people. After the band had proved itself in many other parts of the country, our promoter decided we were ready for…Vegas, baby.

Vegas, Baby

Life in Las Vegas was interesting, to say the least. Las Vegas was a playground for the rich. There was always something exciting to do, even for the not rich, like me. There was lots of great entertainment, both big name and unknown. If you couldn't afford to go to the big shows, there were lots of lesser bands to enjoy. *Lesser* bands? This is a gross misnomer. The bands that played in the many casinos, lounges, and hotel lobbies of this city were first rate. They represented the finest musical talent from all across America. They had perfected stunning shows back home and had brought them to Las Vegas where only the strong survive. They had worked hard and sacrificed much to be there.

There were talent showcases held frequently in Las Vegas. This was an event in which several new bands from out of town gathered to play a free set and hopefully get hired to play somewhere in town. Showcases were usually held on an off night at one of the hotel lounge stages. The showcases were set up by talent agents and were attended by club owners, managers, promoters, and other industry personae. Ordinary people like you and I could go too, if we knew where and when the showcases were held.

Our band played in several showcases during the times we were in Las Vegas. It was good for business. It was the musical equivalent of networking. Whether performing at one or not, I liked going to them. The entertainment was excellent. The groups that were performing knew they were being seen by important people, and they delivered top-notch performances.

You might see a band from Lexington, Kentucky, for instance. Totally unknown to everyone in the room, they were there to break into…Vegas, baby. They would be dazzling. A few weeks later, you'd see their name up on a marquis somewhere. They'd made it; they had their foot in the door.

Even if you couldn't afford to go to the headline shows, you could go to the opening night dress rehearsals of the stars for free. If you saw that somebody well known was opening a three-month engagement at a certain casino, you could just show up that afternoon and sit quietly at the back. Chances are, the entire entourage would be there, performing sound checks or rehearsing. The star would be right in the middle of it, with no makeup and wearing sweats.

Then there were the TV show tapings, which seemed to always be in progress around Las Vegas. They too were free; you could just walk right in. It's a fun way to spend an afternoon if you've never done it.

When we were in Las Vegas, we typically played shows that started at ten o'clock and went until two o'clock in the morning. Occasionally, we played late shows, starting at midnight and going until four. Gradually, our schedules became completely inverted. That is, we'd go to bed at dawn and sleep all day. We got up with the six o'clock evening news, got dressed, ate, and were ready to perform again at ten o'clock. After the show, we'd go to a casino and play cards or go hear some other band. We'd wrap up our day with breakfast in the wee hours and then go to bed as the sun was rising.

Meals were very reasonable in Las Vegas. Most places were in competition to get customers inside, and they did it with incredible meal deals. One place would offer a surprisingly good steak dinner with all the trimmings for $4.49; another place would have king crab legs for $3.99. And *everyone* offered breakfasts for 99¢ —they were all over town.

I was rooming with our drummer in an apartment/hotel in downtown Las Vegas, which rented by the week. Nearby was a small casino called the Orbit Inn, where you could get prime rib, baked potato, and salad for under five dollars. We went there every night for a week. Ah, the folly of youth!

Just as with everywhere we went, we made friends with some of the locals (Vegans?) who we would hang out with—table dealers who worked where we were playing, and such. With them we found out where the locals went to have fun. We sometimes spent days off together, occasionally going to nearby Lake Mead for an afternoon of fun.

. . .

Those days seemed long ago and far away. I occasionally found myself reminiscing about them while I was working. I was working away one day and humming an Elvis song when I managed to hurt my back, putting a swift stop to work. It put me out of commission for a couple of days and served as a wakeup call that I'd better be *really* careful. Not willing to halt progress, I delivered myself to the Quik-Pak to get some help.

Carlos spoke no English, and the only Spanish I knew was from reading the labels of Tequila bottles. Through sounds that had no meaning in either language or crude sign language, I negotiated a deal that could be vaguely characterized as "various carpentry services rendered for the consideration of a nominal wage paid," and off we drove to San Leon. We both made attempts at deeper communication during the ride over to the Oleanders, which generally failed, until I happened to mention J. Lo, the lusty, Latin-American superstar. Instantly, we were both jabbering excitedly, each according to our own tongue, gesticulating wildly and understanding each other perfectly well!

Carlos worked like a Turk. Although I was hobbling around like a little old lady and couldn't really help him much, I could point and demonstrate what needed to be done. Carlos helped me for a couple more days until my back was better, and we got a good deal done. We got all the floor joists nailed on top of the floor sills.

"Floor Joists"

Building a house without a nail gun is slow, slow, slow. Therefore, I rounded up a nail gun and an air compressor. I have healthy amounts of respect for each of these. The air compressor was an ancient, rusty behemoth that clanked, clattered, and wheezed in a tortured manner. But it worked. I talked to it in a reassuring manner, oiled it daily, and pampered it.

The nail gun was an old, unwieldy, and unpredictable abomination. Despite my best efforts, only about half of the nails it fired went all the way into the wood. It also had a scary habit of misfiring into the stratosphere, sometimes even without my finger on the trigger. This it did one Saturday while I was nailing away. It suddenly shot a nail into thin air—and right into my hand! *Ouch!* Fortunately, the nail didn't go very deep and did no lasting harm, but it got my undivided attention. Do musicians have any business ever even touching a nail gun? I strongly doubt this. The nail gun went back to its owner the next day.

It's remarkable that every single person I talked to about nail guns had either hurt themselves with one, or knew someone who did. Add me to those statistics. And this happened even when I was being careful. Nail guns aren't tools, they're weapons. Perhaps they should be included in the "right to bear arms" clause. A person ought to be required to have a weapons permit to own one!

While I was worrying about nail guns, I heard about another tool called a palm nailer. A palm nailer is a small pneumatic device for driving nails. It fits in one hand. I did a little research and found that, although they are not as fast as nail guns, they're much safer. There's almost no way you can get hurt with one. To operate it, you merely hold a nail of any size in place against the board, set the palm nailer on the nail head and push slightly. This activates a rapid, repeating, woodpecker action to drive the nail into the wood. It does not split wood, very seldom bends nails, works with many different nail sizes, and can be used in small spaces.

Well! When I learned this, I took myself down to the local pawnshop, sort of a carpenter's tool mecca, and bought one. I loved my palm nailer almost more than life itself. It was *so* easy to use! I would happily have nailed up an entire subdivision with mine.

By then, I was pleased to note that I fit the criteria for being a carpenter in the following ways:

1. I had the best tan I'd had in years.

2. My language had gotten much worse.

3. I hung out at convenience stores.

4. I sometimes smelled bad.

5. I parked anywhere.

6. My car was full of tools. I look like Fred Sanford (from Sanford and Son on TV) coming down the road!

News Flash:

SAN LEON (AP) Oleander Construction Company, head-quartered in San Leon, Texas, has added a professional carpenter to its payroll, bringing the head count up to one full-time employee. Additional labor will be provided on an as needed basis. The firm's main project, currently, is to build a cabana-style home for a local San Leon resident.

Projections from Oleander Construction are to stand the walls in three days with the entire structure being framed, sided, and roofed within three weeks. The owners of Oleander Construction are pleased with the acquisition and forecast a dramatic rise in productivity in the current project.

• • •

It was true. A carpenter named Gilberto had been retained. His job was to prevent me from performing acts of dumbness, show me the best ways to do things, even though I already know them all, and provide muscle for the bigger jobs. Gilberto was a person with just the right temperament to take a clueless greenhorn, add a pile of lumber, and produce a house. Where did Gilberto come from? My sage, of course! Sages are wonderful entities. I think everybody ought to have one.

Gilberto was an amiable person who had been building houses most of his adult life. He was trained by his father—also a carpenter. Gilberto was organized, experienced, patient, and honest. The first time I mentioned carpenter, he corrected me with, "Not carpenter. *Carpentologist.*"

Okay, I got a comedian too, for the same money. Gilberto was also a musician. Uh-oh, trouble brewing! We struck a deal. Gilberto would begin work the very next Monday.

"We'll start laying the sub-flooring next week. You'd better use the weekend to finish up the plumbing under the house before we begin. Also, we're going to need someone to help us starting Monday," Gilberto said.

I had my work cut out for me. It took me all weekend to get the plumbing put in, with several calls to Justin along the way, but by Sunday evening I had it done.

The next morning, I arrived at the Oleanders early, accompanied by Emilio, procured from the Quik-Pak store. Soon, Gilberto arrived.

"How are you?" I asked, rising to shake his hand.

He looked around indignantly. "Where are the breakfast tacos? And kolaches? And donuts and coffee? I can't work unless I have these things waiting for me every day."

"Uh, yeah, I'll consider that," I said.

Gilberto and me were going to get along fine.

"Three weeks to get this house framed, sided, and roofed?" I asked Gilberto dubiously.

Gilbert glanced at me absently as he was unloading his truck. "It's only a little house. How long did you think it would take?"

I didn't know the answer to this question, but I knew one thing: without some building knowledge and experience it would take longer, and probably turn out badly to boot. I was glad to have Gilberto. His assured manner told me I had nothing to fear. The project was in good hands.

Gilberto inspected the floor joists and pronounced them ready for the sub-floor, or floor decking. This job consisted of cutting and nailing plywood sheets on top of the floor joists. On the subflooring would rest the walls, the finished floors—the whole house.

Soon, the air was filled with all the clamor of a construction zone—radio blasting rock music, skill saws whining, air compressors, and nail guns thwacking. It was obvious to even the most casual of observers that Oleander Construction was open for business, there were three rules to be adhered to by every person at any Oleander Construction job site:

a. Everybody works safe.

b. Nobody yells except to be heard.

c. All personnel leave the construction site with the same number of digits they arrived with.

When Gilberto got out his nail gun, I quelled the urge to turn around and run away. I needed to overcome this cowardice. After observing Gilberto nailing rapidly and with abandon, I decided there was no way around it. I grabbed Gilberto's other nail gun and started nailing. It was newer and safer than the one I had shot my hand with. Twenty nail clips later I was banging away, still intact, although each clip was dispensed with a measure of respect. The subflooring took thirty sheets of plywood. It was finished surprisingly quickly. When we were done, it looked like a stage. Stage, *Hmmm...*

"Floor Decking"

Heave Ho and Up She Rises

The walls were next. We were going up! To build a wall, studs were laid out on the floor (whoa, girls) in a rectangle that was the size and shape of the first wall of the house. More studs were laid out in a row in the middle of the rectangle, on sixteen-and-one-half-inch centers, (this is professional carpenter jargon, only professional carpenters are entitled to use it), and the whole assembly was nailed together.

When it was blessed by Gilberto, the three of us stood it up on the south edge of the house. This was accompanied by encouragement from me, in the form of "Heave ho and up she rises" and "All right you sow bellies, let's get that wall up!" in my best shrill Don Knotts' voice. While Emilio and I held the new wall steady, Gilberto put a level to it and nailed a couple of diagonal braces from the floor to the wall to hold it. The other three walls rose in this manner and were also braced by diagonal studs. When we were done, the four walls were nailed together at the corners. It was starting to look like a house!

"Heave Ho and Up She Rises"

Over the next three weeks, large orders of lumber and other supplies were placed and delivered on an almost daily basis. They all disappeared into the structure that was rising out of the Texas coastal prairie. The driver from the lumber company, Tiny, became a friend and fan. He followed our project closely. Each time he made a delivery, he got out of the truck and walked around to check our progress.

He cheered us on whenever we finished another significant piece of the construction.

Others were beginning to sit up and take notice as well. Every now and then, some acquaintance would drive to San Leon to inspect the house. The curious included sailors, Hoagie Ranchers, and musicians. Some were amazed, others were amused. I doubt if any were impressed! It was fun to see them, and their dropping by afforded us occasional short breaks that were welcomed.

"I didn't know you could build a house," they'd say.

"I didn't either!" would be my reply.

Sometimes a friend would show up with a tool belt and say, "Put me to work." This I did readily, and we'd spend the next few pleasurable hours working together. The unexpected help was appreciated and their friendship and camaraderie was great for my morale. I'd always try to find some way to show my appreciation, like buy dinner when we were done.

The next thing for us to build was two large beams, twenty-two feet long, which would pin the two long sides of the house together. These beams allowed for the big unobstructed room with a vaulted ceiling and no support posts inside. I had originally assumed we would use solid one-piece timbers for the beams, but later found out that this wasn't the best choice. One-piece beams would sag over time. Therefore, we constructed them as follows:

The beams were a laminated assembly constructed out of layers of two-inch by twelve-inch by twelve-foot boards sandwiched by twelve-inch plywood strips, all glued and nailed to a fare-thee-well. The embedded plywood strips would prevent sag. When the beams were finished, they were an awesome piece of work. They also weighed awesomely, as we found out when we tried to muscle them high into the air, one end at a time, and place them atop the walls. Once in place, they were nailed prodigiously into place. Later, the beams would be faced or wrapped with a more handsome wood and refinished.

Next, the window and door openings were cut into the walls and framed with reinforcing two-by-fours. This went easily and quickly over one morning. We were by then into the very hot days of summer. It was long, hard work, with nowhere to hide from the sun, which had climbed high. It became time to break for lunch.

Lunch that day was "San Leon pate," a small tin of potted meat spread on crackers. While we ate, sitting in what little shade the scrawny tree at K1 afforded, I wished there was more shade. If there was ever to be more, I knew that I was either going to have to build it or grow it. That hot Texas sun was no fun. It was a good thing I hadn't planted potatoes. They would have baked right in the ground! I finished lunch and leaned back in my chair.

I thought about the Buffalo River, back in Arkansas. The hills of Arkansas are covered by dense, shady forests. It is beautiful country, and the Buffalo River runs right through it. We grew up swimming in the Buffalo River. At one time I knew every rock in that river by its first name.

The Buffalo River

Back when Mom and Dad were just starting out and our family was much younger, they'd load all us kids up in the car and we'd go over and float the Buffalo for a fun and inexpensive vacation. Each kid got his own inner tube and Dad would follow in a johnboat loaded with lunch, a cooler, and towels. We'd get up early, drive to the river, float and swim down the river for a whole day, and drive home that evening. We called trips like these the "Wonderful One Day."

When I was a little older, we had "Dads and Lads" trips, where several dads and their sons would get together and take longer float trips, usually three or four days, camping out on the gravel bars as we went. Sometimes we'd go the whole way without seeing a single other person. I knew where all of the springs were, bubbling out of perfect hollows, adorned with thick, soft, luxuriant moss and draped with ferns. Back then you could drink the spring water right out of the ground. It was cool and thirst quenching and felt especially good when splashed on your face. Except for the considerable noise we would sometimes make, it was very quiet, especially at night when we would fix big campfires and tell ghost stories.

The Buffalo River is a series of long, tranquil pools, connected by swift rapids. Dense woods covered both banks that were broken by gravel bars and sheer natural limestone bluffs, which sometimes rise to great heights. The river meanders through the hills and valleys and eventually flows into the White River. The river and its surroundings have remained pristine, and today it looks, in many places, just the way it must have looked for eons, thanks to the conservationists of Arkansas.

It probably looked that way to the Indians, too. Whenever I was at the Buffalo River, I felt close to the ancient, native people who had once lived there.

We knew where some caves were located along the river. They were not visible from the river, and you had to climb through some pretty rugged terrain to get to them. Talk about poison ivy; it grew there in abundance with vines over an inch thick. We also knew the best places to hunt for arrowheads, and the places you could find more wild blackberries than you could eat, if you were there at the right time of year.

When we were old enough to drive, us lads would go on Buffalo River float trips of our own. These trips had an entirely different flavor than when our dads had been along. They were perhaps the most fun trips of all! Remove the adult factor and all sorts of wondrous things could happen—most of them fun, not all of them good, and not all of them safe. But nothing truly bad ever happened, and we lived to tell the tales.

I liked canoeing, and became good at it. I got to where I could maneuver a fully loaded canoe down the river by myself for four days and arrive dry. I loved shooting the rapids. After traversing a set of rapids, we'd beach our canoes, grab our snorkels, and walk back upstream. We'd jump in and snorkel the rapids, keeping an eye out for "loot." Sometimes there was a lot to find.

Some of the rapids were wild and wooly. People seldom got seriously hurt in them, but in the wilder and woollier ones, people often capsized and lost gear. This is the loot we were looking for. Items we found included fishing rods, tackle boxes, cooking gear, tents, sunglasses, hats, and cameras. Once we found a rifle. Most of it was ruined, but some of it was in good shape. We had our own share of near misses and capsizes as well. I lost count of how many pairs of my glasses had been claimed by the Buffalo River...

· · ·

"Andy—wake up!"

Somebody was shaking me. I opened my eyes. It was Gilberto.

"Are you just going to screw off the rest of the day?"

It was time to start on the roof. Soon there would be shade! We began with the ridge beam that would run at the peak of the roof from one end of the house to the other. Because of its length, it had to be built out of several pieces of lumber, scarved together to make one continuous timber.

Question: since the ridge beam's final position was, at present, just a point in thin air with nothing yet built to support it, how to know where it should go?

The plans revealed the answer. They showed the height at which the beam should be. All we had to do was to build four temporary cradles to the specified height and then lift the beam into them. The rafters would then be nailed from the wall tops to the beam. Then, the cradles would be dismantled, leaving the roof. Simple! Was I ever glad to have Gilberto. Whereas I would be reinventing a wheel, and wrongly at that, all of this was old hat to him.

The lumber for the rafters had already arrived, and we began. Here was the drill: one man on the ground, one man on a ladder at the top of the wall, and one man on a ladder at the ridge beam. The ground man grabbed a board, cut it to fit, and tossed it up to the other two, who nailed it in place.

There were a lot of rafters. It took a couple of days, but gradually the roof emerged. We raftered up one side of the roof, and then raftered up the other side. At the end of this job, my arms ached mightily. Between the work and the heat, I would only have enough strength to drag myself home at the end of the day, shower, eat, and read a little bit before early bed. Finally, the rafters were all done. Another step closer!

"Roof Rafters Being Installed"

The sun was not "our friend." It sought to make lethargic blobs out of Gilberto and me, and I was eager to get the roof covered. We decked it with OSB, a common building material that resembles plywood and comes in four-by-eight-foot sheets. It is widely used for walls and roofs in our area. I was suspicious of it because it's made essentially of wood fragments and glue, but Gilberto convinced me it was structurally sound. We installed it in much the same way that the subfloor had been done. It was a little harder than the subfloor had been to install because of the up-in-the-air factor. If I ever got through with this house without getting hurt, it would be a miracle. After a couple of close calls with falling boards and unsteady ladders, I came to realize that construction sites, even little ones, are dangerous places.

The roof decking went fairly rapidly, however. When done, it afforded us shade, one of the most valuable of commodities in summertime Texas. What a luxury! I considered the amenities that the Oleanders then had, things that it did not have a year ago. Water. Electricity. Shade. We were fairly racing up the ladder of Maslow's Hierarchy of Needs. It was exciting to see the house in its final size and shape.

"Roof Decking Being Installed"

This propelled me to keep the construction moving along. I was keen to get the house *dried in.* That is, to a point where it would be protected from the elements and lockable at night. We were still having to haul tools and other valuables back and forth every day. Life would be a lot easier if we could leave everything there at night and not have to worry about them either getting wet or sprouting legs and walking off.

The walls were still just two-by-four-foot framing, and we were ready to cover them. Again we used OSB. I ordered a big stack of it. When it arrived, we cut it to fit and nailed it to the studs all the way around the house, preserving the door and window openings.

"OSB Going On"

Once Gilberto and I got to know one another, we talked incessantly about music. He was as knowledgeable (well, almost) about music from the 60s and 70s as I was, and our combined knowledge supplied us with an inexhaustible supply of fodder for discussion. This we did, to the absolute distraction of Emilio or anyone else that had to be around us. We questioned, kidded, quizzed, razzed, and cajoled each other constantly about songs, bands, record albums, Les Paul guitars, Hammond organs, and legions of infinitesimal musical trivia. Discussing these things with him reminded me of the significance of music in my life.

• • •

Music is like a foreign language. A communication. A discourse among musicians. Musicians performing music can be thought of as persons engaged in a dialogue of an unfamiliar tongue, with each musician contributing his part to the "conversation." This communication can occur simultaneously on more than one level: between the musician and his instrument, between the musician and the audience, between several musicians, etc. People enjoy listening to this exchange, either in prerecorded form or in live settings.

Music can be uplifting and joyous. It can also be depressing or annoying. As a matter of fact, music seems to be capable of resonating with many, if not all, of the emotions. With music, some people understand exactly what is being said while others don't have the vaguest idea. It apparently does not matter either way. It's not necessary to understand music to enjoy it, unlike foreign languages. All who are listening to and watching the creation of music can enjoy it, whether they understand how it is being created or not.

This is the essence of a conversation I had once in the darkened parking lot of a jazz club with a drummer friend at three o'clock in the morning, after a gig.

The student of music can learn—and master—the elements of music. You must become familiar with the rules that govern its creation. Once you accomplish this, you can skillfully bend the rules and break them, brilliantly. The two main genres of music taught in music colleges today are classical and jazz. The following can help make the distinction between classical and jazz musicians. Generally, it is this:

If you use all of the elements of music and stridently observe the rules of its creation, you are a classical musician.
If you use all of the elements of music and play both inside *and* outside of the rules of its creation, you are a jazz musician.

I was and still am a student of both, plus a few others.

• • •

I went to pick up the doors and windows that had been ordered and were waiting for me. We installed them quickly and easily in just half a day. When I installed the lockset I'd bought for the front door, I became the possessor of something I hadn't had in five years of living on a boat: a house key. The addition of windows and doors really gave the house its character.

And with that, we were dried in. Another big milestone behind me. I felt great. Hallelujah!

Now it was time for a break. I had been working dawn to dusk seven days a week for three weeks to get dried in. I deserved a vacation day! However, I wasn't going to just kick back on the couch and watch the game. That wasn't my style. No, I had something bigger in mind. Something I'd been wanting to do for a long time.

Have you ever wanted to go out on a shrimp boat, just to see how it's done? Don't you think that would be interesting?

No?

Shrimper Andy

As I have said, I love all things about the sea, the waterfront, and boats. All boats. Even old, rusty shrimpers. Not long after moving to the Gulf Coast of Texas, I got an extraordinary notion— to go out on a shrimper sometime, as a deckhand.

What an adventure. What a great learning opportunity!

This thought resurfaced every once in a while. Usually I was too busy to do anymore than reflect, yet again, on how much I'd like to do that—and then dismiss it

The pesky shrimp boat notion had surfaced again recently. This time, it came with the addendum that my schedule was flexible, the most flexible that it had been for some time. The notion also told me that, now that I had some time on my hands, it was time to make this happen. Once I finished the house and got working again, the window would close. If I was ever to do this, now was the time.

That was it. Into action. Now or probably never. Do or die.

To arms! Time to go out on a shrimp boat.

When my mind started probing the depths of going out on a shrimp boat, I realized I was very interested in—and knew nothing about—shrimping.

Where in the ocean do shrimp live? How do you find them? How are they caught? How do the nets work? How many shrimp can you catch? What other kinds of marine life do shrimpers see in Galveston Bay? A funny song about shrimping started running through my mind as I started looking around for a shrimp boat to go out on:

"Lawdy mercy land of Goshen shades of gray out on the ocean Don't you dare take that boat out to sea ...

there's high seas a-runnin' you will sure enough be done in If you dare take that boat out to sea."

I decided to begin my search with my friend Robert down at the Topwater Grill. They served the best shrimp around. Robert got them from somewhere. He ought to know someone with a shrimp boat. I went to see him that afternoon. Robert listened to what I wanted to do with an amused smile on his face. This wasn't the first odd ball scheme he'd heard from me.

"We used to have three shrimp boats, Andy," he said. "One was sunk, one burned, and one was sold. We're out of the shrimping business."

Then he thought for a minute, and said, "But, I know a guy who might be willing to take you out," and he wrote a name down on a scrap of paper. "Go down to the docks and ask around for this guy."

That's all I needed. I thanked Robert and went looking for Captain Matt. I found him, introduced myself, and described what I wanted to do. Matt, good soul that he was, told me that it would be fine with him and for me to meet him at the dock the following morning at four o'clock. *Four o'clock* —hadn't figured on that! However, I was keen for the adventure, so I set my alarm and went to bed early.

I arrived at the dock the next morning, bleary eyed and clinging to a steaming cup of coffee like a drowning man a life preserver. Even though I was wearing old clothes, I felt like a real city slicker— an outsider—and very conspicuous. I found the boat, the *Sea Hornet*, and sat down to await Matt.

Soon, Captain Matt showed up, followed shortly by Kerry, the deck hand. After brief introductions, we got the boat ready to go and left in the dark. She was a fifty-foot fiberglass boat with a 400 horsepower diesel that roared dully.

"How has the shrimping been?" I inquired.

"Not too good lately. Our catches the last few days have been on the light side."

"Well, you'll be glad to know that I am good luck," I replied (this isn't necessarily true). "We'll catch shrimp today."

Down the channel we chugged, past the little island in the mouth of Dickinson Bayou, past the Topwater Grill, and out into Galveston Bay. I was in the wheelhouse, following our progress on radar. It was fun being back out in the bay, particularly in an unfamiliar vessel such as this.

Galveston Bay, big as it is, is shallow, with an average depth of only nine feet. The Houston Ship Channel is a big ditch that was dug right down the middle of the bay to allow deepwater ships access to the Port of Houston. On any given day you can see ships from all over the world passing through this channel. It is dredged to a depth of forty feet. Ships' hulls extend below the waterline a long way, thirty-five feet or so in some cases. We would be shrimping in the vicinity of the ship channel.

Matt made a pot of coffee, and, as it kicked in, we began talking amiably. I was soon peppering him with questions, which he answered patiently. There were no less than four marine VHF radios in the boat's wheelhouse.

"Why so many?" I asked.

"To be able to get in on all of the gossip," Matt replied. When he saw my raised eyebrows, he continued, "One group of shrimpers might be on one channel, another group might be on another, and so on. Four radios let me keep abreast of all of the chatter, so I can find out where the shrimp are."

"What makes a particular location better for shrimping than any other location?" I queried.

"The best places to catch shrimp are in the middle of the bay. Shrimp are bottom dwellers that swim in schools. Concentrations of shrimp vary with water depth, water temperature, and currents."

I paused thoughtfully. "How often do you go out?"

"With all of the restrictions that govern shrimping, you've got to fish all you can to pay all of your operating expenses and still clear a profit. We typically fish six days a week."

I found all of this interesting. I was getting answers to long-held questions. The predawn air was nippy, but it was comfortable inside the pilothouse. The coffee was warming me up. I was already glad I'd come. To me, this was all high adventure; for Matt, it was an ordinary commute to work. Most of my commuting to work was spent sitting in traffic on the Gulf Freeway, drinking lukewarm coffee, and listening to talk radio.

"What are the restrictions on shrimping?" I asked.

"Well, to begin with, you can't shrimp all year 'round. There are seasons. Then, there are the TEDs. Do you know what a TED is?"

I did. TED stands for turtle excluding device. In the 1970s, there had been a big public awareness of shrimp nets allegedly being responsible for the deaths of porpoises, turtles, and other marine life unfortunate enough to get caught in them. Particularly, air-breathing life such as porpoises and turtles that could easily drown in the hour or more the net is down before it is pulled up. The TED is a government-mandated device that was developed to prevent, or at least minimize, this occurrence.

"How does one work?" I inquired.

"You have a shrimp net that is pulled through the water by a boat. The net is shaped like a giant funnel with a bag at the end to collect the shrimp. Sewn into the net near the bag end is the TED, which is a round grid made of metal, wire, or netting material. It is positioned at an angle. The shrimp pass through the grid and into the bag, but anything bigger is deflected by the grid through an opening in the net."

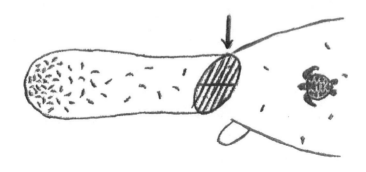

"Turtle-excluding device (TED)"

"Do they work?" I inquired.

"Shrimpers in Galveston Bay hardly ever caught that many turtles to begin with. I've only caught three myself, in forty years of shrimping. None of them made it back in the net as far as the TED. They were all around the net's opening when we pulled it up. Based on this, I can't really claim that the TED saved them. Incidentally, we were able to release all three, unharmed, back into the bay."

I nodded thoughtfully.

"It's one thing if we found lots of dead turtles in our nets before the TEDs became compulsory and none afterward. That would prove the TEDs worked as designed, and saved turtles. That hasn't been the case here."

He took a sip of coffee and continued, "So, how do I know the TEDs are working? I don't. They probably do work. Turtles could be caught in the net and escape through the TED every day and we'd never know it, but I don't think so. Three turtles in forty years is not many turtles.

"The trouble with TEDs is that they let a pretty fair percentage of the catch escape."

"Why is that?" I asked.

"There's no way to prevent the shrimp from getting out through the escape opening. And, if there is a lot of floating debris or seaweed in the water, it clogs the grid. This lets even more shrimp escape. There are some other issues as well, but needless to say, TEDs are a lot of trouble and not very popular with shrimpers. Even so, all the boats around here today have TEDs in place because the law is rigorously enforced."

Matt peered forward into the darkness while I considered his words. Matt obviously didn't want to harm turtles more than anyone else, but I could see the dilemma.

"What are some factors that determine why some days are good for shrimping and others aren't?" I asked.

"It fluctuates according to things like tide, currents, the moon, temperature, wind, and time of year. Shrimping is better than average around a full moon." I'd heard the same thing about fishing.

"What determines the time of day or night that you go out?" I asked, recalling my painful three thirty alarm clock from that morning.

"It's a good idea to go out early, to get a good spot," he replied.

Good spot? This remark raised even more questions.

"It used to be that all the local shrimpers crowded into the best areas. That hurt everyone's catches and occasionally led to skirmishes and even violence. Awhile back, all of the local shrimpers got together and worked out an agreement among themselves to keep the peace. Kind of an unwritten covenant. One of the points in it is that shrimp boats must stay one mile apart. Today, we all pretty much observe this, although there are some who don't play by the rules. Some areas are 'hotter,' or better producers, than others. It's first come first serve. To get to the best producing areas, you have to leave the dock before the others."

"Sounds fair to me," I said. "What are some of the other shrimping restrictions?"

"During the season, there is a seventy-foot length limit on the net. And, you are legally allowed to shrimp from thirty minutes before sunrise to thirty minutes after sunset. But there's nothing stopping you from getting out there to be ready to go when that time arrives. That's why we leave the dock as early as we do. As you can see, it takes awhile for a shrimp boat to get there."

True, it had taken us about an hour and a half to get where we were going. When we did, we still had to wait for the legal time to begin.

"Is there any limit on the amount of shrimp you can catch?"

"No. It's all you can catch between those hours."

It was time to get to work. Enough questions for the time being. First, we lowered the try net in the water. This is a small net that is used to determine if we were in shrimp-bearing waters. It was easier to deploy than the full-sized net. The boat pulled the try net through the water for a few minutes and then we brought it back up. Right off the bat, I could see several small brittle stars, a type of starfish, clinging to it—cool!

Matt cared not for starfish. He was more interested in the contents of the try net. We all crowded around to see what the sea had yielded. Me, for curiosity, and Matt for profit.

Matt studied the assortment of small fish and, yes, shrimp that came up. The results weren't encouraging. We moved down the bay a little ways and then put the try net down again. This time, it came up with more shrimp than before, more small fish, and a fifteen-inch sheepshead. I occasionally caught these while fishing on my Jet Ski. A nice fish in my book.

"Do you want that fish?" Kerry asked.

When fishing in Arkansas, I always kept everything longer than a foot. "If you don't want it, sure!" I yelled. Dinner was assured.

We put the try net out again. Matt was looking for signs. Signs in this case were other marine life typically found in association with shrimp. The presence or absence of certain other organisms in the net can act as a telltale for schools of shrimp. For instance, squid and poagies—a type of small fish—are typically found in association with shrimp, but they normally swim just above them. If you find them in your try net, you are probably fishing too high. Sea bobs, a species of small shrimp, are typically found below schools of shrimp. If you find them in your try net, you are probably fishing too low.

This time, Matt liked what he saw in the net. He nodded in approval.

"Let's go with the big net," he called to Kerry.

Kerry unlashed the net, which began sliding over the stern. The big winch started spinning and I got the hell out of the way. The net was sixty-five feet long and had a triangular opening. I could clearly see the TED as the net went into the water.

The net also had two, big, wooden doors. They were attached to the net's opening with ropes in such a way that the boat's forward motion caused them to "fly" through the water and spread out to either side of the net and hold it open. They also acted as two big scoops to guide shrimp into the net. When the net was all out, the boat's forward progress slowed to about half as she shouldered into her work.

We settled down for the ride. The sun had started to rise by then. It was a beautiful sunrise, fiery and serene. The morning was still mild and calm. We continued talking and drinking coffee and I thought of another question to ask Matt.

"You mentioned the shrimping season. If the season is only at certain times of the year, why can you see fresh shrimp for sale in the seafood markets and grocery stores all year round?"

"Ah, an excellent question. The 'fresh' shrimp you see out of season have been frozen and thawed out. You know, even if shrimp are in season, there's no guarantee that what you see in the store on any given day has not been frozen. It isn't even necessarily local.

"These days, shrimp comes from all sorts of places like Asia and the Far East. Some of it is wild caught and some of it is farmed. Whether shrimp are domestic or imported, wild caught or farmed, they sell it all side by side down in the seafood markets in Seabrook, and the big grocery stores, too."

Hmm. I suddenly felt foolish for the times I have occasionally bought what I assumed were fresh shrimp and taken them home to freeze for another occasion.

"If the weather's bad, do you still go out?"

"Not normally. What sometimes happens is that we are out working and get caught in a storm. Several times we've seen lightning strikes, and close ones. Also waterspouts. That'll get your blood moving! When we see a waterspout forming, we just try and get out of the way. Shrimp boats don't move very fast, particularly with nets in the water."

Hearing this whetted my appetite for some sea stories. I'll bet Matt had had some eye-opening experiences in forty years.

"I'll bet you've had some eye-opening experiences in forty years," I said.

"Well, I've had my share of scrapes. There are snags in the water. Debris, wrecks, etc. They are prone to foul—and ruin—a net. We call them *hangs.* I know where many of them are and can avoid them. Still, I always heave a sigh of relief every time the net comes up un-damaged.

"Sometimes when your net gets hung up on something, it brings the entire boat to a complete stop, almost as if it has hit a solid object. If this happens when you're in the ship channel, you're in a precarious situation. You have to try to get the net free, either by using the winch or maneuvering the boat. If a ship is coming, there you are. Big ships are not very maneuverable."

This, I already knew from my own sailing experiences in Galveston Bay. I'd heard it takes nearly a mile for a large seagoing ship to come to a stop, once she's throttled down.

"One time when we were shrimping, the net caught something solid. I didn't know what it was. While we were trying to get free, an old sunken boat about forty feet long surfaced behind the boat and rolled over. That's what had become tangled up in our net. It took a little doing to get clear of that one."

"How about collisions?"

"I've been hung up and almost run over by ships or barges several times. That gets a little exciting. We were nearly hit by a big ship one time even when we weren't hung up on anything."

"Really? What happened?"

"Well, I'll tell you. We were shrimping in the channel, nets were in the water."

"Isn't that against the law?" I asked. Ever since I began sailing in Galveston Bay I had sometimes seen shrimp boats working in the Houston Ship Channel, and it seemed unsafe to me. "No, it's not against the law," Matt replied. "Sometimes that's where the shrimp are, and that's where we were shrimping that day. Ship traffic was coming and going as it always does. Ship traffic is usually not a bother to shrimpers. Everybody communicates on the radio and generally stays out of each other's way. On this day, a ship was coming down the channel. Everything was fine until the ship veered and started heading inexplicably toward us. The next moment, the skipper of the ship called us on the radio. They had a big problem: they had lost power and were out of control. They had no steerage, and were coasting, rapidly, right at us. We were squarely in the way. Their problem became ours!"

"Wow," I exclaimed. "What did you do?"

"We immediately started taking in the nets and trying to get out of the way. Neither of these operations can be done in a split second on a shrimp boat. By the time we got the ship's radio message, we didn't have very much time. The ship was already far too close and traveling fast. We worked as fast as we could, but by then the ship's bow was then only one hundred yards away and still coming right at us. I remember that there were a couple of crewmen on the bow of the ship watching us, high over our heads. I could clearly hear one say to the other, 'They're not going to make it!'"

"This ship, like many do, had a large, bulbous mass at the front of the keel at the waterline—"

"What are those there for?" I interjected.

"They're for increased speed and efficiency through the water, through fluid dynamics (I had assumed they were for deflecting debris and slow-moving sailboats).

"As I was saying, I watched that bulb get closer and closer. It barely missed us and passed behind, and then the ship ran aground on the edge of the ship channel. As the bow hit, it rode up out of the water. Draped over the bulb was our net. What a close call!"

"Bet that put a few gray hairs on you," I noted.

Matt grinned wryly. "Time to haul up," he said.

Kerry flipped on the switch to the big winch and I got the hell out of the way. The net came up gradually out of the water and up over the deck where it hung for a moment, water cascading down. In it was a glistening, dripping heap of…something.

"Hey, Matt, come take a look," Kerry called. But Matt was already on his way back from the wheelhouse. His face broke out into a broad grin. He said to Kerry, "That's more than we've seen in the last few days, isn't it?"

"…Told you I was good luck," I said. "Oh, by the way, did I forget to mention to you my nominal shrimp locator fee of fifty dollars?"

Kerry and Matt glanced at each other and rolled their eyes.

"We'll talk about that later. Time to get to work, gentlemen," Matt said.

I grinned, as Kerry released the opening at the bottom of the net and its contents all sloshed down into a big holding tank with aerated, circulating, seawater inside.

Back went the net into the sea. The winch sang and I got the hell out of the way.

It was our task to sort through the catch. Kerry placed a tray on top of the tank to use as a work surface. He reached for a hand net and scooped up a load of wriggling shrimp and other things and poured them in the tray.

I watched expectantly to see what all we had caught: butter fish, croakers, baby gaff top catfish baby stingrays, and squid. There were ribbonfish, also called silver eels, with mouthfuls of small, needle-sharp teeth. There also were some interesting small fish called look-downs, an occasional small crab, jellyfish, cigar minnows, and more. There were also some juveniles of bigger species. I had always heard that bays and estuaries were nurseries for larger, seagoing fish, but here was the living proof—right on the tray in front of me.

Kerry showed me how to pick the live shrimp out and put them in a second holding tank. Shrimp are delicate, and some had already expired. Even so, they were fresh and harvestable, and they went into a cooler with ice. Squid are good fishing bait and they were reserved as well. The other marine life is referred to as *bycatch*. Since the catch was never out of seawater for more than a few seconds, most of it was still alive and was returned to the bay.

As much as I'd like to have seen *all* of the bycatch go back into the water alive, I could see it just wasn't possible Conscientious shrimpers do what they can, and I reconciled that was about the best I could do as well. By then, a big flock of seagulls was on hand, along with a pelican or two, to feast on the casualties. Nothing goes to waste in the sea.

We went through the catch one scoop at a time. In one batch, to my delight, was a small puffer fish. It did what puffer fish do when they are scared, puffing up to about the size of a baseball. I held it in my hand for a fascinating moment and then carefully returned it to the bay.

Several things in the catch could hurt you. Some of the jellyfish were the stinging kinds. Portuguese man 'o' war jellyfish were the worst, although we found none that day. Those gaff tops were bad news. There were a lot of small ones. In their fins are long, brittle spines that the fish flicks rapidly when it's alarmed. If your finger is unlucky enough to be in the way, the spine will easily pierce it, right through a glove, and then break off in your hand. These wounds are more painful than, say, a splinter, and are prone to ugly infections later. We stayed well clear of the stingrays too. Although I've never been stung by one, I've heard their stings are extremely painful. Luckily, there weren't that many of them.

It took us over an hour to cull the first catch. Kerry produced a license plate bent over at a forty-five degree angle that worked well for scooping up the live shrimp off of the tray and flipping them into the tank. I noted that they'd spared no expense with the equipment, and Kerry grinned.

A deck hand gets paid twenty percent of gross. It is a good deal for both the boat owner and the deck hand. Shrimping is either feast or famine, depending on if you found shrimp that day. We were primarily after live shrimp, to be sold as bait. Matt could get four dollars a pound for it at the bait camps. The iced shrimp went to restaurants and seafood markets. It only fetched a dollar a pound. I would try and remember that the next time I was enjoying a $12.95 shrimp entrée for dinner at a restaurant somewhere!

While Kerry and I were busy culling, Matt was on the phone with bait camps and seafood markets, lining up customers for that afternoon. Wheeling and dealing. Commerce on the high seas.

Presently we were finished culling the shrimp. Time to bring up the big net again. The winch spun and I got the hell out of the way. Pay dirt again. *Woo-hoo!*

"You know, Matt," I began. "The shrimping has been way better for you today, because of me. I've been working too cheap. I may have to raise my shrimp locator fee."

"Fine," Matt shot back. "I'm still working out what I'm going to charge you for this nice boat ride. Besides, don't sheepshead get about five dollars a pound down at Rose's Seafood Market?"

That settled my hash!

The sun was shimmering on the tranquil water, it was a golden morning and pleasantly warm. Kerry and I took a break and ate our sandwiches and then began culling the new catch. While we worked, we talked. About the usual stuff—girls, trucks, deer leases, sports, and rock 'n' roll. Man stuff; gnarly stuff. Did you think we shrimpers sit around discussing things like the *inner child* or trying to "find" ourselves?

I asked Kerry what was some of the other more unusual marine life he saw while out shrimping.

"Oh, sometimes we get sea horses. Those are pretty neat. When we get some, I take one or two home to dry out for my nieces."

Seahorses—how wonderful! I had no idea they lived right here in Galveston Bay.

"What else?" I persisted.

"Sometimes there are small sharks."

I myself have never seen a shark in Galveston Bay, but that doesn't mean there aren't any.

"Man, I hope we get one today," I replied, although we didn't. We *did* get another nice sheepshead later. Well, all right!

We spent another pleasant hour, talking as we culled. In a moment of inattention I got pricked by a baby gaff top, but, in accordance with the Shrimper's Code, I didn't flinch (well, not much). If that was the worst that would happen, it would be a pretty good day. It was both.

We took a third drag with the net and then headed home. We culled the last catch on the way in. When we arrived, we weighed the shrimp and began cleaning up the boat. We ended up with 300 pounds of live shrimp and 300 pounds of dead shrimp. I helped Matt and Kerry clean up. The live shrimp went into a special trailer that had a covered holding tank with a re-circulating pump, powered by a small gasoline motor.

When we were through, I said, "Gentlemen, I'm not a rich man, but it would be my pleasure for us all to go have dinner at the Topwater Grill, on my nickel."

They thought that was a grand idea, and we parted friends. As I was leaving, Matt gave me a bag of shrimp to take home.

• • •

Dried in the house may be; however, it was still vulnerable to the weather, like a patch of bare hide around a few million San Leon mosquitoes at dusk. Plywood and OSB do not like to get wet. Time for a little protection. The day after my shrimping adventure, we got back to work. First, we shingled the roof. This is the only job I didn't want any part of. I'm afraid of heights. A couple of weeks back, a roofer had come by looking for work. I had gotten his telephone number, and I gave him a call.

Shingles, the traditional asphalt kind, were bought and delivered, along with tarpaper. Jim, the roofer, got to work. Roofers work an alternative schedule in the heat of the year. Jim roofed early in the morning and quit around ten a.m. He came back about dinnertime and roofed till dark. In three or four days he was done. The brand new roof looked splendid, and Jim had earned a tip.

Now to cover the outside walls. I chose a product known as Hardi siding. I was initially wary when I found out it was made of a mixture of cement and paper. This material was, in fact, known to be durable, easy to work with, and nice looking. It was also one of the more expensive options.

Cement and paper? What the heck, the Mongols living in the Himalayas use felt for building houses. *Felt!* Felt is made from yak hair. If yurts made of yak hair could withstand the fierce elements in the Himalayas, then maybe concrete and paper could fare well in San Leon. Not only that, I wasn't sure I could locate a supplier of yak hair in the Houston market. I *felt* better about the whole thing when I placed a scrap of the siding material in a puddle of water as an experiment and noted its condition. It held up well and only became waterlogged and unusable after several days of immersion.

The siding arrived in a big load of boards. Gilberto and I nailed up tarpaper on the walls of the house to serve as a moisture barrier and then spent the next several days nailing the siding onto the house. The pieces were textured to resemble real boards, and looked nice, even unpainted.

"Siding Completed"

With the walls completed, we could add the wood trim around the gables and soffits. We also added wood trim around the windows and doors. How skillfully these details are executed has a lot to do with how "finished" a house looks. Gilberto knew how to do this job right.

And that is how the infrastructure of the Oleanders came to be. *Built by musicians for musicians.*

Chapter 11

The Ladies of San Leon

"Confucius say: man who runs behind car soon gets exhausted."

"All right, you maggots!" I yelled cheerfully as Gilberto and Chris climbed their ladders to go up to the gables. "Make it snappy and keep me happy!"

Chris was out helping me this day. I was glad he was there. It was mid-August by then. The house was fitted with a roof, doors, and windows. It was a beautiful morning. A flock of noisy parrots was having a prayer breakfast in a nearby tree. It was deliciously cool and a light breeze was coming in off of Galveston Bay, ruffling my faded Jimmy Buffett T-shirt. The aspirin I had taken earlier for my tortured muscles would be kicking in soon. I puffed up and strutted over closer so as to make a better impression and yelled shrilly, "Now use your level on that soffit!"

We were finishing up the soffits early because these days, by ten o'clock, it was already hotter than the hinges of hell. The hideous brown recluses, denizens of the night, would be scuttling off into their dark crevices—about where Chris and Gilberto were working—to hide from the sun. Recluses are poisonous. They are also house spiders, and I'd already seen some here. How did they know there was a house there where one had never been before? They must have looked on a *web* site!

I whistled a little song and swatted a mosquito. Construction was progressing well. Perhaps soon I could move a few things in and begin sleeping there, 'ere the cold north wind started to howl and knot my knickers.

Gilberto broke my reverie.

"This coffee tastes like dirt," he exclaimed.

"Well it was just *ground* this morning," I retorted.

Gilberto and I had just built a world-class porch. Forty-two feet long, it faced onto what would become a pretty landscaped yard full of paths and gardens. I couldn't wait for that day, far in the distant future, when there wouldn't be any more building to do, and I could just go out onto the porch and sit in my rocker and do...nothing.

I told Gilberto about the porch becoming a stage for Sunday afternoon concerts. He thought that was a great idea and immediately claimed a spot to set up his guitar amplifier on the porch.

While working on the porch, Gilberto showed me what he called a Mexican table saw. This is a circular saw with a pair of vise-grips clamped onto the saw's deck to act as a guide. This allows you to make a straight cut in boards several feet long, with the vise-grips guide keeping the saw perfectly straight.

Mucho bueno, si?

• • •

While listening to the whine of the skill saw, I was reminded that, while loud and obnoxious, the sound was a definite musical pitch. It made me think of perfect pitch. Perfect pitch, also called "absolute pitch," is the ability to hear a note, chord, or song and be able to tell, accurately, exactly what the notes are. Perfect pitch is coveted among musicians and is a rare natural phenomenon. "Rare as hens' teeth," as my grandmother would have said. People with perfect pitch can recognize and reproduce notes, apparently right out of thin air. I have perfect pitch. I thank my Maker each and every day for this gift, and "gift" would surely be the correct term for it.

Many sounds in everyday life that aren't typically thought of as musical notes, but like my skill saw, actually are. A running car engine. The ping of a hammer on metal. For most people, these sounds are just indiscriminate noise. Persons with perfect pitch can listen to them and name the note or notes that comprise them. Some sounds are obvious, others not so. The whine of my circular saw was a B-flat.

When I was a young beginning piano student, I didn't know what perfect pitch was and had never heard of it. Here is how it was discovered that I had it:

My piano teacher, dear old Mrs. Humphreys, would assign me a piece to learn, and we'd go through it, slowly. She would then play the piece so I could hear how it was supposed to sound. I would go home and sit at the piano and play it. Not from the music that would still be on the floor where it had landed when I got home, but from memory. I could remember the key, all the notes in the proper sequence, everything.

I saw nothing extraordinary in this. I thought everyone could do it. All I had to do was play the song through a few times, and I had it down. Cool, let's go play some baseball! It was easier and faster for me to hear someone else play the piece and mimic it than it was to read the notes from the printed page.

One day while playing a lesson piece for Mrs. Humphreys, things were going along fine, until she heard something that got her attention; namely, notes that were not in the piece. She stopped me, took the music away, and asked me to play the piece over again from the beginning. At this point, a student who was really reading the piece would not have been able to get very far, yet there I was, playing the piece, if anything, *better* than the first time!

Mrs. Humphreys stared in amazement. She smiled and exclaimed, "Andy, I wonder if you have perfect pitch?"

People with perfect pitch can hear music and recognize notes as easily as you can recognize colors in a picture. For instance, you know the dress in the picture is red, the sky is blue, and the grass is green. The musician with perfect pitch hears music, and he *knows* the violin played an A, the tuba played a low E, the flute played a C#, and the tympani drum played a low A. The musician with perfect pitch can tell by listening that Led Zeppelin performed the song *Stairway to Heaven* in the key of A and so on. Musicians without perfect pitch hear the same music but would not be able to say with confidence what notes are being played.

Many people with perfect pitch also have an expanded capacity for remembering long sequences of notes and chords. For them, memorization of even lengthy pieces is no problem. By the time they've mastered a piece to performance level, it is already memorized. When a musician without perfect pitch has mastered a song, he must often put in additional hours memorizing it.

Think of how useful perfect pitch is to a vocalist. Before he even goes on stage, he *knows* beyond the shadow of a doubt what the first note of the first song is. He can sing it correctly even before the band plays a single chord.

It is just as useful to the musical arranger. He hears a recording of a song only a couple of times, and he knows the key the song is in, the chords played by the guitar, and the notes played by the horns in the brass section. He already has the hard part done; it is in his head. All that remains is to write it all down.

To test the theory of perfect pitch on me, Mrs. Humphreys asked me to step into the adjoining room, and then she played some random notes on the piano. I was able to name every note with 100-percent accuracy[4], without seeing the keyboard. I had perfect pitch! From that day forward, Mrs. Humphreys would have me perform a live demonstration of perfect pitch during recitals.

---

4 Perfect pitch is not always perfect. Accuracy can be reduced or impaired by fatigue, distractions, or other factors.

There are many more practical applications in music for perfect pitch.

There are no practical applications in house building for perfect pitch!

. . .

More construction lore:

Tubes of caulking and buckets of paint,
Make carpenters out of men that ain't.

One day, I was boring Gilberto with my concern for level. He suggested that, just for fun, we check the level of my foundation with an old-fashioned water level. According to Gilberto, water levels have been around since biblical times. Here is how you use one:

Suppose you are building something, like a cabana. Supposing also you want to see if your floor is level. Standing outside, take one end of a length of clear plastic tubing and hold it up to the surface of the floor on one end of the house. While your pretty young assistant holds this end of the tube steady, walk the other end of the tube all the way around to the other end of the house and hold it up to the surface of the floor there.

Recall that water always seeks its own level. With the two of you keeping very still, pour water into one end of the tube, observing its level. Use your largest pitcher; you're filling nearly the entire piece of tubing. Stop adding water when the level in the tube is even with top edge of the floor.

Ask your assistant to look at the water level at her end. If it is exactly at the top edge of the floor there also, your floor is level. Your assistant will be impressed. There's no telling what might happen next. On the other hand, if the water level is even with the floor on one end, but not on the other, your floor is not level. Take your assistant home. Better yet, call her a cab. You will have no relationship. There's no future for you and her. Better luck next time.

May I take this opportunity to say that the levelness of the floor that I worried so much about was only one-quarter inch out of level? *Woo-hoo!* By the way, where did they get plastic tubing in biblical times?

Now that the cabana was enclosed and lockable, I concerned myself with air conditioning. Due to the cabana's small size and open concept, I could use either a conventional central heat and air system, or an in-wall unit. I grappled long and hard with the decision of which to choose. I ultimately decided on an in-wall unit for these reasons:

1. I could get the same size in BTU's in an in-wall unit as in a central unit,

2. I reckoned that I could get the same results with an in-wall unit and a couple of ceiling fans as I could with central heat and air,

3. I would have to install ducts and a separate outside compressor for a central heat and air system

4. The in-wall unit was less than half the price of a central heat and air system.

The price difference clinched the deal[5].

5 What I had not studied enough was its operating costs.

I drove to Houston and picked up my new in-wall unit, which looked like the world's largest window unit air conditioner, and took it to the house where Gilberto and I promptly installed it. That blast of cool air blowing strongly in my face when I turned it on for the first time felt like the absolute height of luxury.

The air conditioner worked and worked well. It cooled down the cabana in no time on a hot day, even without insulation in the walls. It had an economy feature that turned the compressor on and off as needed, saving money. The unit also contained a heater element that, supposedly, would be all I needed to get me through the winter months in which squirrels look up nervously at the gathering clouds and deer paw the snow for tender young shoots.

One day a small house trailer appeared in the empty lot across the street. It looked like I was going to have a new neighbor. Over the next few days, I saw the occupant of the trailer engaged in various pursuits of carpentry. I decided to take a break and ambled over to introduce myself.

"Hi," I said and, extending my hand, introduced myself. "I guess I'm as close as you'll get to the San Leon Welcome Wagon."

The person had a slight build, curly hair, and wire rim glasses that gave him a studious look. "My name is Ivan," he said, with a Slavic accent. "I'm pleased to meet you."

"What are you building?" I inquired.

"It's a cradle for a boat," he replied.

Ivan was an interesting person. He was an engineer. He had sold his house and bought a sailboat. The boat needed a lot of work. Ivan planned to live in the little trailer while he worked on it. He was outfitting it for extended ocean voyaging. I like meeting people with diverse interests and goals. I was interested in his project. Maybe when the house was done, I would restore a sailboat next!

Ivan was a nice guy, friendly, and intelligent. I was glad to have him as a neighbor. I imagined I would someday have to prevail upon his engineering skills. I was happy at the thought of having a neighbor who was also a sailor.

I got back to building. A couple of days later I heard a rumbling noise. I looked up and saw a large truck with an even larger sailboat on it. A crane arrived presently that carefully picked up the boat and placed it in the wooden cradle where it towered over the neighborhood. That suited me fine. I had no objections to looking down my driveway each morning to see a sailboat.

We became friends. Ivan possessed a wealth of practical knowledge. He also possessed a wealth of tools. From time to time he would walk over to inspect whatever I happened to be working on at the time, and vice versa. We had long conversations in which we debated the finer points of this or that detail of our respective projects. Ivan also came in handy during those times when I had just broken my last three-sixteenths drill bit.

One day, I was feeling charitable. Wouldn't it be a nice gesture to do something special for lunch for Gilberto, and whoever was helping the next Saturday? Ivan could come, too. What to do? Bring out a BBQ grill and throw some sausages on it? Or maybe prepare chili ahead of time and just warm it up at noon? I looked in my recipe folder to see what I might find. I came across a recipe for chili that I reprint here, for your inspection:

Alligator Chili

1. Line up a buddy with a small boat.

2. Find a farmer who will sell you three or four chickens, fresh dead. No need to remove the feathers.

3. At dusk, meet your buddy at the boat ramp. You'll be wearing shorts because it will be hot and steamy. Do bring your insect repellant. Bring your snakebite kit as well. When we used to float the Buffalo River, we always brought along our snakebite kit that consisted of a bottle of Tequila (we also packed along one small snake too, just in case).

4. Put the boat in the water and motor up the bayou into the gathering gloom. Don't forget your chickens, and a flashlight.

5. When properly dark, nose your boat up to the bank into the thick vegetation. Tie it off to one of the overhanging limbs. Watch for water moccasins that are known for lurking on branches and falling into boats at night in swamps.

6. Convince your buddy to get out of the boat into the tea-colored, waist deep water with a freshly deceased chicken. If you can't convince him, you'll have to.

7. Since he won't get out of the boat, take your chicken and slide down into the water and mud. Wade a few feet out from the boat and tie the chicken with string onto an overhanging tree branch. Try not to notice the nightlife around you that is beginning to take notice. Jiggle the dead chicken around a few times to simulate a wounded animal that will seem like easy prey to any hungry alligators.

8. Tie the remaining chickens in similar fashion onto branches in an area where you can keep an eye on them. Be sure to watch for alligators.

9. Get back into the boat to wait. Beware of snakes, which are plentiful at this time of year.

10. There is a lot of commotion when an alligator strikes the bait. When one does, get back in the water and make your way over to it hastily, lest it get away.

11. Have your buddy shoot the alligator. If he won't, you'll have to.

12. Since your buddy won't, you must shoot the alligator between the eyes, dispatching it.

13. Wondering why you asked this particular buddy to accompany you, go over to the gator and pull its tail.

Your task is twofold: you must make sure your alligator has expired, and you must make sure no other alligators have come to consume your gator, or you.

14. If pulling the alligator's tail elicits another round of violent thrashing, instruct your buddy to shoot the alligator again. He *must not fail* with this.

15. If, however, your alligator is limp, tie a rope around him and get back into the boat, pulling your alligator in after you. Don't take all day with this.

16. This recipe started seeming a bit ambitious for my available time and inclination.

17. Back home, rinse and dry your alligator. Dinner is not far away.

18. Cut your alligator up into pieces that will fit in your largest pot. Place gator pieces in pot and add water to cover. Add one medium sized onion, chili powder, and a bottle of ketchup.

19. Cover and simmer until alligator is fork tender. Salt to taste. Serves 10-20 depending on size of the alligator.

You know, this recipe wasn't sounding all that good. I'd better go with the BBQ and sausages!

Boy, It's Green

It was time to consider paint. I went to the paint store and got samples. It didn't take me long to select the overall color: green. My grandfather had painted everything green and white around their house when I was young, and I've always liked the combination. This house would be green with white trim. I selected a cheery shade of green. Not a nice, tasteful forest green like others might have selected, but a bright, robust green. The green of growing things. The name of the color on the label was *Grass Green*.

The white trim was a little harder. There are probably hundreds of shades of white paint, each subtly different. They all have cute names designed to appeal to gushy newlyweds picking out paint for their first house, or pregnant mothers-to-be outfitting a baby's room. Names like *Whisper White, Snowflake,* and *Wedding Cake.* As humorist Dave Barry might say, these paints all began life as basic white paint. They attained their subtle differences by the percentage of rodent droppings that found their way into the vats during formulation. Thus, *Lacy Veil White* is actually known as *Rodent Dropping #26* and *Oyster Shell* is *Rodent Dropping #42* and so on. I selected *Icy Tundra White (Rodent Dropping #15)* as my trim paint.

I let a friend of mine spray the green paint on because he had an industrial paint sprayer and could do the whole house quickly, whereas little me, armed with only my brush, would take forever. On the day the house was to be painted, I couldn't get there until after dark. I couldn't wait to see it! When I drove up it first appeared like someone had stolen the house because the green blended in with the trees. I swung down the drive and beheld—green. It was *very* green. Not army green or hospital green. It was bright green. I loved it. It was not in the least obnoxious. Most of the neighbors liked it, or said they did. I didn't have the courage to ask Ivan, who lived directly across the street, how he liked it.

Not long thereafter, Gilberto and I set about painting the white trim, with brushes. The painting was easy and straightforward. When we finished, the cabana looked splendid.

Time to stop and take stock—find out where I was on the building list. The windows and doors were installed. All exterior trim was installed. The air conditioner was installed and trimmed around. Everything was painted, too. As a matter of fact, the exterior of the house was almost completely done.

The house was weatherproof and theft-proof as well. With this milestone achieved, life suddenly got a lot easier. Now, we wouldn't have to wait out rainy days. No more did we have to pack up the tools and take them back and forth each day. We could lock everything up in the house at night. Work on the house was shifting to the inside, and we could now work there in relative comfort. Gratefully, we framed the interior wall around the bathroom the next day in air-conditioned bliss.

There was still a *lot* to do before the house would be finished. There was the interior ceiling, walls, and floors. The kitchen and bathroom had to be built too. Right then though, I was in dire need of a couple of things in particular—an indoor toilet and indoor electricity. The first shouldn't need any explanation other than I was tired of running to the woods and the second because I was tired of running extension cords out of a window to the utility pole for power tools.

First things first. I went commode hunting. The one I came back with was green. No surprise there! It wasn't bright green, but *Sea Foam Green*, which really doesn't look as bad as it sounds. It features an aerodynamically designed, elongated bowl.

I began its installation by cutting holes in the floor for the sewer and water pipes, and then setting the toilet in place, using a wax barrier ring. For the time being, the toilet would be installed on the plywood sub floor. It would have to be removed and re-installed later when the bathroom floor was put in, but that was fine with me. I then went under the house and made the PVC sewer and water connections to the toilet. Back inside, I bolted it down. Installing a water shutoff valve finished the job, after which the toilet was promptly field-tested without pomp and circumstance.

The toilet came without a seat. Until a seat could be purchased, one had to employ a technique borrowed from the fairer sex (there's *nothing* fair about that sex) known as *hovering*. The addition of a toilet may just have been the most celebrated amenity added to the cabana thus far. Back to the store to look at toilet seats.

"Money is no object!" I declared expansively to the man behind the counter, and placed the order.

Rock, No Roll

I have always loved natural stone. In addition to arrowheads, I was always collecting rocks and fossils as a boy. Places like Hot Springs, Arkansas, are a real rock hound's delight. Quartz crystals are naturally occurring around those parts. You can pick them up right off the ground.

There are also crystal mines in the surrounding hills where you can go and dig your own. You can take home all you want. There are little, six-sided crystals that fit in your hand, and I've seen some beautiful quartz clusters as big as coffee tables. Our family made a trip to Hot Springs when I was young. While there, I accumulated a pile of crystals that would have filled the trunk of the car, but my father set a limit of "one shoebox full only."

I can't mention Arkansas quartz without also mentioning the only naturally-occurring diamond mine in the United States, which is located not far from Hot Springs. It is fun to go there and dig for diamonds. I have never found one, but people regularly do. Some are both large and valuable. I am ever hopeful though, and I go back there, once in a while. (Later, after I had finished the house and was getting married, I took my fiancée there, and teased that if she wanted a diamond in her engagement ring, she would have to dig it herself.).

Diamonds aside, I have always admired beautiful objects made from marble, granite, and other natural stone. Countertops and floors included. I learned that there was a granite and marble auction that was held a couple of times a year in a warehouse not far from the Port of Houston. The auction was held to liquidate granite and other stone building products that were remnants from building sites located all over the United States. There may be a batch of black marble left over from building a hotel lobby in Kansas City, or some pretty speckled granite from a new office tower floor in Oregon.

I had the date of the next auction marked in my calendar and eagerly awaited it. It was to be held the very next Sunday. I went to it with great anticipation, armed with the dimensions of my floors and countertops. The auction was wonderful. I never saw so much pretty stone all in one place—I could have happily bought one piece of everything. I looked at about a hundred different kinds of stone. For an auction like this you had to go with an open mind about what you would accept. For example, it would have been too restrictive to decide you wanted "pink granite" and nothing else would do. Better would be to go looking for *light-colored* granite. You were almost certain to find something you'd be happy with.

I wanted real marble countertops in the kitchen. I also needed another kind of decorative stone for the bathroom countertop, plus something for the kitchen and bathroom floors. Except for the marble, I had no preconceived notions of what to get; I just needed to look and get some ideas. I saw maybe fifteen different colors of marble there. I was in heaven!

I was very happy to discover some beautiful, dark green marble, with white veins. The color was listed as Imperial Green. It could only be described as sexy. What great luck! The auction began and we went around the room, the auctioneer barking and a crowd of people bidding. When we got to the green marble, I bid and played to win. The marble came in twelve-inch by twelve-inch squares. I was able to get enough for my job plus a margin of extra too, at a good price.

While there, I saw some stunning Mexican onyx, also in twelve-inch by twelve-inch squares. Each square was highly polished, had an overall cream color, and was translucent when held up to the light. It featured rich, swirling brown veins in it. Beautiful! I decided to get this for the bathroom countertop. I spent a little more for it, but I only needed twelve squares for the countertop and backsplash.

I also found some real slate that was attractive. It was grey with mottled browns. It came in twelve-inch by twelve-inch squares too. I got enough of this to do both the bathroom and kitchen floors. This I got for a fabulous bargain, about what you'd have to pay for cheap linoleum.

That evening when I got back, I had a surprise waiting for me: a flagpole. Not just any flagpole, mind you—the very best kind—a sailboat mast. My friend, Marcel was a well-known local sailor. He had been following my building progress with great interest. The mast was his contribution to the Oleanders. It was lying beside the driveway when I got home. This was great! Upon its halyards would fly flags from Bermuda, Arkansas, the Bahamas, the Jolly Roger, and any other flags I might happen across. I had just the spot for it, too. Right beside the driveway where it would be visible when I drove up.

I didn't need any help setting it up. I used what I'd learned when we set the pilings: two bracing two by fours, attached to the mast at a ninety-degree angle, leveled and staked down, and set in cement. What do you know; I got it straight! The first flag I flew on the new flagpole had been made for me by a sister of my sailboat. It was inspired from the *Wizard of Oz*, and read: *I'd turn back if I were you.*

And now, I mustn't write another word, for to do so would be robbing from the next chapter. Not only that, I must go hover.

As far as the ladies of San Leon are concerned, what did you want to know about them? Why do you want to know?

Chapter 12
Going Shopping

"When the going gets tough, the tough go shopping."

I went shopping for showers. I needed a model with lots of neon, smoked Plexiglas, an MP3 player, an enhanced surround sound system, and water jets that pulsated in time to the music. The plumbing was all ready for it; the requisite supporting layer had been installed in the corner where it would go. I went to the home improvement store to order it.

While I was at it, I picked up my special order toilet seat (Arkansas picture frame) that was already in. It was a sight to behold, polished wood with brass fittings and a dark mahogany finish. I gave it ten years, after which it would likely crack and pinch some unlucky soul in a private place one cold morning.

During these days, amenities were flying onto the house thick and fast. It was very exciting to see it coming together, but I was getting tired of building. I was still painfully reminded that everything that was to be built would only get built if I made it happen. Many were the days that I would rather have done other things than build, but I couldn't stop. I was constantly either continuing a job, finishing a job, or starting a new one. And, I was having to go so slowly. Everything took me a lot longer than it would a seasoned carpenter.

I was lamenting this to a friend one night, who offered the following encouraging words:

"Remember, the Titanic was built by professionals, and the Ark was built by amateurs."

The next thing to address was proper indoor electricity. The chief feature of this would be the electrical service panel and box. This was the box to which the power lines from the light company were connected, as well as all of the wall outlets, light fixtures, and appliances within the house. I would like to have hidden this panel inside a convenient closet, but alas, there were none handy. I had to mount it in one of the walls of the main room. This would detract from the good looks of my knotty pine walls but not half as bad as the velvet Elvis painting I would have to get to cover it up!

I installed the box and panel with no trouble. Then I dug a ditch between the house and the pole for the wires. Underground, the wires would be hurricane-proof and safe. When I was finished, I called my electrician friend Wayne.

Wayne came over the next Saturday. He carefully disconnected the electric power, and we removed the temporary outlets I had been using. We routed the new wiring from the meter on the pole down into the ditch, over to the house and up into the service panel. The wiring was routed through PVC pipe for safety.

When we were finished, Wayne carefully made the final connections to the live power. I flipped the main breaker switch in the house, and my test light came on. You guessed it—money and alcohol changed hands, along with my profuse thanks. When Wayne left, I tidied up the box for a safe installation that was also clean and neat. The service panel was ready for action. No more extension cords running out the window!

In the meantime, Gilberto had to move onward and upward. At least that is what he said. I took this to mean he would be working on a house that was up on stilts. Actually he got a more lucrative contract than what I could pay him. I bid him a fond farewell and pressed on, alone. That was okay; I had plenty to do. Onward into the abyss I trudged. My, how time flies when you don't know what you're doing!

It was lonely with Gilberto gone. There was nobody there to squabble over the radio with. It was too quiet. In fact, I missed all of my friends. Building the house had taken me out of circulation. On Saturdays, I thought about all of my sailing friends, out enjoying the bay while I was stuck here, banging nails, sawing boards, and generally imperiling my health. I thought back again to my friend, Tim—Tim the pirate—and wondered what he was up to.

Tim the Pirate

"Mother, mother ocean, I have heard you call,
Wanted to sail upon your waters since I was three feet tall"

—Jimmy Buffett, A Pirate Looks at Forty

Tim was one of the regular Hoagie Ranchers. He kept a sailboat at Marina D'Amigos, just down the road. He was carefree, funny, and likable. Tim was indeed a real, live, modern-day pirate. One day he got the opportunity to buy three very nice large sailboats, for a small fraction of what they were worth. There was a catch: the boats were being held, illegally, in Mexico. Someone would have to go there, somehow get possession of them, and sail them back. The boats were originally owned by Americans and had been placed in the Mexican charter industry, but the charter company had failed to perform their obligations as set forth in the contract. A dispute between them and the American owners ensued. The Mexican charter company severed ties but kept the boats and continued to charter them.

With no income from the Mexican charter company, the owners had no choice but to default on the boat loans, which reverted back to the local bank that was financing the operation. In an effort to close the books on the loss, the bank advertised the boats for sale at extremely low rates, no doubt having reservations about anyone ever being able to actually succeed in getting the boats back. When Tim heard about it, he jumped at the chance.

Tim assembled some friends for crew and went to Mexico to reconnoiter things. One boat had been wrecked on a reef and was not salvageable. The other two were being chartered regularly by unsuspecting vacationers in a beautiful tropical paradise. They were moored in a little bay in front of the charter company owner's home and in plain sight. This would make any recovery of the boats tough!

They eventually decided on a plan that involved arranging a charter of one of the two boats. Unfortunately, they were required to take a local skipper on board. Therefore, they would have to begin the charter and overpower the skipper at an opportune moment. Then they would sail over to the other boat, put half of the crew on it and sail both boats back to Texas.

The next day, the charter began. They had gotten away from the dock and were just preparing to take over the boat when the skipper unexpectedly turned into a hotel to pick up some more passengers. Uh-oh! Tim couldn't very well commandeer a boat with other people on it and perhaps put their lives in jeopardy, so he went below to think. While he did, he looked around and noted the condition of the boat and supplies. It was a good thing, for he discovered that the mainsail had a four-foot tear in it and would never make it back to Texas. He decided it would be wise to scuttle the mission, fly back to Texas and try again at another time. When they were ready for the second attempt, they flew back to Mexico, new mainsail in hand. Tim had dyed his hair and shaved his moustache so as to not be recognized. Their plan was basically the same. This time they were much better prepared.

They arranged a three-day charter. Once underway, they commandeered the boat from the surprised skipper. This was thankfully accomplished without violence. Tim carefully explained to the skipper, Francesco, what they were doing and why. He gave Francesco the choice of either going with them, or getting into the dinghy and going ashore. They were still not too far from land at this point. Franscesco's response was, "Oh no, Mon. I'm going with *you!*"

This made everyone on board laugh, and Tim told Francesco he would buy him a plane ticket home when they got to Texas.

They waited till dark and then quietly made their way over to where the other vessel was moored. They stealthily went aboard, hot-wired the motor to get it started, and both boats slipped away in the moonlight to begin the trip back to Texas.

When he discovered the loss, the owner of the charter company called the Federales to report a theft and kidnapping. Tim and the crews had made it to open water, but they were subsequently located by the Mexican Navy and arrested at gunpoint on the high seas. The boats were confiscated, and Tim and the crew were put in jail.

The story of being in a Mexican jail and finally getting out was not a pretty one. It included dangerous other prisoners, unsanitary conditions, and corrupt officials demanding bribes. They finally got released, only for Tim to have to endure a protracted ordeal of proving his ownership of the boats. After much time had gone by and several fruitless trips to Mexico, it was finally proven to the satisfaction of the Federales that Tim was the rightful owner, and he was cleared to recover the boats. Tim assembled two crews and flew to Mexico to sail the two boats back.

It was by then November of that year. November is a tempestuous time in the Gulf of Mexico. The weather is frequently punctuated by strong squalls. The boats and crews took quite a beating. One boat lost power and subsequently the use of the motor, radio, lights, and stove. They couldn't get fresh water out of the tanks and had to live on Spam, crackers, and cereal. The other boat developed a severe leak and the steering system came apart. They weathered storm after storm, and the two boats became separated and lost contact.

Finally, Tim's boat made it to Galveston, Texas, after eight days at sea. The other boat limped in a day later. When Tim and crew sailed into Kemah, there were about thirty people waiting at the marina to catch the dock lines. What a joyous reunion! Beers were tossed to the bedraggled but triumphant crew. Word had leaked around the sailing community via the "coconut telegraph," and everybody wanted to hear the story of the adventure.

When I heard Tim's story one night at the Hoagie ranch after it was all over, I just looked at him and grinned. I realized that I was indeed looking at a real live, modern-day pirate.

"Tim the pirate, in staged pirate regalia"

• • •

Back to work. One fine morning, the phone at Oleander Construction rang. It startled me, causing me to spit out my peanuts and almost capsize the chair I was leaning back in. The caller turned out to be another carpenter, looking for work. He had seen the sign in the yard for "Oleander Construction"— ha! I invited him to drop by, and he did, a short while later. Yes, he had been in construction for several years. Yes, he was familiar with electrical. Yes, he could help me do the wood vaulted ceiling. And he had some cool tools. And he was a lead guitarist. Remember, this house was "built by musicians for musicians." I hired him on the spot. He would start the next morning.

It's a good idea to be cautious about walk-up types like this. San Leon is what it is, and it ain't what it ain't. However, Larry and I got along famously from the start. Larry was nearly one generation younger than me, and about six or seven musical generations younger. Larry had the advantage of youth and skill, which contrasted nicely with…well, me. It didn't take long before I realized he was indeed knowledgeable about the jobs to be done. He lived nearby and was willing to work on an as-needed basis. He later proved to be honest and dependable.

We began working. Hark—what was that noise? My first load of oyster shell arriving by dump truck. Another step closer to the little Port Aransas fishing cottage look.

Port Aransas

Port Aransas will always hold a special place in my heart. I first went there as a child, on a family driving vacation from Arkansas. I fell in love with it immediately. We stayed at a little motel there in the dunes, right on the beach. Each morning I couldn't wait to go outside. I'd be up at dawn. My sisters and I were allowed to go play on the beach before Mom and Dad were up, but we could not get in the water. I'd go down with my sisters to look for shells. Sand dollars were rare and celebrated finds.

We'd walk all the way down to the long pier that stretched out into the Gulf. On the way we'd examine with great interest all of the flotsam and jetsam the sea had delivered the night before. We'd walk out on the pier to see how the fishermen were doing. Often there would be big fish that had been caught, sharks even, that made me green with envy. Eventually, we'd scurry back to the motel, lest we get in trouble for being gone too long.

We'd have breakfast in the room and then all go back to the beach for the morning swim. I'd take my fishing rod along and wade out into the surf to fish, using frozen shrimp for bait. I'd catch sand trout every day. One night we'd cook them up for dinner in the little kitchenette. After the morning swim, we'd have lunch and then explore the island. We'd go into the little shops that sold *curios* and souvenirs. I had saved up my allowance to buy shells to take home. Not many shell shops in Arkansas! Then, we'd go back to the beach for the afternoon swim. If we'd had lunch out that day, we'd eat supper from things we'd bought at the little island grocery. If we'd had lunch in, we'd go out for supper. I can still taste those delicious fried shrimp, stuffed crabs, and hush puppies!

We actually had some family roots in Port Aransas. My grandfather, the one with the wooden leg, loved to fish. He would regale us with stories about fishing there with friends in the 1930s. They would stay in the Tarpon Inn, a rambling, wooden hotel.

Tarpon fishing was in its heyday in those days. It was the custom back then that when you caught a tarpon, you removed one of its scales, signed and dated it, and nailed it to the wall in the lobby of the Tarpon Inn. Tarpon scales are around three inches in diameter. The lobby walls of the Tarpon Inn eventually became so covered with scales they had to stop. There are maybe a couple thousand tarpon scales on the walls, signed and dated. Two of them were put there by my grandfather. One is dated 1937 and the other is 1939.

On that first family trip to Port Aransas, we went to the Tarpon Inn and found the scales for the first time. From then right on up to the present, whenever anyone from our family goes to Port Aransas, they are automatically charged with going to the Tarpon Inn and finding Grandpa's fish scales. They are easy to find, if you know where to look.

• • •

Oh yes, the oyster shells. My load of oyster shells was dumped in an odiferous pile. Soon, the Oleanders would look like a little fishing camp. Not all of the shells were exactly vacated by their original occupants, and for a while, the Oleanders *smelled* like a fishing camp as well. This would bring every cat in the county over to investigate. If Ivan, next door, had any objections (and he surely did), he didn't say anything about it. The pile of shells was pretty big. Until Mike got there with his tractor to spread them out, the pile sported a sign that read: "Shells 2 /$1.00."

No takers. When Larry parked next to the pile one day, I warned him sternly, "Don't make me have to check your truck for shells when you leave here!" Poor Larry.

Larry was a good carpenter. He had once built custom furniture for a living. One day, he made us a worktable out of an old pallet. The table was fairly crude, but it would be useful. Upon seeing it, I allowed as how it had probably been a shrewd business decision to get out of the custom furniture business.

At this point, I would like to make the following observation: house carpentry is completely different from boat carpentry. It is possible to build houses that are level and square. With boats, throw away your level; it won't be. Lose your square; it can't be. Nothing on a boat is ever level or square. My preoccupation with level was driven by a fear that people driving by would see the house and say things like, "He must have thrown away his level," or "Maybe he lost his square."

Because of my teasing, Larry learned early on to seize his little victories wherever he could. One day, he said, "Hey Andy, go look in my toolbox and bring me a sky hook."

I obediently put down my coffee and started pawing around in the toolbox. After a few minutes of fruitless searching, I returned with a blank expression on my face to Larry, who was wearing a broad grin. Sometimes, I'm not the sharpest knife in the drawer, but this time, nobody had to draw me a picture that I'd been taken.

"All right, you," I growled. "Remember, I've got neckties older than you are."

Skyhooks are in the same category as *henweighs*. "What's a henweigh?" you may ask.

Oh, about three pounds.

The Critical Path

I sat uncomfortably in a hard chair in the stark office of Miss Abigail Oglethorpe. Miss Oglethorpe was the very portrait of a loan officer: single, too thin, and with an abysmal wardrobe. And those glasses...! I took all this in as she frowned over the paperwork I had just delivered to her.

"What is your budget?" she wanted to know. "What's the time frame? Where is the critical path?"

"The critical path has only been lightly traveled since the toilet got installed," I replied.

This humor is completely lost on persons like Miss Oglethorpe. She sighed disappointedly.

"Mr. Upchurch," she began. "You have exactly ninety-three days to complete this house before your construction loan term expires. You identified no less than fifty-one tasks that you must complete within that time."

She leaned forward, removed her glasses, and clasped her hands in front of her. "Now, just how do you plan to accomplish this?"

"Don't worry. It will all get done," I said, marshalling my confidence. "I've got some good people helping me. I am 'way ahead of the construction loan in the dollars spent projection. If time starts getting short, I can bring in more skilled labor to speed things up. I'm not going to let anything stand in the way of me finishing this house."

"Well, good luck," she sighed, in a way that sounded as if she had already written me off. "I wish you success." Then she warned, "Better get with it. We'd hate to see you lose your house or damage your credit."

I thanked her, said good-bye and slunk out of the office. It would all get done too, if it didn't kill me first. This house was *meant to be*! I was going to have to work harder, smarter, and faster. I drove off to the hardware store. I had received a call earlier that day: My shower had arrived.

There was something wrong with the shower. There was no smoked Plexiglas. No neon. No fancy electronics either. I pouted, but loaded it up anyway to take to the Oleanders for installation.

The installation started off fairly well. I maneuvered the shower into place and then marked it. I pulled the shower back. I maneuvered it into place again to verify my marks. I repeated this another time or two—it had to be right; there wouldn't be any second chances. When I was satisfied that all was ready, I moved the shower back into position. This time, underneath it was a pile of wet cement that would support the bottom. The shower did not seat correctly. Something was holding it up on one side. I felt around the perimeter, feeling for what could be holding it up. I didn't feel anything, so I stuck my finger underneath the shower. This constituted an act of dumbness. The good news was that it only fell one inch. The bad news was that the weight of the whole shower landed squarely on the end of my finger, breaking it.

At this point, a seasoned carpenter would merely have winced and kept going. Those guys are tough! I, however, hopped around the bathroom, howling piteously, and then danced all around the main room as if in some kind of wondrous tarantella, swinging an imaginary partner to and fro as I dipped and whirled among the tools and sawdust. I danced over near the cooler and plunged my injured digit, which was starting to swell, into the ice water. My startled helper took all of this in, and then asked, "What happened?"

"I think I've broken my finger," I replied, trying to sound nonchalant. "What do you say we call it a day?"

After a few minutes, my finger became numb, and my heart rate returned to normal. Further construction had lost its appeal for the day. I finished getting the shower seated anyway and lightly tacked it to the wall. It was past suppertime by then. I called a doctor friend of mine to see what could be done for a broken finger. He said that about all I could do would be to splint it and let it start healing. This I did, and I began wondering how I was going to play the piano, something I was slated to do the very next evening. For money.

The short answer was that I could still play the piano after a fashion, although my playing was a little sloppy in the left hand.

With this particular band I was set up in front of a brass section. On one song, I kept hearing wrong notes every time we got to the bridge. *Boy*, I thought. *I need to check out those brass parts in our next rehearsal.* The last time through the bridge, however, I happened to look down and discovered the source of the offending sounds: my finger splint was dragging on the black keys!

My finger didn't hurt so bad as to stop me from having a little fun later on in the evening. When it was time to begin the middle set, we all got on stage. The singer counted the opening piece down, and off we went. Or were supposed to. The song, which featured a strong brass introduction, attempted to take wing and soar. However, the song was mortally wounded and never even got off the ground. The brass section couldn't play a single note, because I, unnoticed, had stolen all of their mouthpieces. The band ground to a clangorous halt. Amid the ensuing chaos, I pulled four mouthpieces out of my pocket.

The brass section, a villainous lot that now had vengeance on their minds, paid me back later, or tried to. But I was wary. As I was getting ready to sit down at the piano to play the last set, I happened to see out of the corner of my eye a large, delicious, chocolate éclair—sitting right on my piano seat! I barely saw it in time.

My broken finger slowed me down with construction, but it didn't stop me. I prevailed with the shower. After I attached the glass shower doors, it looked grand. The next order of business was to get a hot water heater. I had decided to make the house all-electric, because I didn't want to risk blowing myself up with an amateur installation of natural gas lines. I purchased a hot water heater and installed it. There weren't any sinks or other fixtures that could utilize the hot water except for the shower, but that was okay. I went under the house and connected the plumbing. This was followed by the first shower in the new house. *Aaaah!*

Now it was time to toil through the installation of the wood ceiling. To see what perils lay ahead during this job, you too must toil onward to the next section.

The Next Section

"We are the Champions."

—*Freddie Mercury*

The ceiling operation started off with the *installation of the insulation*, a task that left me itching for days, and more than a little irritable once the minute fiberglass fibers worked their way into my knickers. What a miserable job.

The ceiling was to be vaulted and faced with an attractive wood that came in long, narrow slats. This wood is called "beadboard," but I have also heard it referred to as "car siding" too because in the olden days, wood like this was used to line the inside of railroad cars.

I placed an order for some. While I was waiting for it, I added some wiring for ceiling fans and smoke detectors. Fires can and do happen in houses under construction. I was keen to get smoke detectors operational as soon as I could.

The lumber arrived, a small forest's worth. Larry and I started nailing it up. Even though the house was not very big, the entire ceiling was getting this treatment, and it took a long time. When done, it looked positively smashing, even unfinished.

Now, to refinish it. The various tasks that had to be done to it included a complete sanding, and applying coats of wood conditioner, stain, and polyurethane. All counted, the whole ceiling had to be gone over nine times. I worked all day long and into the nights. I'd put on a coat of whatever was being applied at the time and then do other tasks to give it time to dry, and then apply the next coat. I bought a floodlight so that I could work at night. The days and nights blended together. I had my little portable CD player, my cooler, and a small microwave. That's all I needed. I'd play CDs to keep me company and was happy.

Dinner was out of cans. If anybody had asked me what cologne I was wearing during these days, the response would have been Aroma Therapy, because that was the brand of dish detergent I used to wash up with each night before I left to go home to the boat.

Brush by brush, coat by coat, I worked steadily toward finishing it, and then one day, it was. I got Ivan to come over and take a look. It was worth all the work. It turned out a warm, lustrous blond color. Of all of the jobs involved in building the house, the ceiling was one of which I was the proudest.

When I was finished with the ceiling, I could feel the stealth of what I'll call "builder paralysis" setting in. I would find myself sometimes just sitting and staring, thinking about all of the things that still needed to be done and not knowing exactly where to start or what order they should be done in.

I felt overwhelmed. Should I put in the bathroom wall or the bathroom sink cabinet first? What about the bathroom ceiling? When should I start on the kitchen? Oh wait; I can't do that until I do the kitchen electrical wiring. And hold up, I'm about out of money. Time to request another draw from the construction loan…

Larry saved the day. "Relax," he soothed. "First we'll do the bathroom ceiling, then the bathroom walls, then the sink cabinet and the sink. Then we'll finish up the electrical wiring, put in the kitchen walls, and then install the kitchen cabinets."

And that is just what we did. See? Anybody can build a house. You just have to take things slowly, one step at a time.

> Dear Mom—
> How are you? I am fine. The house is coming along. The other morning I had to go to the hardware store where they all know me by name. When I walked in the door, a couple of the guys who work there, who I thought were my friends, smirked at each other and then one said, "What kind of paint is that on your house? Would that be John Deere paint?"
> They snickered, and then Derrick said, "Is that shade 'Mobile Home Green' or something?" Then Clint said, "Did somebody *give* you all of that paint?" and they all laughed. It's okay, because we're all big construction bud-

dies, and they were laughing *with* me, and not at me. At least, that's what they said, but Mom, I wasn't laughing. I didn't think it was so funny. I sort of got my feelings hurt.
All for now,
Your loving son

I had to maintain a stiff upper lip around all of my man friends. Mustn't let them see that you're wounded. I subscribe to the *Man Rules.*

Burnt Toast

Remember Clayton? My cousin, the one who was with me when we found all of those arrowheads when we were young? Clayton is a great cousin. He called to offer his services with all of the house wiring.

"Yes, come," I enthused, "At your earliest convenience."

Clayton arrived the next weekend with a complete entourage, including his father and two sons. The whole crew went under the name of Burnt Toast Electrical Service. They arrived ready to work, but first, a big seafood dinner at Topwater Grill was in order. The next morning, bright and early, we got to work. The place was abuzz. We drilled holes in studs, snaked wires through them, and wired up the electrical outlets. The wires ran from the electrical service panel to all of the outlets, light fixtures, and appliances.

Uncle Jim, wiser than the others, found a not-too-dirty chair and supplied the play-by-play, with a cup of construction coffee (that's instant coffee with a pinch of sawdust in it) in his hand. They worked hard for a whole weekend, and then they were gone. What a great help! Prior to departing, everybody signed their names on the interior wall studs. Signing the walls became a tradition at the Oleanders for everyone who worked on the house. I waved goodbye to them, fondly. It had been a fun weekend.

Going back inside, I suddenly saw for the first time the glimmer of light. The light at the end of the tunnel! It was very faint, but it was *visible, unmistakable.* For the first time, I could see the end. It was in sight.

I had a humorous thought about beers having a "born-on" date. Maybe this house needed a born-on date, too! What should that date be? Would it be the date that I actually started building, or the completion date? Or perhaps the move-in date?

I wanted to start spending nights in the house as soon as construction was far enough along and save the drive to and from the boat, which was getting old. The date for this should be simple enough to establish. It would be the day that the house had acquired more amenities than currently existed on the boat. The house was still missing things like a sink and a bed. So far, the boat was infinitely more comfortable than the house would be, in those fall-ish days.

When would the house be finished? I didn't know. The construction loan term was supposed to be over in three months. I guess that would be when I would be finished. What if I wasn't? I knew I'd better have something to show for it when I had to go and face Miss Oglethorpe again. This evoked the quintessential and philosophical question:

"If a woman could have a baby in nine months, could nine women have a baby in one month?"

Unlike the riddle, the answer for me was "yes." If it looked like I wasn't going to be done in time, I could always get more professional help and speed things up so that it would be. However, that wouldn't be the Oleander Way. I still wanted to do all of the building myself.

By then I was getting very tired of building. I didn't take days off. I was tired of hanging out in hardware stores and researching building supplies. Almost every day, I was doing things I didn't know how to do even the year before. I was living in the unknown; I met it on a daily basis. This was not a bad thing. How was I to learn if I never have any new experiences? If I always stayed within my comfort zone, I never would have undertaken the building of a house.

I also would never have had one of my best adventures of all, a couple of years before I started building the house. The one where I decided to take my sailboat, Mañana on a voyage different than any I had taken before—offshore, overnight, and alone.

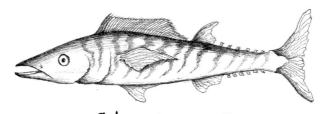

Chapter 13

Single-handed to Port Aransas!

I sat, contemplating life. I was back home. The bruises and my sunburn were fading, and the saltwater sores were nearly gone. I had just returned from a trip I'd been wanting to make for a long time—a sailing trip to Port Aransas—in my own boat, offshore, and by myself.

Mañana, my sailboat, was well built for coastal sailing. I wanted to see if I was! I regarded this trip as the next step in my continuing development as a sailor. I'd been to Port Aransas before via the ICW, and I'd been there offshore as well, on other's boats. I wasn't ready to do this trip even a year ago, but I was now. This voyage's time had come.

I broke out my charts, offshore as well as ICW just in case, and studied them. I input waypoints into my GPS for the intermediate ports, should I need to find one due to weather or boat problems. I then paid a visit to a sailing friend whose judgment I trusted, to avail myself of his knowledge and experience. After that, it was only a matter of checking out the boat, buying groceries, and…departing.

This I did one sunny Saturday morning in August. It started with the easy and familiar trip from Kemah to Galveston. The leg was remarkable only because the mainsail developed a twelve-inch tear. Not because of weather, but age. The sail was just tired. In Galveston, I was met by Excitable Crew, who drove over to meet me for dinner. After a nice meal in this historic old seaport town, I got out a big needle and some dental floss, and Excitable Crew stitched the sail back together.

The next morning, bright and early, I arose and prepared to put to sea, on what was to be my greatest adventure yet. I was excited at the prospect of being offshore by myself for the first time and looked forward to spending my first night at sea alone, if slightly nervous about it all. I figured August was a good month to stage the trip because, hurricanes notwithstanding, I could count on settled weather. August is not typically a very windy month, and, this first time out of the box I would rather have had too little wind than too much of it. I wouldn't want to try the trip in October with its Blue Northers blasting through, or in March with its spring squalls. As it turned out, light wind, plus getting lost, made for a longer trip than it normally would have been.

I got the boat underway, after a tot of rum over the side for Neptune and a small utterance for my deliverance. I raised full main and jib in the protected waters of Galveston Harbor and headed out to the jetties.

I sailed out of the jetties and into the Gulf. I originally planned to sail the depth contours, staying in about fifty feet of water. That would keep me from either going too far out to sea or getting too close to shore. But because of the nice reach I was on I changed my mind and kept going. I put on my safety harness.

It was exhilarating being out in really big water. The color changed to a deep, rich indigo. Gradually, all vestiges of the shore slipped away and I was totally alone. I felt no fear, only excitement.

After about four hours, I tacked back toward Port Aransas. By this time I was in eighty and ninety feet of water. It turned out that I never had to tack again the whole trip. The weather was settled. I was making good time and sailing in the right direction. Because I was new to ocean sailing, I was not expecting a particularly fast run. Just getting there in one piece would be good enough. All in all, I figured it would take me about thirty-five hours to make the 176 nautical mile trip. That would put me in Port Aransas at suppertime the next evening. *Charge!*

The luncheon hour afforded me cheese and Braunschweiger on crackers. By mid-afternoon it was hot. Very. I was chain-drinking Gatorades. The wind died and I turned on the motor. I sailed by my compass heading and checked the GPS about every two hours to make sure of where I was. Freeport loomed ahead and to starboard, thirty miles off. Life was good.

I was keen to do some fishing. You never know what you may catch out in waters like this. I'd be a fool *not* to try! I had bought some frozen ballyhoo, a type of saltwater baitfish that was good for trolling, in Galveston before I left. I rigged up my trolling rod.

All of a sudden, the reel started singing and line started paying out. I leapt to my station, hitting my head and crashing into the stern railing. I grabbed the fishing rod and started cranking. I had a solid hookup! I cranked, corrected course, cranked, corrected course, etc., until my prize was in sight. You could not imagine my excitement as I got the fish in the last few yards. I squinted at the water, bursting with curiosity to see what I'd caught. A tuna? I had wasabi and soy aboard for just this occasion. I'm talking *fresh* sushi! If not tuna, perhaps a wahoo? Dolphin? Giant squid? Sea serpent?

When the fish was close enough I carefully grabbed the line and hoisted it aboard. A fifteen-pound mackerel. *Well, all right!* Yikes, it had teeth! He was dispatched with the winch handle and committed to the ice chest. *Ha!* Onward to Port Aransas!

Catching this fish made me remember the time I went fishing and "caught" lunch for some boat neighbors, Jim and Linda. It turned into a funny joke, and thinking about it made me laugh out loud. It went like this:

• • •

One Saturday morning not long after I had first moved aboard the sailboat, I decided to jump on the Jet Ski and do a little fishing. I gathered my fishing gear, got on the ski, and headed out to the bay. On the way out of the marina, I saw some friends, Jim and Linda, enjoying coffee in the cockpit of their boat. I puttered over to say hello.

"Where are you off to?" Jim inquired.

"Fishing," I replied. "Do you like fish?"

"Love it," said Linda. "We eat it once or twice a week."

"Me too. What is your favorite?"

"Flounder," Jim and Linda both said, together.

We all laughed, and then I said, "Would you like me to catch you some?"

"Sure," said Jim, humoring me.

"Okay—I'll catch you some flounders. Where will you be in a couple of hours?"

Jim could tell that his chain was being jerked, but he said, "Right here. Just bring 'em on over, and we'll put them on the grill for lunch."

"Okay. Don't go out to eat," I said, and I started the Scalded Hog and putted off to get bait.

The fishing, which had been generally good of late, was not good that morning. I didn't know why—my bait was fresh, the weather was nice, and there was a favorable tide. Sometimes fishing can be like that. I fished up most of my bait without much action and decided to call it a day.

Now I had a problem: I had pompously told Jim and Linda that I would catch them some fish, but I was empty handed. By the time I was back in the channel heading home, I had come up with a backup plan. I rode the Jet Ski around to a fish market where I bought four nice flounders. Laughing to myself, I put them on my fish stringer. Never mind that they had already been scaled and cleaned! I got back on my Jet Ski and went back to the marina.

Linda was lounging on the boat, reading a book. I idled over, lifted up the stringer of fish for her to take, and grinned.

Linda stared in amazement. "Jim! Come and see what Andy's caught."

Jim's head popped up out of the companionway. He saw the fish and broke into a broad smile.

"Well I'll be! Where did you catch those things?" he asked.

"Right over there behind Mirabelle's," I replied, trying to keep a straight face.

"Wow, thanks. Cleaned and everything. Can I give you some money for them?" asked Linda.

"Oh, no, this is a gift. *Bon appétit!*" And with that I started the Scalded Hog and went back to my own boat. Not a moment too soon, because I was laughing almost before I was out of hearing.

I laughed on and off about it for the rest of the day, and the next several days. Another neighbor told me later that he had heard about the fish I'd caught for Jim and Linda, causing me to start laughing all over again. It was all in good fun. I didn't tell them the truth for a long time. One day I finally did, with a few neighbors standing around.

• • •

The mackerel turned out to be the only fish I caught on the way to Port Aransas. I got four more good hookups but was unable to boat them. I had bought the rod and reel at a nautical flea market for ten dollars and it kept malfunctioning in the heat of the battle, allowing the fish to throw the hook. Heartbreaking. Fishing is a kind of torture...

After awhile, I put my rod away. I began having sort of a *sinking* spell. The cockpit was by then an unholy mixture of slimy ballyhoo, suntan lotion, spilled potato chips, tangled lines, and empty Gatorade bottles. The wind was off, it was very hot, and I had just heard on the radio about hurricane Alberto in the Atlantic. Alberto wasn't particularly threatening the Gulf of Mexico area, but when you're hot and tired, you don't always think clearly and things bother you more.

I actually considered scrubbing the offshore trip and going ashore at Freeport. I continued in this funk for a couple of hours and almost succumbed to it. After a few minutes of considering it, I thought, *what are you thinking? You can't do that!*—and snapped out of it. I rallied and made up my mind to continue. I'm glad I did. My GPS told me that I was abreast of Freeport, and then as I worked my way southwest, Freeport slipped off astern.

Single-handing Mañana, which has no autopilot or self-steering, means you can't leave the wheel for long. She won't go more than a minute unattended before the waves or wind have slapped her off course. I got to where I wouldn't leave the wheel for just "one reason." I'd wait until I had about five accumulated tasks to do. Then I'd put the wheel brake on to keep the boat sailing the same heading, and then make a mad dash around the boat to do my tasks and get back to the helm before Mañana took over and had us sailing back the direction in which we'd come. Tasks like getting a Gatorade, grabbing something to eat, throwing away the trash on the cabin floor where it had been tossed , turning on the radio, turning off the radio, etc., etc.

You can trim a sailboat so that she stops sailing forward and looks after herself. This is called "heaving to." Heaving to is a method of setting the sails and rudder so that the boat lies more or less in place in the water. Mariners have used this practice for eons while sailing long distances across open water in order to get some rest. With a boat hove to and no one on watch, she is less apt to run into whales, other vessels, oil platforms, or floating junk, or get into other trouble. I had heard that large, room-sized shipping containers sometimes fall off ships and drift just under the surface around the oceans of the world.

Heaving to is a drill that causes the boat to go into a slow, undulating dance wherein she goes forward and then backwards in slow, graceful arcs, like a fluttering leaf. The overall effect is that the boat stays relatively put. At least, she is not charging ahead.

I hove to the boat. I was inexperienced at this and didn't quite have the hang of it, but I got it close enough. I sat and watched her for a couple of minutes to make sure she would behave and then left the wheel. With the boat gently working to and fro, I could spend as long as I wanted away from the helm. I spent several minutes fixing my position on the chart. So far, so good. I tidied the boat up a little, stretched some, turned on navigation lights, updated the log, and got some supper ready to eat. Food, while I was underway, was generally whatever was easy to fix and sounded good.

When I was ready, I went back to the helm and put Mañana back on her course. I leisurely enjoyed my Spartan supper. I don't remember what it was, except that it was out of a can. It tasted good and I was thankful to have it. Sometimes the simplest of pleasures can be so satisfying...

I prepared to spend my first night at sea. The sun set gloriously, and for a moment I wished I had someone there to share it with. It soon became dark and the moon rose. It was full, and I was surprised at how well I could see. The oil and gas platforms were plainly visible. They were plentiful in this part of the Gulf, and there were always eight or ten in sight. They were mostly well lit; however, I did see a few structures that weren't. This was concerning! One of my biggest fears was colliding with an unlit structure in the dark. Gradually, I began to feel at ease. I was wide awake. The night was not without its few tense moments though.

Uh-oh, what was that up ahead? Red and green lights on what I thought was a stationary platform. Red and green lights at sea indicate a vessel underway. I couldn't make the object out. Was it a ship? It had to be a ship... it was headed my way. How big? Couldn't tell. Maybe huge. It looked like it was on a collision course! I needed to get out of the way. Was I ready to tack? *Okay! Hurry*...tack. *Now!*

I spun the wheel hard over. The boat spun wildly around, winches clattering, lines flailing and sails flapping, and I put her on a course that I hoped would take me out of the path of the perceived danger. A few anxious minutes passed. When it appeared that I was no longer in harm's way, I relaxed a little and put Mañana back on course.

What had happened? When my heart settled down, I realized that my own boat's movement had created an illusion. The object was not moving. Yet the red and green lights signify movement. Could they belong to a supply boat tied up to a platform with its navigation lights left burning? I couldn't wait to become a more seasoned mariner and be able to figure more of these things out on my own.

Onward I sailed. The night was beautiful. It was mild and quiet. Serene. Spiritual, even. The hours went by. I reflected on the good as well as the bad things in my life. I noted my position in the log every hour but only checked my position on the chart every two hours. Kind of like investments: if you check their performance less often, it shows more performance! The stars were out and I could see my old friend the Big Dipper. It looked so low that my mast could touch it.

And then the meteors started! That's right; it was August, the best month for viewing meteors. There were no showers, but I saw several dazzling meteors, presented for my eyes only. I'll never forget sitting there at three o'clock in the morning, Mañana sailing contentedly along, the gentle swishing of water against the hull, a sky full of stars, the moon illuminating the waves, and the calmness I felt.

An hour later, I was beginning to flag. I hove to the boat to see if I could get a little rest. I set my egg timer for twenty minutes—there were oil and gas rigs around that I could run into if I were dozing. All too soon, the timer went off. I got some coffee and put us back on course.

Coffee—I couldn't cook anything while underway. It would have been unsafe to start the stove and leave it unattended to heat water while I went back up to steer. Yet I needed caffeine. I splashed some water into a cup and (I can't believe I did this) dumped in some instant coffee and drank it—cold. Whatever gets you through the night. It did the trick though, restoring me to alertness.

I set my egg timer for every hour. It startled me every time it went off. This helped me keep track of time. Every other time it went off I would turn on the GPS to find out where I was, and make a note or two in the log. On that night, I'm afraid the log was rather skimpy! I discovered that my little stereo had stopped working. I didn't feel like going down below and finding out why, although I could have used a little musical stimulus.

I didn't really need it. An endless loop of music created by my mind is always running through my head, whether I want it to or not. Now playing was my songwriter friend Kelly McGuire. Nearly all of his original songs about sailing lent themselves to my trip. Songs like *Therapy Cruise* and *Sailing Across the Gulf On My Own* (*"...like standing in the shower for five hundred hours...got me to thinkin' wishin' I was home a-drinkin' in a dry pair of underwear"*). These songs, mixed up with Jimmy Buffett's and a whole host of others kept playing—and replaying—in my mind. And kept me awake.

I started looking for dawn around five o'clock. It didn't come until six. When it did, the words from the Wizard of Oz, where Dorothy left the scary forest and beheld the Emerald City for the first time; claimed my mind:

"We're out of the woods, we're out of the woods, na-nana-na na..."

I had survived my first night at sea!

Somehow, in all my preparations, I had neglected to make sure I had good, working flashlights aboard. I discovered I had just one. It was too small, and it kept flickering. Very bad for a sailor! Without a flashlight I couldn't see the sails well enough. When it was light, I looked aloft. The repaired mainsail, which had developed an audible flutter, had not survived the night. It was ripped in a new place, nearly in half. Down she came, never to draw again. I had to complete the trip without it. That wouldn't do much to help me get to Port Aransas any quicker!

Soon, I felt an overpowering urge to close my eyes. Reasoning that any other boat traffic in the area could now see me, I hove to and lay down, still behind the wheel for a snooze. Mañana slowly meandered back and forth, and I got a little rest.

The nice wind I had all night died mid-morning. It became hot and still. I furled the jib and started the motor. There was a new vibration that didn't feel quite right. Bent prop shaft? An alignment problem? A loose strut perhaps? What if the strut was detaching from the hull? What kind of damage could *that* do? Pull loose, leaving a hole in the hull and flooding the boat, in ninety feet of water?

I'm so neurotic. Too often, I find myself "pole vaulting over mouse turds." Sometimes this is about the only exercise I ever get, that and jumping to conclusions! At any rate, there was no sense in hyperventilating over it. There was nothing I could do about it in the middle of the ocean.

The wind was still dead calm and it got even hotter. I killed the motor, put on my life vest, and jumped overboard for a swim (My sails were furled). The water felt glorious! It was a gorgeous shade of deep blue and was as calm as Clear Lake, save for gentle swells. I lollygagged in the cool water for about twenty minutes, staying right by the ladder.

The water was very clear. I wanted to get my mask and examine the prop and strut while I could see them clearly, but was afraid to do so. The stern was rising and falling, and if it fell on me while I was under water, it could knock me colder than the mackerel down in the fridge. When I had cooled off, I climbed back aboard, refreshed, and put Mañana back on her course…for Port Aransas!

A major culinary event followed the morning swim: an elegant luncheon, consisting of a can of Chili Del Sol. It was plenty warm enough and delicious, with a dollop of ketchup and some sliced onion and cheese mixed in. While I savored lunch, I enjoyed the cloud art. I can conjure up most anything when looking at clouds!

High noon found me twenty-nine nautical miles away from Port O'Connor, seventy-four miles to go to Port Aransas. My projected ETA there was two o'clock the next morning. I was about six hours behind schedule. The wind came back and soon we were again romping, toward Port Aransas. There was a clean, audible hiss as

Mañana's hull cut through the water. Her bow rose and fell gracefully as she went along, making me just about the proudest sailor there ever was.

The trip was taking its toll. I was cut, bruised, my back hurt, I had a sunburn and leg cramps. *Leg cramps?* Maybe my potassium level was low due to water loss. I had already eaten my last banana and I wished for some milk. The wind dropped a little and it became dreadfully hot again. When my speed fell below five knots, I started the motor.

A couple more times that day I felt overwhelmingly tired and hove to the boat to catch a few winks. The day wore on. Suppertime brought some surprisingly good canned Greek dolmas in olive oil, and feta cheese. By eight o'clock that evening I had only thirty-seven nautical miles to go to Port Aransas. My ETA was still two o'clock, six more hours. I wasn't keen on a jetty entrance in the dark, but that's when I was arriving, like it or not. I thought that if I got close and could see well and felt comfortable about it I might give it a try. Else, I could just loiter around outside the jetties until the sun came up. If I could stay awake.

Right about dusk, I started having hallucinations. Not serious ones like the tie-dyed Jimi Hendrix-worshipping hippies of the sixties, but odd, harmless ones. I kept imagining I was hearing music. And people talking. I went downstairs *three different times* to see if I'd left the radio on. I kept imagining I saw out of the corner of my eye someone else aboard, leaning up against the mast or sitting in the cockpit. It was very weird.

It got dark. When the moon arose this second night, it shone on the waves around me and looked for all the world like waves breaking on rocks. This was totally unnerving and I had to force myself to not look at them. There were no rocks. I was still in seventy feet of water.

At midnight I tried to heave to again and rest, but the wind was a little stronger. I locked the helm over and lay back, but the boat's motion was too distracting. *Crash! Boom! Bang! Rattle-Rattle-Rattle-Rattle-Rattle! Shake-Shake-Shake-Shake-Shake!* A few seconds of silence and then the sequence repeated itself. There was no sleep for it. Giving up, I got some "coffee" and pressed on.

Around two a.m., according to the GPS, I was seven miles away from the sea buoy, marking the entrance of the channel leading to Port Aransas. I was again wide-awake from the coffee, and very jittery. Somehow, nothing looked right. I seemed to be in an industrial area, but I was still in seventy feet of water. Could I be in a cluster of oil platforms? To make matters worse, clouds started rolling in, greatly reducing visibility. Just what I didn't need! A light rain began to fall. By then, all I wanted was to get there. I fired up the motor.

I motored directly to the location where the GPS said the sea buoy should be. As I got close to the location, I peered expectantly into the darkness ahead. I checked the GPS. It showed that I was right on top of it, but it was not there. I circled around the area for several minutes, but no sea buoy. Not good. Now what? What if I had made a mistake inputting the waypoint into the GPS before I left? I had double-checked them. I was lost!

I sailed west toward the coastline, trying to see if I could find a landmark, keeping an eye on my depth gauge. Presently, I discerned what I took to be a set of channel markers. Could they be the ones for the Port Aransas jetties? I made for a pair farthest east for insurance. When I got there and turned to go in, nothing looked right. I would have loved for a ship to come along right then to lead me in, but no such luck.

Just then I saw a very bright light. It was accompanied by red and green running lights. It was a boat, and judging from the lights was coming my way. Was I fixing to go to Davy Jones's Locker? It kept coming. I bumped the throttle all the way up and turned to try to get the hell out of the way, sweating. The object turned out to be a small open boat, night fishing, with bright lights to attract fish. The lights completely destroyed my night vision. It was by now close by, so I motored over to try to find out where I was. Aboard was an Asian couple, who couldn't understand a single word of English.

I was lost, tired, and disoriented. I tried to make sense out of my surroundings again. At least the small boat's presence meant that Port Aransas must be close by. All of this had taken two hours. It was five o'clock by then. It would be light soon. I'd best stay put and wait for daylight, and then I'd be able to sort everything out.

I sailed around in lazy circles, staying well out into deep water, waiting until the sun came up. When it did, I set off west. When I got closer, I could see a low smudge on the horizon that was land. I started looking for landmarks: the jetties, St. Joseph's Lighthouse, Horace Caldwell Pier, and condos. I saw no jetties, no lighthouse, no pier, no condos.

What I did see was a boat in the distance.

I went below and raised them on the radio. It turns out I was seven miles south of the jetties. I had sailed past them in the dark. I had evidently been too far out to sea to find them. I thanked the helpful skipper and turned around. It was then 8:30 a.m. Would I *ever* get to Port Aransas?

I was relieved to know where I was, and that the trip would be over soon. I closed in until I could see land better, being careful not to stray into shallow water. Following the coast back northeast, I started coming across…condos, the Horace Caldwell Pier, and…the jetties. I knew where I was—I was nearly there!

I sailed over to the ends of the jetties, giving them a very respectable margin of safety and then turned to go in between them. I felt my grandfather's presence as I proudly motored in. There were all the landmarks of this place that were so special to me. Down the channel I went and then turned into the city marina.

I had made it!

I was not in good shape. I was tired, weak, sore, jittery, sunburned, dirty, and hot. My hands were shaking. The boat was a complete disaster inside and out. I tied up along the wall and took a hose shower. I then collected my wallet, put on a clean shirt, and walked to the office.

I couldn't rest just yet—there was some work to do. I needed fuel and ice, and to arrange for a slip to stay in for a couple of days. After these things were accomplished, I motored over to the slip and tied up. It was nine thirty. It had taken me fifty-one hours. I was sixteen hours late.

I threw everything from the cockpit down below. With the boat stationary, it was blazing hot. Another hose shower. The bed was piled high with shore power cords, dirty clothes, etc. The air conditioner was first priority. I hooked up the shore power and got it running. Then I cleared the floor so I could walk, and then the bed. Another hose shower.

The next priority was to phone news of my safe arrival. My cell phone would not work so I went to a pay phone. Excitable Crew was not at her desk at work and a series of local and long-distance operators would not allow me to leave a message or call her pager either. At this I'm afraid I became a little snippy! I would need to get a phone card. Another hose shower. After grappling with all of the above tasks, I was inexplicably not tired anymore. I must have gotten my fifteenth or sixteenth wind. I thought that maybe if I ate a big meal, I could fall asleep afterward. I wanted to eat the fish I'd caught, but I didn't feel like cooking it. I changed clothes, stuffed the fish in a plastic sack, and caught the free trolley around to Trout Street where there was a restaurant that would cook your catch.

I walked in and encountered a pretty young hostess, who appraised my bag with the fish's snout sticking out of it with an amused smile.

"Can you cook this fish for me? I'll pay handsomely!"

She laughed and said, "Sure! You have to clean it, though."

No worries. I borrowed a knife from the kitchen and walked next door to Woody's Boat Basin where there was a fish-cleaning table. I filleted my fish in my Hawaiian shirt and returned with two big fillets, which I gave to a waiter.

"Grill and serve with lemons, please?"

The fish came out on two platters; there was so much of it. It was accompanied by a salad and baked potato. I ordered a celebratory piña colada to compliment the meal. I don't remember ever enjoying a fish dinner so much!

I did my best, but barely made a dent in all of that fish. It was delicious, and I took most of it back to the boat. It would be delicious chilled,
flaked, and mixed up with a little mayonnaise and pickle relish, like tuna
salad. On the way back, I got a phone card and called Excitable Crew to
let her know I had arrived. This time I got through. She had, of course,
been worried because I was so late getting in. For some inexplicable reason, I *still* wasn't tired, so I rattled around cleaning up some more until I
was. When I did finally lie down, I fell into a long, deep sleep. I awoke
late the next morning. Sunlight was streaming in the window. The boat
was not pitching and rolling. I looked around me. The cabin was clean
and straight. I was rested. The day was beautiful. It was cool inside. I
made a cup of espresso and turned on the little five-inch TV I'd bought
at a grocery store and watched the news. Life was *great!*

After that luxurious cup, I went outside to give Mañana a proper
scrubbing. While I was at it, I plugged the cockpit drains, filled the
cockpit with water, and enjoyed a soapy bath. I even unrolled the jib and
rinsed it. When I was done, I went around lubricating all the hardware
and inspected the rigging for wear and missing cotter pins. I found one
and replaced it. You can lose a mast over something like that.

I then put on street clothes and caught the free trolley. I was content to just ride around the island in the air conditioning and visit
with Evelyn, the driver. I got off at the grocery store to lay in some
supplies. I took too long in the store and missed the next trolley. It's
never a problem snagging a ride in a beach town, and a kind soul
gave me one back to the boat. Groceries stowed, I again caught the
trolley to finish my ride around the island.

This time I got off at the Tarpon Inn and went in to look for
Grandpa's fish scales. Then, I walked across the street to Mustang
Rod and Reel. I emerged an hour later with a brand new, deep-sea
trolling rod and reel. I walked to Virginia's, another little waterfront
restaurant, where I lunched on some delicious fresh fried calamari and
an ice cold beer. I spent the rest of the afternoon and evening studying
charts, writing up the log, and doing a little fishing. What a wonderful

day! The next day was spent in similar Bohemian fashion. I had to get ready for Excitable Crew, who was driving down from Kemah.

After she arrived, we had nothing but fun. We took a day and drove to Corpus Christi. We went fishing, swimming, and shopping. We rode the free trolley and drove to the Maritime Museum in Rockport for an interesting tour.

One night I bought fresh shrimp off of the deep-sea shrimper Pollyanna who was in port nearby. That night we had boiled shrimp in the cockpit of Mañana. Yum!

I would have loved to stay in Port Aransas for another week. All too soon, the leaving day arrived. We went to Virginia's for a final lunch and to watch the weather channel. There was a tropical depression in the Gulf. Wonderful. We went to the store where I provisioned, and then put Excitable Crew on the road. The rest of the day was spent preparing for sea.

Monday, Tropical Depression #5 spoiled my plans for going offshore and threw *me* into a tropical depression. It was not threatening the immediate area, but it was something to watch. I didn't want to be offshore if the weather took a turn for the worse. Should I wait a day and go offshore anyway or go up the ICW and be sixty miles closer to home by dark? I decided to be the prudent mariner and chose the latter.

I said good-bye to Port Aransas and left the next morning. I sailed to Port O'Connor and spent the night. There was access to the open Gulf there. The forecast was for nice weather for the next couple of days, so I decided to go offshore again and come in at Galveston. I was eager to try out my new fishing rod. I sailed out of the Matagorda Ship Channel into the open Gulf and got out the rod. Licking my chops, I baited up a ballyhoo. As I cast far out into the Gulf, I was reminded of a funny fishing episode of yore.

• • •

One day during the preceding summer, fishing had been on my mind at work. It was a Friday, the weather was very nice, and I had developed a case of office fever. I successfully fended it off for most of the day, but by mid-afternoon, I decided enough was enough. Fend no more. I gave in.

I left work early and went home to get ready to go fishing. I got on the Jet Ski and rode over to see if Stephanie had any live shrimp. She did, and I was happy to take them off her hands. I decided to go try my luck at the wall. When I got there I heaved my little anchor over, practically in the shadow of the Kemah Boardwalk. Being a nice Friday afternoon, people were coming from all over to eat at the restaurants by the water. They strolled by overhead, enjoying the evening. I began fishing. I overheard someone say, "I can't believe he's actually *fishing* off of that thing."

I fished. Boats of all kinds vroomed in and out of the channel. Life was good. Almost immediately I got a nibble and then an honest-to-goodness bite. The fish ran with my shrimp, causing my rod to dip sharply, but as soon as I started to reel, the line went slack.

Over the next several minutes, I got several more bites and then… *Wham—hookup!* I had a fish on the line. I reeled rapidly. The reel drag protested. I carefully worked the fish up to the surface and there was a momentary flash of black and silver When the fish was near, I reached down and grabbed the line and…hauled up a five pound black drum. A small round of applause went up from the people on the boardwalk.

I put dinner on the stringer. Now, if anyone laughed, I had some ammunition. I retrieved another shrimp, baited my hook and cast, landing it right next to the base of the boardwalk. Suddenly, I felt a promising tug. What could this be? Wouldn't it be fun to catch some kind of wonderful big fish, with an audience right there?

It was a solid hookup. The fish ran and I adjusted my drag. The fight was on. The fish pulled strongly. This was a quality fish! I reeled in and let it run time after time. This went on for several minutes.

Finally, the fish began to tire, and I carefully brought it up to the Jet Ski. It was a big sheepshead. I could see the brilliant black and silver stripes and the large human-like front teeth. It had to be over ten pounds. I clipped my rod on so it wouldn't go overboard and picked up my landing net. The fish was laying calmly at the water's surface beside me. I tried to net it, but the fish was too big for the net—*ha!*

I grabbed the leader and started to lift the fish up out of the water. And then, disaster. The fish was heavy enough to cause my snap swivel to open up. It straightened out like a broken diaper pin. The big fish dropped back into the water and was gone.

There was a chorus of "Awww" from above.

I attempted to stand up on the bobbing Jet Ski for a theatrical bow and very nearly capsized the Scalded Hog in the process. This brought laughter and cheering.

By this time it was starting to get dark. I hauled up my anchor and headed back to the marina to light the grill. Remembering this story made me smile as I contemplated the ballyhoo, now trailing behind the boat. Great moments in fishing!

• • •

After an hour, no fish. As it turns out, I didn't get a single strike the whole way back. How disappointing! Fishing is a kind of torture...

The wind went light and I turned on the motor. I had to motor quite a bit that day. At about four o'clock that afternoon, the wind returned and I killed the diesel. The stereo was blasting Jack Mack and the Heart Attack, and it was hard to keep from jumping up in the cockpit and dancing. At dusk, I got ready for a night at sea. I was eighty-three miles from Galveston. My ETA was noon the next day.

It got dark, and I started having trouble staying awake. I tried to heave to and rest, but there was too much wind and the boat's motion kept me awake. Giving up, I got some coffee and pressed on. It was a long, weary night. At one point I was overtaken by a large ship, but it passed harmlessly by a mile away.

Just for fun, I scribbled out a note of my adventure, put it in a bottle, and heaved it overboard. Around three o'clock a.m., I got my little TV to see if I could tune in anything to watch. I found a rerun of Nightline, which was airing the story of a doomed Russian submarine. It was an atomic sub that had just gone down in deep water. It was unknown if there was life aboard or not, but there was little hope. I felt badly for my fellow sailors.

Finally, morning guilded the skies. Twenty-seven miles to Galveston, ETA still noon. It took all morning to work my way up the Coast of Galveston Island. As I got closer, I sighted the one skyscraper on Galveston Island, where Excitable Crew worked. When noon rolled around, I had the Galveston channel markers in sight, but it was still nearly two o'clock by the time I had negotiated the Galveston jetties and was in the harbor. I got a slip at the Yacht Basin, fueled up and iced down. I straightened up a little bit, called Excitable Crew, who had seen me coming in with her binoculars, and got some rest. She drove over after work and we went out to a triumphant dinner.

I slept late the next morning. It was the last day. I arose and made a cup of steaming espresso. While the day was cool I straightened up and got ready for the short, easy trip to Kemah. It was a nice day for sailing—not as hot as it had been. When I was ready I wistfully departed Galveston. It was good to be back in my own back yard. I was ready for a few days of hiding from the sun, but I was sad the voyage was ending. On the way, I reflected on the trip. It had been wonderful and a good learning experience. I was infinitely glad that I had chosen to make it happen, instead of just dreaming about it.

As I peeled out of the Houston Ship Channel and pointed Mañana toward the Kemah Bridge, the Sailor's Prayer suddenly popped into my mind:

From rocks and sand and every ill,
May God preserve the sailor still.

I was home. I had cheated death once again!

Chapter 14

Trouble in Paradise

"Everything you need to know is printed on a jar of mayonnaise: keep cool, do not freeze." (Source unknown)

Color Conniptions

Recall that the vaulted ceiling was made of long thin boards, refinished in a light blond color. The walls would be ten-inch-wide, knotty, pine boards that would be set vertically and refinished a medium color to contrast with the ceiling. Lastly, there would be a wood floor of three-inch boards with a dark finish to contrast the walls and ceiling. Even though that was a lot of wood, there would be different colors and textures that would set the walls, floor, and ceiling off from each other and add interest. The exposed beams, windowsills, baseboards, and other wood trim would be stained dark to match the floor and help tie everything together.

Was there such a thing as too much wood? Would it all look good together? Could I find three different finishes that would complement each other? I lost sleep over this. My fears turned out to be ungrounded. As it turned out, it looked beyond great. It was not too much wood after all, and the three shades I ended up with worked perfectly together.

While I worried about color conniptions, work in other areas continued. I found a pretty hammered copper sink at a Mexican import shop that was perfect for the bathroom. I went to a home-building center and designed a kitchen on the computer.

Since the whole rest of the house's interior was natural wood, I could get away with simple, white painted cabinets in the kitchen and bathroom, and it would look fine. It was preferable, really. I needed to find ways to break up all that wood wherever I could. A picture of a similar kitchen with this look in a design catalog reinforced my decision. Happily, white painted cabinets were also cheaper than stained wood ones.

I placed an order for the kitchen and bathroom cabinets. They arrived disassembled in a stack of boxes. Their installation would have to wait until the interior walls were done.

While walls were open and exposed, it was a good time to run wires for stereo speakers and an alarm system. One day I made a pot of coffee and did just that. With coffee, all things are possible. My coffee is high voltage. Larry noted that it was strong enough to float a horseshoe in.

Outside, Larry and I built the front porch steps and arboretum. The arboretum consisted of four-inch-by-four-inch treated posts, supporting a ceiling of wood lattice that would cover the patio. I wasn't aiming to keep this area dry, just shady. I already had a nice, oversized porch for staying dry under. The plants would like it on the shady patio, out of the fierce Texas sun. As soon as I could get around to it, I would make the patio floor out of bricks.

We also poured the slab for a hot tub. This was easy to do. We built a ten-foot-by-ten-foot wooden form out of two-by-six-inch boards that were nailed together and staked to the ground. We leveled it as we went, but then made one side slightly lower on purpose to allow water to run off. We put heavy wire in the bottom of the form for internal strength. When the frame was ready, we ordered cement.

The next day, a cement truck arrived. Over the next hour we used wheelbarrows to transport cement from the churning truck to the hot tub slab. Larry was the brains of the operation; I was the dumb labor. He had made a wooden "float" that he used to work the cement as I poured it in, load by load. Presently, the form was full of wet cement. Larry worked it to a nice, flat surface, and we left it to dry. *Yes!* A hot tub had always been part of the plans, but I reasoned that if I ran out of money and couldn't afford one I could hang a mirror ball over the slab and make it into a dance floor.

Now the Oleanders had heat, air conditioning, hot water, a toilet, a shower, electricity, and a telephone. I could start sleeping there. Another milestone! I could even hook up my computer and get online. I brought a mattress to the Oleanders so I could begin staying there full time. Ah, but this was not to be. The bunking was primitive, to say the least. Each evening I would have to clear a place amid the tools, sawdust, and general rubble. I would lay a tarp down, put the mattress on top of it, make up the bed, and get into it.

It was dreadful. After a night rendered sleepless because I couldn't breathe for all the dust, I would arise, stuff the sheets in a clean trash bag, and lean the mattress up against the wall. If I had to get up in the middle of the night, I risked running into or stepping on things. Sawdust got everywhere. The whole experience became so tedious that after a few nights I pronounced the experiment a failure and aborted the mission. The "anchorage was untenable." I resorted back to the boat that was infinitely more comfortable, inviting, and *clean.* I would try again when I was a little further along. It had been unrealistic to think that I could move there so soon.

December arrived. Christmas did not go unobserved at the Oleanders. I bought a little pine tree in a pail that could be planted outside later. I placed it amid the chaos inside on a pile of wood where it cheered me. It had one string of lights on it and one ornament. When it was cold and grey outside, inside it was warm and comforting. I played Christmas music on the radio and kept working steadily. Still sometimes, loneliness would creep in and give me the blues. When that happened, I turned on every light in the place, turned up the Christmas music loud, and made a cup of coffee. That usually did the trick, and I would be back to my old self soon.

Christmas also meant the Christmas Boat Parade, the one diversion I did allow for. Of course this effort was a building distraction, but it was a meaningful experience that I was unwilling to forfeit.

That year we did a giant planet on a large sailboat. The planet featured continents, all outlined in lights. The whole thing rotated. There was also a large, bright, shooting star on the masthead with a long lit tail that ran down behind it. There were over six thousand lights on the boat, powered by three generators. Our theme? "Peace on Earth."

The judges were impressed, and we garnered an award for "Most Original."

"Christmas Boat Parades"

December also meant that the plant nurseries had big sales. I had created a little room in my construction budget for landscaping, so one day I borrowed a trailer and visited several of them, filling up the trailer with palm trees and other tropical fare.

My Christmas gift was the chance to build the house. Even on bad days I felt very fortunate to be able to have this experience. Christmas came and went, and then it was time to get back to serious work.

I was ready to start on the interior walls. The first task of this operation was to install insulation. I found a great deal on some excess rolls of insulation left over from a commercial job. The R-factor was right and it was soundproof as well. There was enough to do the walls of the entire house, and I bought it for almost nothing. At least, I was not working over my head this time. While dealing with insulation is never comfortable, walls were a lot easier to work on than ceilings.

In the meantime, I had located a mill that still produced knotty pine boards like the ones in my grandmother's house. I placed an order for enough to do the walls.

Andy and the Dreamsicles

I had a couple of friends who asked me if I would play with them in a band. I initially told them that I was too busy building, and then mentioned my construction deadline.

They said, "What if we come help build to get you finished quicker? Then can you?"

How could I refuse such a generous, timely, and needed offer for help? I grinned and said, "Okay, you win!"

Ben and Frank hit the Oleanders like a tidal wave. They arrived with fistfuls of CDs, which we crammed in the dusty old CD player and played one right after another, at volume ten. This was great, since I was tired of mine and had given up on all of the radio stations within range. The knotty pine flew onto the walls. Those were fun days. When we were finished, the change to the interior of the house was dramatic, even unfinished.

We began refinishing the new walls without skipping a beat. As with the ceiling, this involved several iterations of sanding, conditioning, staining, and polyurethaning. Ben and Frank hung in there and helped. We got this big job done in record time. Soon, there was beautiful, refinished, knotty pine everywhere. It looked even better than I had imagined it would. As hoped, it contrasted very nicely with the ceiling.

Ben and Frank were a huge help and were appreciated more than they know. I kept my end of the bargain, and we started performing. The name of the new band? "Andy and the Dreamsicles!"

"Back Wall"

Grovel

I sat in the lobby of the bank. My shoes were shined. My fingernails were clean. My hair was combed. I was there because I was in trouble. It was the middle of February. My construction loan was ending in two weeks and I wasn't going to be finished with the house in time. I put on a humble face and tried to make myself small.

Miss Abigail Oglethorpe skittered out into the lobby and I stood to greet her.

"How are you," she asked.

"Uh, okay."

"This way, please," she said. We went back into her office, and I took a seat. Miss Oglethorpe had my file out already and had been reading through it. "I hope you're here to tell me that you are finished with your house."

I fidgeted, looked down. "Well, not exactly," I said. "I'm pretty close, but still not done. On the bright side, since I was laid off, I've had lots of time to build…"

"*Laid off?*" she spluttered. "When did that happen?"

I started telling her about the blessing in disguise that being laid off had been, and about how I was able to devote all of my time to construction.

Miss Oglethorpe shook her head slowly. "This is why we don't grant construction loans to people who are not qualified," and gave me a baleful stare.

It was so comical, I had to bite my lip to keep from smiling. Mustn't laugh, I scolded myself. It'll just make things worse. I had to concentrate hard on not smiling as she went on. Suddenly it became quiet, and she was looking at me. Uh-oh, she had just asked me a question.

"Uh, could you repeat that, please?" I asked, feeling dumb.

"I *said*, where are you on the critical path?"

"I have just gotten the interior walls done. What is left to build is the kitchen and bathroom, and install the hardwood floor."

"And how long do you think it will take to get these things done?" she inquired.

Truthfully, I didn't know.

"Truthfully, I don't know," I said.

Miss Oglethorpe frowned. "Just a minute," she said, and got up, disappearing in the direction of Dave Bloom's office. She was gone several long minutes. When she returned, she said primly, "Mr. Bloom has decided to grant you a three-month extension. Will that give you enough time to finish?"

"Yes, thank you, Miss Oglethorpe. I'm sure I can be done by then," I said.

Miss Oglethorpe got up and said, "I hope so. Now get out there and finish that house."

I'll bet Miss Oglethorpe was loads of fun on a date.

Back in the car, I relaxed a little. An extension—what a relief! I had better get going. Even driving away from the bank that day, I started to feel new enthusiasm coursing through my body. Builder paralysis no more! Bend on all sail! Your best possible speed, helmsman. *Charge!* And onward into the unknown I tumbled, pell-mell.

Chapter 15
The End Is Near

"Success comes in cans, not in cant's."

Time to "man up." Where was the checklist? Over there, under yesterday's half a baloney sandwich. Where was my gnarly tool belt, frayed and worn by the work of countless jobs? By then, tasks innumerable had been tackled, demystified, and conquered. Each one completed made me feel successful and boosted my confidence. Each one meant another check mark on the checklist and brought me closer to completion.

I was like a horse smelling the barn. It was hard to keep from cutting corners in my froth to get done, but I held my horses and saw each job through to completion the right way.

I turned my attention to the floor. Wood, of course, nothing else would do. I wanted a good, solid, honest wood, no cheap substitutions, please. I started hunting. I have always been good at looking under rocks for things. Frequently, I have succeeded in locating the un-locatable. Finding real wood for my floor shouldn't be any big deal.

My search led me to a company in nearby Texas City that salvaged wood from buildings that were being demolished. They took beams, rafters, walls, ceilings, anything wood. Many of the planks were very rough, and some of them were quite large. When milled down, these same planks yielded wood that was pretty, strong, and of higher quality than what was available new in hardware stores. And it was cheaper. The very essence of recycling! It seemed worthwhile to take a road trip to visit them.

I was met by the owner of the company. He took me outside into the mill yard that contained vast piles of old, weathered, and you would have thought worthless wood. We then went back inside where he showed me the finished product. I was impressed. Using this wood was appealing to me. I described the kind of wood I was looking for and the amount that I would need. He took me to a pile of freshly milled tongue-and-groove boards three inches wide that were stacked neatly. This wood would do fine!

It so happened that this particular wood was out of an old historic landmark from the Port of Galveston, built in the early 1900s. I bought this wood, not because of its illustrious past, but because it was the right color and width to make a beautiful floor. Still, I liked that it had some history to it. In Arkansas they'd say "Hell, son, that wood's still *new* if it ain't been used in at least three barns before now!"

The wood came to the Oleanders on my friend's flatbed trailer. I unloaded the wood into a large neat pile in the middle of the house.

Now for the show stopper: the wood had to sit and acclimate for six weeks in conditioned air. *Six weeks?* I hadn't counted on that. I was cautioned not to ignore this advice. To do so could likely cause the floor to swell and warp, spoiling the job.

In building this house I tried always to apply this hard-won lesson: *Seek, and then heed, the advice of the experts.*

I resolutely left the wood alone to sit for the full length of time. Luckily, there were plenty of other things I could be doing while I waited.

Larry and I built the bar that completed the U-shaped kitchen. We made it stout enough for three dance hall girls to dance on. I then started assembling the kitchen cabinets. They were made out of particleboard and covered with a white finish resembling plastic.

I didn't consider particleboard to be of particularly high quality, even though the cabinets had been expensive. Hopefully, they would look all right when they were mounted.

I dislike working with particle wood. Like OSB, particleboard is essentially a mixture of sawdust and glue. It can break easily during assembly. However, I was very careful with it and the cabinets all went together without much trouble. I wondered how sawdust and glue would react to a slight plumbing leak. How about hurricane floodwaters?

Now to mount the cabinets. First, the lower cabinets were all moved into place, shimmed level, and screwed down. Then, I made the counter and bar tops out of plywood to make a suitable foundation for the green marble. Lastly, the upper cabinets were all hung in a neat row. So far, so good. I then assembled and installed the bathroom sink cabinet. Larry inspected my installation and gave me a passing grade.

When the kitchen and bathroom were ready for the marble, I hunted down a professional tile installer. I didn't want to spoil all that beautiful marble with an inept installation. I might have gotten the job done by myself, but I knew nothing of the latent pitfalls of working with marble that I might encounter.

There did turn out to be one. I found out that green marble squares have a propensity for warping when they get wet. Yes, marble *bends*! Other shades of marble weren't as prone to this. This doesn't mean green marble was unsuitable for kitchen countertops, but it did mean that I would have to take some precautions. The fronts and backs of each square had to be sealed before mounting them. Otherwise the marble would be apt to curl up slightly on the edges. That could be enough to break it loose from its mortar.

Had I not asked the right questions, or had I asked the right questions of the "wrong" persons I would never have known this. Lest there be any other hidden "gotchas" with regard to working with marble, I found someone who had a lot of experience with marble.

I knew I had the right man when Rene mentioned, unprompted, this fact about working with green marble. We made a deal whereby instead of him bringing a second man to help him, I would be his helper. This saved me hundreds of dollars.

Rene showed up on time on the appointed day. When I heard his truck in the driveway, I drained my coffee and went out on the porch to meet him. Rene would do most of the installation and I would operate the tile saw.

After Rene gave me a few minutes' instruction with the saw, we were ready to start. With Rene doing the placing and me doing the sawing, we installed, first, the Mexican onyx on the bathroom lavatory. With the beautiful translucency of the onyx I got the notion to mount an electric light in the cabinet underneath, shining up through it. Great idea, but perhaps a little ostentatious for the cabana. Besides, I didn't want it to look as if it came out of a brothel!

Next we moved on to the kitchen and bar countertops. Rene suggested we set the marble in black grout, which turned out to be the perfect choice. I selected the prettiest of the marble squares and laid them out. Rene carefully set them in place, including the backsplash.

Last, we put down the natural slate squares on the kitchen and bathroom floors. All of this took only three days, after which Rene drove off, leaving me breathless in the presence of all of the new-found beauty around me. I am a sucker when it comes to natural stone. It came out even better than I had imagined. When I added dark stained wood trim around the edges, it was stunning. For several minutes, all I could do was walk around and admire. I had to run right over and get Ivan to come take a look.

I installed the copper sink into the top of the bathroom cabinet, along with brass faucets. They looked wonderful against the onyx. Encouraged by this little victory, I went on to install the kitchen sink. My parents had remodeled their kitchen a couple of years before, and I came away with their old, big, stainless steel sink, the same one that I had washed dishes in under duress when I was young. It was still in great condition. In fact, the stainless steel in this sink was of better quality than the new ones I had seen in the stores

I also got Mom's range top and dishwasher, which were still serviceable. Their color was Harvest Gold, which for some unknown reason was popular at one time. Alas, they looked ghastly with all of that beautiful green marble! I just couldn't bring myself to install the range top, even if it *was* free. I broke down and bought a new range top and vent hood, in stainless steel. Much better! The dishwasher had a front panel that was reversible, and it was painted white on the other side. Luckily.

"Bathroom"

"Kitchen"

After this whirlwind of construction, it was still too soon to start on the wood floor, so we began installing the interior window and door trim. When we were done, I went ahead and refinished it. Waiting until after the floor was installed would have meant having to worry about spills. We moved on to the light fixtures. The fluorescent fixture I picked out for the kitchen was as close as I could get to one I had been admiring in my favorite sushi bar. I suspended it from the vaulted ceiling by four decorative chains.

I borrowed my neighbor's flatbed trailer one more time, this time to pick up a couple of tons of brick pavers to make a patio. I began the patio by making a frame out of treated two-by-fours, twenty feet square. Just like for the hot tub slab, I used my string level to get it even. I then ordered a load of sand, which I used to make a bed for the pavers. I packed it down, and then started carefully placing the bricks, checking each one with my level as I went. Brick by brick, the patio began to grow. When I was finished, I spread the remaining sand over the surface and set a sprinkler to wash the sand down in the cracks to form a tight, weed-proof matrix. No mortar was needed. The patio was perfect. Perhaps someday it would also serve as a dance floor!

I studied my checklist. Kitchen? Completed. Bathroom? Completed! And both beautiful. Ceilings and walls? Done. I was getting *close*! At the end of six weeks, Ben, Frank, and Larry all came back over to help me lay the floor. We got it done in one weekend. It looked great once it was down, and squeaked cozily when tread upon in some places. It squeaked a little too cozily in other places. This needed to be fixed. There were apparently voids in some places between the new wood floor and the subfloor that were causing the squeaks when the hardwood floor flexed. I learned that the fix was this: drill several small holes right into the floor in the area of the squeaks. Using a caulking gun, inject subfloor adhesive into the holes to fill the voids. The process worked well. Soon, there was nary a squeak as you traveled from point to point.

Now to fill the old nail holes and injection holes. How? By a laborious process on hands and knees, with wood filler, that's how! There were lots of them. When I was finally done, the entire floor got a wet sanding, followed by a scrupulous cleaning with an old towel and paint thinner. There then commenced a furious floor-refinishing effort, beginning with stain. I was aiming for a warm, rich finish. When I was done with the stain, the floor was dark and dramatic. It completely changed the look of the house.

I will at this point reveal a *possible builder error* (PBE): Before I stained the whole floor I figured that the filler I had used to fill the nail holes would take the stain like the rest of the wood and blend in. Not so! I was wrong. They stood out. Now what?

I tried touching up a couple with a Q-tip moistened with an even darker stain. Not too bad, but when I realized that many of the natural imperfections in the floor were very nearly black, I had another idea—a black magic marker. This I tried on a few of the filled nail holes and it looked great! If I skillfully made the magic marker touchups irregular and then blended in the edges with a bit of moistened rag, you couldn't even tell from your knees which ones were natural and which weren't. Perfect! I went over the whole floor several times, making sure to get them all.

Problem solved. Now for some protection. I applied four coats of polyurethane. This gave the floor a soft, lustrous glow and afforded it protection from scuffs, water, parrots, electric pianos, drum kits, golf shoes, and all manner of floor traumas that were apt to come along. The floor was then smooth, dry, and clean enough to perform surgeries on. It looked marvelous.

I was getting very close to being finished. I mean, *completely* finished. Wait until Abigail heard this!

I cut, stained, and installed the baseboards and all remaining interior wood trim. As an experiment, I put up a wood shelf on one wall about a foot down from the ceiling to hold books, ship models, and the like. It looked so good that I decided to let the shelves carry on around the perimeter of the entire big room. When stained dark and set about with various nautical items, it would really give the room a warm and cozy character.

Interior design is not really my strong suit. Things like curtains didn't interest me; bored me, in fact. Yet I was going to have to go find something to cover the windows with. They were at the moment still covered by the old sheets we had hung over them the day the windows were installed. The next weekend I broke off from building and went to a nice home interior design center to see what I could see. Places like that were not within my normal orbit, but now that I had a house to make into a home, I found much to interest me.

Over the next couple of weeks. I made the rounds, looking for home accents. I ended up with an area rug with a pretty palm tree motif, a bamboo coffee table and matching end table, a gazebo in kit form to put over the hot tub, some African print bar stools, some island theme lamps and pictures, and, oh yes, what I'd gone in for in the first place: curtains!

The curtains I picked were not in the drapery department. They were actually shower curtains, but not the inexpensive plastic kind. They were fabric, and featured a subdued palm tree motif in shades of muted greens and beiges on a cream-colored background. They were perfect for the Oleanders. They had *the look*!

I bought enough for all of the windows. I hung them with dark wood curtain rings on thick, round wooden rods, sanded smooth and stained dark to match the wood trim. They looked very nice. You would never know they were shower curtains.

Don't rush, don't rush, don't rush. This became my mantra. I had been building a little over a year and I was anxious to be done, but I forced myself to be thorough and careful. The list of remaining tasks was dwindling rapidly. By now the list was dirty, stained, tattered, crossed out, added to, re-numbered, and falling apart. It had performed its function as the project roadmap since the beginning. As I read it this happy day, I realized that there were no more big jobs to do—they had all been done! I was going to make my construction loan deadline with time to spare. I gave Miss Oglethorpe a call to let her know.

The house was now clean and empty. I loved walking inside the next morning. The freshly refinished floor was gleaming and gave it a most pleasing aroma. I was circling the inside walls with a Q-tip and a can of stain, touching up any blemishes I could find when it suddenly dawned on me: when I finished this final touch-up, there was nothing to keep me from moving in. That could conceivably be as early as the *next day!* I now had my born-on date. I grabbed my big carpenter's marker, went around to the back of the house, and wrote it on the foundation. *Woo-hoo!*

Before I could move, there were still a few non-building details to take care of. I arranged for a final inspection by the county and a final survey. I called Miss Oglethorpe to set the date for a closing, in which the construction loan would be converted to a permanent mortgage. I was happy to learn that the prevailing interest rates were favorable. Better yet, due to all of the money I'd saved, my monthly mortgage payment was ridiculously low, lower than my car payment.

Another big moment had arrived. It was time to get a hot tub. I had not gotten one sooner for the same reason that my hammock stayed packed away in a box. I didn't need hammocks and hot tubs competing for building time. I knew very well where that would lead!

Shopping for hot tubs was fun. At least it was, the way I did it. I put on a bathing suit, jumped in my car, and spent the entire day driving around to every hot tub showroom in town. At each stop, I got in and "field tested" them. The tub at the second stop was so wonderful that I wanted to stop right there, but I made myself complete my route just the same. I came back to that one at the end of the day. It had a terrific, strong water flow that reminded me of the Buffalo River. I ordered one in blue, the color of water. They would build it there and deliver it in one week. I could scarcely wait for it to arrive.

I looked forward to morning coffees and moonlit evenings in it. Incidentally, Caribbean rules would be strictly observed at all times.

Caribbean Rules

Bathing suits are absolutely required, unless one of the following circumstances applies: Vegetation is thick enough, no one else is around, or it's dark.

I also started thinking about having a housewarming party. I had not forgotten! That vision had been what kept me going on a few of those cold, bleak days of building when nothing was going right, and I was overwhelmed with doubt.

• • •

The next thing on my agenda was to go visit my parents in Arkansas, something I had been wanting to do. There were some things they had been keeping for me there and I could bring them back, now that I wasn't going to be living on the boat anymore. The boat... had it all been a dream, living aboard? The next morning I headed for Arkansas.

You Can Take the Boy Out of Arkansas...

It was a nice trip to Arkansas that was long overdue. When I got there we got in some good visiting. By happy coincidence, my sister and her young family were there visiting as well. I had been keeping Mom and Dad abreast of the building progress, but they wanted to hear all about it again. I would have liked nothing better than for them to be able to see the house first hand, but they were up in years and would probably never get to see the house in person. This thought made me sad, and it, in fact, turned out to be true. I spent a few days there so that I could do a lot of visiting, and help Mom and Dad around the house.

They still lived in the same house that I grew up in. The house was built in 1919 by my great-grandfather. It was by no means a mansion, but it was a largish, wooden, four-bedroom structure with high ceilings. It had originally had a wood-burning stove in the kitchen, and three fireplaces for heat. Growing up in this house was plenty of fun. The house had at least one secret: a hidden room in the basement with no doors or windows.

I always looked forward to visiting Mom and Dad. I was going to bring some furniture and other items back to San Leon in Dad's trailer. The last time I had seen the trailer it was newer, with shiny red paint. That had been several years ago, and before the trailer could take anything anywhere, it was going to need some work. A few new tires and a repair bill later, it was ready for the road. However, it looked tired. It was scratched, rusty in places, and the paint was faded.

The trailer had an open top. Not what I wanted to be trans-porting pretty antiques in, but if I was careful, and if I had a clear forecast, it might be okay. I carefully loaded the trailer with some furniture, boxes, and the real prize, a grandfather clock. When I was done I secured it all with a tarp. With a lumpy tarp, in addition to the trailer's aforementioned condition, it would look like the Beverly Hillbillies were hitting the road.

The next morning, I arose and got an early start to make the drive back to San Leon. It was windy that day and I nervously monitored the tarp in the rearview mirror. I didn't even make it twenty miles before the tarp started to flutter. I pulled over to check on it and the tarp had *already* started to tear. Oh my! This could be a long day! Over the next fifteen minutes I carefully retied the tarp and began wondering where I could get another one. I needed a good heavy canvas one. Where was I going to find one like that, on a Sunday? Maybe a truck stop?

I pulled off at the first one I came to. The only tarps they had were lightweight and flimsy. By this time, the original tarp was shredded, so I bought two plastic tarps. I put one on the trailer, keeping the other one in reserve.

Again I set off. Fifteen minutes passed and the new tarp began fluttering in the wind. I knew that, just like a sail in irons, it would not take much of that. I pulled over and re-tied it, but was unable to stop the fluttering. Maybe duct tape would work. I got some duct tape (also known as *Arkansas Chrome*) and applied it in an artistic criss-cross pattern.

The trailer looked *really* great, then, but at least I was underway once again. There's a place in Texas designated for people like me. It's called San Leon! I'm sure the Arkansas plates on the trailer answered a lot of questions for those sharing the road with me that day. Just then I was passed by someone I knew. Oh, what could be worse? It was my sister and her family. They were all laughing and pointing.

I had to drive slowly and stop to check the tarp about every hour, just like when you're sailing all night and you have to go forward in the dark to check the sails. The new tarp began fraying after only one hour. I knew it would never make it all the way. I stopped at three or four more truck stops, but I was never able to find a heavy trucker's tarp. Oh well, I still had the flimsy tarp in reserve. At least it wasn't raining. I was okay—for the time being.

South I went through Arkansas, west to Oklahoma, and then south again to Texas. The tarp was in a gradual but steady state of decline. The duct tape started coming loose and streaming back, looking like remoras on a shark. Cars passed warily, giving me a wide berth.

At suppertime I discovered a large and terminal rip. The tarp was a goner. Thirty minutes later I was moving again with the third and last tarp snugged down. I had another four hours to go. It got dark and I tried to reason with myself that, if I could no longer see the tarp in the dark it must be okay. There were no further mishaps, and after several more check stops, I rolled gratefully into the Oleanders.

And there you have it. Proof positive:

You can take the boy out of Arkansas but you can't take the Arkansas out of the boy!

. . .

Upon my return, I became quite busy. I lined up some movers to bring everything from my storage area to the Oleanders. I turned my attention to the party. I couldn't think of a better time to have one than right then, at the end of construction. I had already put the word out on the street before I'd left for Arkansas. I arrived back to find that the Coconut Telegraph had been working.

Everyone was excited! I began getting inquires, plus offers to help. The ball was rolling and gathering momentum quickly. Soon it was out of my hands. There was going to be a party, whether I wanted one or not. It would be held the next Sunday afternoon. Would I be ready?

Chapter 16
Party!

"Play hard, live fast, die young and have a beautiful corpse!"

The following notice was circulated to the greater (and lesser) Clear Lake area:

Press Release
Oleanders Completed

San Leon, Texas (AP)—The long-anticipated project at the Oleanders has been completed according to Andy Upchurch, President and CEO of Oleander Construction. The project consists of a cabana, built on a tract of land near the water. It was mostly self-built, with a little help from friends. The cabana took over a year to build and features indoor plumbing with flush toilets.

"She was a long time a-buildin', and now I'm looking to party!" said Upchurch. To celebrate its completion, there will be an OLEANDER PARTY next Sunday. Music, tropical clothing, and fun will be the order of the day. Everyone is invited who wants to attend. There will be live music from two o'clock until dark. An eclectic mix of people will be in attendance: musicians, music lovers, sailors and the occasional pirate—a recipe for fun!

"I'm going to BBQ some hams and Marcel is going to smoke a couple of sacks of oysters. We're providing a keg of beer, soft drinks and a lavish buffet. Partygoers should bring something delicious to put on the lavish buffet, lawn chairs, your own suitable libation and a smile. If you are so inclined, a palm tree, hibiscus or other tropical plant to assist with the Oleanders Reforestation Program would be appreciated. The organizers of the Oleander Party hope to see everyone there."

The party was on. It would be held on a Sunday because that is when the musicians could make it. I called in a few favors from my musician friends and, as advertised, was able to field no less than five bands to perform. It was the beginning of May. It was the perfect time of the year for a party. Everything outside was fresh and green and growing. As a bonus, *all* of the oleanders were blooming prodigiously.

I got busy. I found some fake dinner rolls at the dollar store that looked very convincing. I got a pretty little basket, lined it with a clean, plaid, kitchen towel and nestled the rolls seductively into it. The basket would be put on the lavish buffet with the rest of the food.

The hot tub I had ordered arrived. It was delivered by three big, ex-rugby players. They set it on its slab and got it ready for action. While they were working, I noted with a straight face that, now when I caught fish in the bay I could keep them alive in the hot tub until I was ready to cook them.

The day before the party, lots of people came over to help. We built a long table for the lavish buffet out of plywood and saw horses. We set up smaller tables and lawn chairs. We set up a drink area, and erected pop-up tents. We set up the oyster pit for smoking oysters. Soon, The Oleanders looked quite festive!

The oysters would be slow-smoked over hickory. Then, they would be opened and brushed with melted butter and sprinkled with parmesan cheese and garlic salt. They would be served and eaten on the half shell. I knew they would be a big hit.

Sunday morning. Time for a party! I arose early to light the smoker. By seven o'clock, I already had one hour invested in the day. The house was clean and neat. The yard was pristine and braced for the onslaught. I got another cup of coffee and lollygagged for a moment, savoring the peace and quiet. I knew that when I started moving, I wouldn't stop for a long time.

Before long, friends started arriving to help. We cleared the porch and transformed it into a stage on which nearly forty musicians would play that day. Then, we adorned it with flower leis, tropical fish cutouts, crepe paper, and all manner of festivia. Ivan watched this activity dubiously and shook his head.

We had to throw the party out of coolers because the Oleanders did not yet have a refrigerator. I went down to the Topwater Grill where my friend Robert donated ice.

The first guests started arriving around one o'clock, catching me shaving. Show time! A tropical rock band called "Ocean Breeze" kicked us off. The party was underway! After an hour, people were arriving in a steady stream. When "Ocean Breeze" finished their set, "Andy and the Dreamsicles" took the stage.

The next band was the Kemah Bums, in all of their decadence. There were many Hoagie Ranchers in the audience, and since this band didn't play so often anymore, the audience enjoyed this unexpected treat. I was playing keyboards with all of the bands. Even though this kept me very busy, I didn't care. I was having the time of my life.

After the Kemah Bums played, the San Jacinto Junior College Steel Drum Ensemble played. There were thirteen steel drums. It looked like a whole army on the porch. You would have thought we were in Jamaica instead of San Leon!

By this time, the crowd was quite large. There were groups of people talking, eating, and drinking all around.

"Party!"

"What Is Hip" was the last band to play. They were a ten-piece soul/R&B/funk band. By their second song, everybody jumped up, scooted the tables and chairs out of the way, and danced like mad until a little after dark. Nobody was ready to quit, but all good things must come to an end sometime. The band played their last notes and people reluctantly began to disperse.

I was exhausted. With my last ounce of strength, I drove off to get one last cooler full of ice for the leftover food and then lurched into the hot tub. I stretched out and relaxed in the swirling waters and gazed up at the stars above. I ruled the evening a success. What a great party it had been!

All of the bands had been wonderful. I felt like the luckiest guy around to have so many talented friends who were willing to play at the Oleander Party. I could never repay them for their kindnesses, but I knew that I would be doing musical favors for whoever needed it for a long time. Between one hundred and two hundred people showed up. I knew many of them, but there were several there that I'd never met. There had even been some people who just happened to be driving by, saw the party in progress, and asked if they could make a donation for the food and beer and stay!

Everybody there had a larrapin' good time, but nobody had more fun than I did. The house had been properly warmed, but if it ever started cooling off a little bit, we might have to warm it back up again sometime!

Many people were curious to see the house that I had been working on, and most everyone went inside for a look. I received many nice compliments. Everyone had brought great food, and the buffet was indeed lavish. I'm sure the can of Spam that I'd placed conspicuously in the middle of the buffet table raised some eyebrows. The basket of fake dinner rolls claimed a victim—one of them had teeth marks in it! Many people brought plants. This was good; I had a lot of San Leon scrub growth to replace with tropical paradise. I ended up with an entire jungle. All of the green offerings were appreciated except for Gene's, which was a sprig of poison ivy in a pretty planter, tied with a festive ribbon. I was thankful to have them. I would have to plant a few of them each day

The Oleanders looked like a bomb had gone off in the yard, but I didn't care. It was the kind of housewarming I had been looking for. I was full of gratitude. At length, I dragged my unwilling self out of the hot tub. What a fun day. We had "bent the needle on the fun meter!"

The next morning, I slept in. I wasn't in a hurry to go anywhere or do anything. When I awoke, I made coffee and went out on the porch to sit in my rocking chair.

Neither the house nor the yard were the worse off for the wear, although it took me a couple of days to get everything back to its pre-party condition. It was clear that there would have to be another Oleander party sometime. How about next spring? By then I'd be ready for another one. I wondered if I could pull off a luau, complete with a whole pig roasted underground. Who did I know who had ever given one?

Chapter 17
Twilight

"It's not the miles you travel; it's the roads you go over."

"Front Porch"

I sat on my front porch. It was dusk. The nighttime creatures were about to come on shift as the daytime shift punched out. I sat in total solitary contentment in the deepening crepuscule, marveling at how I got here.

Was the house really done? I couldn't believe it was actually finished. The tools were put away, I was all moved in, and the music and laughter of the party had died away. The ancient, wheezy old air compressor that I had borrowed and kept throughout the entire project had been returned to its owner, refurbished, and accompanied by a gift. Things were settling down into a state of normalcy.

I loved the little house. It suited me. It was everything I wanted it to be when I drew it up on a sheet of notebook paper one night on the sailboat. That day seemed so very long ago. I had grown a lot, lived a lot, learned a lot since then.

Most aspects of the house turned out as anticipated. Some did not. One example of this was the thin lattice material I'd bought for the patio covering. It had been attractive, but it was flimsy and rickety, and started falling apart almost as soon as we finished putting it up. It would have to be replaced with something a little bit more robust. But not soon.

There were a few building errors as well. They were not problems that were serious enough to fix, and some were actually a little comical. One of these was that I got two of the lower kitchen cabinets switched and subsequently, the countertops on each leg of the U-shaped kitchen were different lengths. This did not mightily bother me. A good thing, it would be major surgery to fix.

Another mistake was with the upper kitchen cabinets. When I mounted them, the determining factor for their height was the height of the refrigerator. Since I was buying the refrigerator from a friend, I called her to ask its dimensions. She obliged, but gave me the wrong height. When it arrived, it was two inches taller than the space allotted for it. The fastidious fix would be to raise *all* of the upper cabinets two inches so they'd be even at the top. I, however, raised only the one over the refrigerator and left the rest alone. I was happy with it. It was not noticeable to anyone else unless I pointed it out.

Some parts of the house turned out much better than I imagined. For all the worrying I did about too much wood in the interior, it turned out to be fine. The dark trim throughout the house set the wood off and yet tied it all together in a pleasing way. The trim looked particularly striking against the green marble. The vaulted ceiling was perfect for the house, and the natural stone was beautiful.

When I started out building the house, I didn't know how these choices would look together. I just had to close my eyes and take a leap of faith. Just like a little boy, standing on the garage roof with a flour sack cape tied around his neck, trying to get up the nerve to jump off—armed with a mental image of Superman, who always trusted his cape. I had to trust my own cape, and it was, many times, all I had. And the little house, the fruits of my labors, came out well and it brought me much pleasure.

Merely finishing the house did not mean that I was done. You are never *really* finished with houses. There was the pit in the backyard, the Black Hole of Calcutta that needed to be filled in, all manner of junk that needed to be carted off, there was a mountain of construction scraps to be burned, the Oleander bushes themselves were in dire need of trimming and the shed/storeroom/shop needed to be built out back.

Building the shop, hauling off junk, and making the yard pretty were all things that I could fit in around the rest of my schedule. They would get done when they would get done.

Would there ever be a Phase II? I still have the vision of a second house, medium-sized, with conventional rooms and walls, built up on stilts with decks above and parking underneath, sharing the courtyard with the cottage.

I wanted to eventually build this house and let the little cottage become a home office, guest bedroom, or rehearsal room. For the time being, I needed a break from construction. Not only that, the tide had gone out of my bank account! At the moment, I was quite happy to just sit. I had pushed to keep building, always building for so long, I was looking forward to a little down time. Some time to relax, take it easy. The hot tub kicked on, reminding me it was nearly time for a soak.

I was filled with gratitude. Gratitude for the chance to build the house, and gratitude for being able to finish it. Gratitude that it turned out well, gratitude for all the experiences I had along the way, and all the things I had learned.

A flock of wild parrots whizzed noisily past, and I heard my own parrot stir in the house. I scratched an ant bite and went inside to find a towel and my drink.

Day is done.

My voyage was completed.

"The Oleander Hot Tub"

Epilogue
Hurricane

If you don't live in a coastal area and have never had to deal with a hurricane, the following might be of interest to you.

The week that Hurricane Ike struck the Texas coast began like any other week, although on the Sunday night news we[6] noted that there was a tropical storm in the Atlantic. During the hurricane season, tropical storms normally aren't a concern unless two things occur: they enter the Gulf of Mexico and they become tropical depressions. It was September, right in the middle of hurricane season. This storm grew into a tropical depression and, subsequently, strengthened into a category four hurricane that was given the name Ike. It had then entered the Caribbean Sea and was heading northeast toward the United States.

On Tuesday, Ike grazed Cuba and weakened to a category two. We kept our eye on it and went on about the week. By Wednesday morning, it had strengthened again over open water and entered the Gulf of Mexico. Time to sit up and take notice. Although still far away, the projected path of the storm was to come across the Gulf and hit somewhere along the Texas coast Friday night. Galveston was uncomfortably near the center of the so-called "cone of uncer-

---

6 Since building the Oleanders, I had acquired a mate, Vicki. The Oleanders had a new mistress. Vicki already had a townhouse, and we lived part time at both places.

tainty," the projected area of the most likely landfall. San Leon is only twenty-five miles from Galveston. Uh-oh.

Even though Ike was still only a category two storm, it was spreading out and becoming uncharacteristically large on the weather map. It was bigger than other storms. Its swirling pattern seemed to fill the entire Gulf. Texas coastal residents went on high alert. We might have to batten down the hatches and evacuate. Ike had my undivided attention.

On Wednesday morning I noted with alarm that the cone of uncertainty had not changed much, except for narrowing somewhat. It was still centering on Galveston. This was not happy news. Ike had increased to a category three and because of its above average size, coastal flooding was likely. Landfall was still projected for Friday night. I became fearful. My little house, the Oleanders of San Leon, could be in peril.

Should we stay or should we go? Watching the news that night, it became clear that we should go. The forecast had not changed. Where we decided to go was influenced by a couple of different factors. Each storm is a little different. With this one, we weren't so much nervous about the winds, but we were about the storm surge. We knew we had to run, but we didn't figure we had to run far—just away from the immediate coast.

We found a medium-large hotel about fifty miles inland that was out of the storm surge area. We made a reservation for Friday night and got the hotel's last room. We went to bed early that night because we knew the next day would be a full one.

Thursday was a very long day. I took off work. We had to prepare the Oleanders, the townhouse, and the sailboat for a major storm. We arose early and began battening down. We went to the Oleanders first.

Inside the house, we packed a cooler with ice, drinks, perishable food from the refrigerator, and canned goods. We could survive for a few days on this larder if we had to. We packed up a few valuables and possessions I wanted to save in case everything was swept away. We also packed practical items such as flashlights, clothes, tools, and paper towels.

Here is how God works: I had, just one month before, bought a cargo trailer to haul band equipment. We were able to use it to evacuate. Among my most cherished possessions was a vintage Hammond organ. It was large and heavy. It went into the trailer with plenty of room to spare. Taking it with us turned out to be fortuitous indeed. It would have been ruined if it were left behind.

Outside, we tied all the lawn furniture together. We brought all of the outside items we could into the house and shop, including the hot tub lid. We lay the fountain down so it wouldn't fall over and break. I had recently bought a Hobie catamaran, and it was sitting beside the house on its trailer. We looped a rope around it and the foundation, lest it sail away during the storm. We boarded up the windows and doors of the house and the little shop out back that I had built; with plywood. When we were finished, I screwed the last plywood sheet across the front door of the Oleanders. We looked wistfully around, and then left.

Off to the marina to take care of the sailboat. There, we doubled up the dock lines and stowed sails on Mañana. We added more lines to the Jet Ski, which was floating beside the sailboat on her little dock. That's about all we could do. We finished up and left them to fend for themselves. The water was already rising ominously.

We went on to the townhouse. There, we put plywood over all the windows we could reach. We also packed up more perishable food and possessions, and two parrots.

These three jobs took us all the way up to ten o'clock. We knew we should leave right then and take our chances with the evacuation traffic, which would only get worse with each passing hour until the storm struck.

Ike was still a category three hurricane, powerful enough to inflict plenty of damage. The high storm surge was still being emphasized. The hurricane was getting closer and was still heading straight toward Galveston. The mayor there had ordered a mandatory evacuation.

We stashed Vicki's car in a safe place and drove to her sister Terri's apartment, which was located out of harm's way. There we spent the first night. The traffic was not yet bad. We arrived exhausted and fell gratefully into bed. We were officially refugees. The next day was Friday. The storm was predicted to strike late that night. It was taking a bead on Galveston and closing in relentlessly. We arose, had a nice big breakfast with Terri, and drove the short distance to the hotel to hunker down.

On the way I looked for gas for the car and ice for the cooler, but I found neither. The storm was front-page news to everyone. People were going about their day, calmly, if not somewhat nervously. They were buying food, candles, water, and making storm preparations of their own. We heard about shortages of plywood and some food staples on the car radio.

We checked into our hotel. There was nothing to do but try not to worry. I spent a luxurious hour in the hotel's hot tub, until it started to rain. I was glad later that I had. It would be a long while till I could again.

The storm drew closer. On TV, we saw a national news team broadcasting live from a restaurant that was very close to the Oleanders. Not a good sign! Behind the broadcaster, big waves were crashing against the shore. We also saw images of air rescues already being made along the coast. Parts of Galveston were flooding. I felt impending doom.

I intended to stay up as the storm made landfall, but I couldn't stay awake. Ike roared ashore at Galveston at around two o'clock Saturday morning. We awoke before dawn to no electricity and terrific wind and rain. I grabbed a flashlight and went on a reconnaissance. There were many people milling around the darkened hotel lobby. The roof of the hotel across the street had partially collapsed from the rain and many of those people had come to our hotel (there were no injuries). We learned that the eye of the hurricane had gone right over Galveston—and San Leon. It made landfall as a category two hurricane.

There we all were. Without electricity, the hotel's kitchen was useless, but the staff put out all of their sweet rolls and sandwiches, and accommodated their guests the best they could. People were stuck there and making the best of it.

We had breakfast and visited with the other evacuees. Around mid-morning, after listening to battery-powered radios for a couple of hours, Vicki announced that we should leave to go back home.

"No way," I protested.

I didn't think we would be able to make it, but Vicki was optimistic, and persuaded me that it was worth a try. I decided to take a leap of faith and we checked out, me wondering if we would have to turn around and come right back.

We set off toward home. The road, a freeway, was open and clear...until it wasn't. We came to a roadblock and had to turn around. We took another road that went around the blockage and proceeded until that road became blocked as well by high water.

We backtracked again around to the original road, which was back open at that point. On it, we eventually got all the way back to Clear Lake.

We saw flooding, along with downed power lines and trees, beside the access road. Some exits were under water. Would ours be? It wasn't, but the area looked swamped. Aside from trees and power lines, there wasn't a lot of visible structural damage. Neither was there much traffic, but a few souls were venturing out like us.

The electricity was off and the traffic lights were out. I didn't realize how much we rely on traffic lights. You have to be *very* careful driving around in a city when they are not working. People do not expect ungoverned intersections and whiz right through them without looking. If you are not alert, *you* will miss them, too. It's bad during daylight hours and worse after dark.

We went first to the townhouse. It seemed okay, but the underground parking area contained water and a flooded car. We entered the townhouse and made a check. Everything was fine, thank goodness, except for there being no electricity. And it was hot.

We got the townhouse un-boarded by dusk, and then went for a short drive to look around. Galveston Bay had invaded Kemah. Even though the water was receding, it was still up and covering many areas. The radio in the car was the only news source we had. We listened to it as we drove.

The gaze of the nation was fixed on the Texas coast. For a small slice of time, we were the day's headlines. I was glad that cell phones still worked. Family and friends began checking in to see if we were okay. Loved ones from out of town offered their spare bedrooms. Lots of people wanted to help. Having friends and relatives who cared gave us a warm feeling.

We had a supper from the cooler by candlelight and went to bed, grateful. The only real discomforts we had to deal with so far were no air conditioning and mosquitoes. I wished that—and doubted that—everyone else was so lucky.

The next morning, we got up early and headed toward San Leon, full of trepidation. It's normally only a twenty-minute drive, but it took much longer that day. The damage grew steadily worse as we worked our way south. When we got there, we saw *many* houses with damage, several of which had been moved around, and others that were total losses. One house had been blown, or washed, right into the middle of a street. Boats and cars littered yards and the road. The area of town around the Topwater Grill looked like a tornado had touched down. My heart sank.

There was destruction all around and debris everywhere. There were dangling electrical and telephone lines, some of which lay in the road. I had no choice but to drive over them, telling myself that the electricity was off and fervently hoping it was true. A foul odor permeated the air, and we smelled natural gas here and there. There was lots of mud. It was everywhere. There were people out in it, moving about—cleaning, fixing, or just staring...

It was slow going and dangerous at times. We finally got to the Oleanders. There was the house, still standing. It initially appeared intact. We breathed a big sigh of relief. There was an eerie calm. It was still all around. The yard looked drowned.

The driveway was blocked by boards, tree limbs, toys, household goods, and other odd trash. We parked the car and the trailer that I was still towing on the street and got out. The driveway was covered with a layer of mud. We walked down the driveway to the carport. It contained only about half of the things that had been there when we evacuated. We walked up the steps onto the porch. It had a slippery layer of mud on it as well. I removed the plywood covering the door and unlocked it. The door was swollen and stuck shut, and it took me awhile to get it open. Vicki went to check on all of the plants in the yard.

I finally got the door open and went in. It was dark inside because of the plywood on the windows. Needless to say, there was no electricity to turn on the lights. For a second, it was comical—the furniture and other things were moved around, as if someone was playing a joke on me. Then I saw the quarter inch of slimy mud all over the floor and I realized that water had been in the house, and the objects had been *floating*.

Galveston bay had just been in my living room. The wood floor glistened in the dim light as if it had just been washed. The big palm tree rug was soaked and caked with mud. It would have to come out.

Suddenly, I didn't know what to do first. The things under the bed? Soaked boxes that had been left on the floor? The contents of the lower cabinets in the kitchen and bathroom? The file cabinet lower drawers? What about the shop out back and all of the things stored in it? And my record collection on the floor of the closet? Oh no…

We went right to work. There was no sense getting into a hurry, this was going to take awhile. First, we got everything up off the floor, taking most things out to the porch, patio, carport, and yard. It started raining, which didn't help. The rain continued off and on, all day.

There was no running water. We cleaned as much mud off of the floor as we could, using buckets, towels, and water from the hot tub, which was semi-fresh. When we were done, we went back to the shop and pulled everything out of it as well. The yard took on the appearance of a flea market. Then began the big job of attempting to care for and dry the long list of things that had gotten wet. Not just a little damp, total immersion in muddy salt water.

At the top of the list was getting any food out of the fridge and freezer. Luckily there had not been much there, but we had to throw out some frozen food we didn't have any way of preparing. The ice cream in the freezer was still a little frozen, and I had no reservations about having some before it too was tossed. Vicki opened the dryer and discovered a load of clothes that were a muddy mess.

There were lots of things to go through: clothes, towels, books, tools, pictures, and more. All clamored for attention at once. Most of the band equipment I had removed from the band trailer and left at the Oleanders had gotten wet—speakers, amplifiers, etc. Ouch!

Of all the painful discoveries we made that day, my flooded music collection hurt the most. There were around six hundred LP records. All of them were coated with a fine layer of mud. The cardboard jackets had disintegrated, and mold had already started growing on the vinyls. They were surely ruined. There were also two hundred reel-to-reel audiotapes. Each one of them had two record albums recorded on them. All of the tapes had to be thrown away; they would never again be playable. Several of the recordings were irreplaceable.

My favorite music, going all the way back to my youth, that had been carefully preserved for years was an unholy mess, and it made me sad. Among the many musical treasures in the collection was a complete set of Beatles albums, in their original shrink-wrap, and unopened. I just couldn't bring myself to take any of the records up to the street for trash pickup. I made a place for them on the porch.

The kitchen and bathroom cabinets were constructed of particleboard. I was painfully reminded of why I refer to this as a "dishonest" building material. They were swelling and disintegrating into sawdust, and the marble countertops they supported were beginning to sag. I wanted to save the countertops, but they needed prompt attention.

The house had gotten eighteen inches of water in it. The water line was readily apparent on many objects such as the walls and furniture. The water seemed to have come up and then gone back down fairly soon. The walls had gotten water behind them. They needed to be dried out, and soon.

Outside, the lawn mower was beyond recall. The sailboat that we had tied to the house had been moved around, but it appeared okay. The hot tub had also been moved several feet off of its pad and its components flooded. The heavy steel barbecue pit in the yard was already beginning to rust. The red scooter that I had put on the porch for safekeeping had gotten flooded anyway and would not start. I took it to a shop for repairs later, but it could not be brought back. The yard had been covered by four and a half feet of water. I drove a nail into a back corner of the house at the waterline to mark the spot.

We cleaned and dried and did as much as we could all that day. In the midst of this dirty, hard work occurred this amusing event: I knew there might be snakes about, dislodged by the floodwaters. I'm not particularly afraid of snakes, although I do have the proper respect for any I see. Vicki is terrified of all snakes. As it happened, one small, bedraggled, non-poisonous snake did turn up, inside the house. Its discovery was made, unfortunately, by Vicki.

We worked until dark and left because of a curfew that had been imposed. I locked the front door but had to leave the screened windows open for ventilation. Everything we had taken outside was vulnerable to theft and the weather, but there was no alternative.

We couldn't have stayed much longer at the Oleanders anyway because at dusk, the mosquitoes became horrific. Hurricanes blow millions of mosquitoes out of the nearby marshes. Those coupled with the ones that breed in standing storm waters would make the toughest of men turn and run!

When we got back to the townhouse in League City, wonder of wonders, the electricity was back on. *Woo-hoo!* This meant hot showers, air conditioning, and no mosquitoes. It also meant...hot coffee. And TV, so that we could see images of the destruction that was all around us.

We had so much to do in San Leon that there was no time for sightseeing or watching TV. We still had to go to the marina to check on the sailboat when the water receded. When we were able to get there, we found the parking lot blocked by a huge pile of debris. We parked on the road outside and walked in. We had to climb over the debris to get to the docks. Right in the middle of the debris pile I spotted my dinghy. I clambered in and retrieved it, dragging it over to the side. I was glad that I had taken the time to put my name and telephone number on it in magic marker before the storm.

The docks were twisted and strewn with debris. Boards were missing in spots. Most of the boats were intact, although some had been sunk in their slips. When I got to the sailboat, it and the Jet Ski were still floating, to my relief. The Jet Ski looked fine. The sailboat, however, had been dismasted. The mast had fallen over onto the next boat and lay broken in two pieces in a tangle of cables and lines. The jib sail, which had been wound up and tightly bound with extra line, was shredded. We checked around for other damages, but found none, apart from the ruined mast. We couldn't move the mast by ourselves and had to leave.

I came back the next morning with two friends, who helped me saw the mast in two at the break point and lash them to the boat. There she would have to wait until later for any further attention.

I still hadn't found a place to get gas or ice, nor were there any immediate prospects for getting any. Most businesses were closed and couldn't open, which included gas stations and grocery stores. We would have to make do with what we had left. We were okay for the time being, but at some point I would need to fill up the gas tank. Gradually, over the next several days, the roads were cleared and electricity and water were restored. Businesses began re-opening as they were able.

Back at the Oleanders, cleaning and drying continued. We became creatures of the mud. It was everywhere. As we worked, different friends and neighbors dropped by to see how we'd fared.

We heard many reports of both good and bad humanity. One local restaurant cooked up all the food in their freezer on a charcoal grill before it spoiled and was serving it free to anyone who was hungry. On the dark side, there were also reports of looting.

Everyone wanted to hear each other's storm experiences. Each person had their own story of how they fared during the hurricane. We heard accounts ranging from minimal damage to losing everything. One friend, Doug, didn't believe the storm would do much damage. He evacuated anyway, carrying only a small overnight bag. He returned after the storm to find that his house was completely gone! The only thing he recognized were some pieces of his former living room floor, lying in the street.

A neighbor, Lori, lived alone across the street from the Oleanders. She had decided not to evacuate, and rode out the storm in her house trailer. She told us it was the scariest thing she'd ever done. As the storm approached, the rain began and the wind blew hard. Her trailer was buffeted by the wind. When she looked outside, she couldn't see any ground—only water. The electricity went off and the water kept rising.

When the water started coming inside the trailer, Lori got up on her kitchen cabinets with her dogs and cats. The trailer began to sway and rock from wave action. If it had tipped over, she could have drowned. She realized she might not make it through the storm. She might not have, had the hurricane been stronger than a category two. Hurricane Ike did in fact claim several victims, some in San Leon.

The eye passed over San Leon and the wind suddenly died down, but Lori stayed inside. Everything in the trailer was soaking wet and floating around in four feet of water.

When the wind returned, she got back up on the kitchen counter and said a prayer. It blew very hard again for what seemed like a long time. When she looked outside again, she was in the middle of a huge, angry lake. The trailer was still being rocked by waves. Too bad for the three cars parked in her driveway.

Gradually, the storm eased up. The water level stopped rising. It was still inside of Lori's trailer when daylight finally arrived, but the level started dropping soon after, and was out of the trailer by mid-afternoon. The yard remained under water for awhile longer. It had been a terrifying night. Everything she owned was lost, wet or ruined, but she was lucky.

And she had walked over to the Oleanders to see if *we* needed any help!

Everybody helps each other. That's the way it works. Or should. Lori helped us pull the waterlogged rug out of the house and we gave her something to eat and dry clothes. She said she was okay for the time being and had a place to stay.

My boss at work was very understanding. Our company had not been extensively damaged, and he gave me time off. That meant no paycheck, but it was a true blessing to be able to take care of the house.

Aid began arriving in San Leon in the form of the National Guard, the Red Cross, and other organizations. Many people in San Leon were without food and shelter. The local churches set up large tents with cots, bedding, and fans.

Driving through San Leon was a challenge. Several roads were down to a two-lane track through the debris, and others were completely blocked. During the first week after the storm, my car incurred three flat tires from nails, screws, or other debris. I got two additional flats in the second week.

The fourth morning after the storm, I was heading to San Leon to work on the Oleanders. Overnight, a roadblock had been set up, manned by the National Guard. They were there to control looting and for general security. They weren't letting people into San Leon without some proof that they lived there. Uh-oh, I didn't have anything with me that proved I lived there! My driver's license had never been updated with my San Leon address.

I *almost* didn't get in at all. I tried the straightforward approach. I pleaded my case with the guard and showed him a bunch of muddy things and tools in the back of the car. Miraculously, he believed me and let me through. The first thing I did after arriving back at the house was to find a water bill that showed the service address. The bill was waterlogged and I had to dry it out—ha! I put it in the glove compartment to show later.

For the first week I still had to go in and out of the house through the window on account of the swollen front door. It wasn't back to normal for a good six weeks.

During the next several days I cleaned and dried numerous items. It was slow and sometimes sad work. It was also hot, dirty work. We set up Oleander party tables in the yard and put books on them to dry in the sun. We took all of the flooded pictures out of their frames and attempted to save the ones we could. One had been a very good portrait of me that had been hand-painted by a friend.

I resolved to save, clean, and fix everything I could. For instance, the set of cookware, which was rather expensive, was muddy and slightly discolored from the salt. To me, however, it was still good and would be safe to use, after a good cleaning.

It was easy to get depressed during this time. It seemed that everything I owned needed to be dried, cleaned, repaired, thrown out, or replaced. Whenever I became sad about some particular item, I tried to arrest those thoughts and replace them with joy at something else that I had been able to save. Some things were beyond salvage. They couldn't be brought back, regardless of how much time and money I was willing to spend.

"Ruined keyboard"

It appeared that many people just carted everything that got wet to the street, whether it was actually damaged or not. Perhaps they didn't have the time or inclination to resurrect them. Soon, all the streets in San Leon were lined with huge piles of debris. There were piles of splintered lumber that had been entire houses, which had been bulldozed and pushed to the street. There were not only tree branches, but entire trees. Also, appliances, furniture, toys, books, clothes, dishes, tools, lamps—every single trapping of American existence was set out for the garbage trucks to pick up. Before long there were people walking the streets, salvaging what they could from the trash. So long as their intentions were good I was happy for them to take all that they could use.

After a hurricane, I found out that lots of damaged items can be brought back, if you are willing to take the time. I was ultimately able to save many things. This included tools. My five-drawer tool chest had been completely submerged. The tools were rusty, some more than others, but in most cases still serviceable. I rinsed each tool in water and then cleaned it with an oily rag. I was able to save the tool chest itself as well.

To my surprise, several of my power tools, which had been completely immersed in salt water, were fine. I decided to test them after the power came back on. Amazingly, a saw, orbital sander, and electric drill all ran! I was unsure about how long they'd continue to run, but I'm glad I checked. I cleaned and oiled them and put them away.

I rented a climate controlled storage area temporarily to move some things into. This was for security and to help them to dry faster. There wouldn't be room inside the house for everything once I began repairs.

Occasionally, friends would show up to help. One friend appeared with a chain saw, and removed all of the downed tree limbs for us. We used my come-along to ratchet some palm trees back upright that had been pushed over by the wind.

I needed help getting the house fixed, but I knew carpenters were going to be hard to find. I finally found a contracting company that thought they could squeeze me in. They were extremely busy (ha, imagine that). And expensive. They looked at the house and quoted me a rather high price for a tear-out and rebuild. This included the kitchen and bathroom cabinets and the interior walls. In other words, gutting the house.

I saw no reason why the knotty pine walls and marble counter tops couldn't be salvaged. Although the contractor was against it because of the extra time it would entail, I specified that we save them.

We began with the walls. We started by marking a straight line completely around the interior of the house four feet high. This was so that we could neatly saw and remove the lower halves of the wall-boards. I planned to clean and dry each board and then put them all back. The cut line could be easily hidden with a narrow strip of wood trim that would resemble a chair rail when we were done. The walls of the shop out back needed this same treatment, but those interior walls were only raw plywood and need not look nice.

With this strategy, it would be relatively easy to fix the walls the same way if and when there was ever another flood. Even though the water had only gotten eighteen inches deep in the house, making the cut line at the four foot level would provide a margin of safety in case water got even higher the next time.

We carefully removed the baseboards and the bottom half of the wallboards, numbering them as we went. We also removed the soaked insulation so the interior wall cavities could start to dry. At the same time, I replaced all of the electrical outlets.

Then we carefully removed the cabinets underneath the marble countertops in the kitchen and bathroom, building temporary two by four braces to support them. We used saws and sometimes, hammer and chisel for this work. Later we would slide new cabinets underneath the countertops. Again, this was amid the protests of the contractors, who said it would never work. Nonetheless, we completed the task and got the countertops braced without incident.

After this work was done, I bade the contractors an early farewell. They had no confidence in saving the countertops, and were entirely in too much of a hurry. I didn't think that they would be careful enough with the rebuild. I avoid negative people.

The concern after a house gets flooded is black mold. Black mold is associated with alarming health risks. It is a serious enough threat that some houses have to be torn completely down because of it. Black mold can grow on damp surfaces in poorly ventilated places, such as inside the walls of houses that have been flooded.

I started researching black mold. Using what I learned, I prepared a solution of bleach and water to kill the developing mold.

The interior walls received two applications of this, using sponges, brushes, and mops. The wall in the shop out back had to get this treatment as well.

The municipal water came back on after a week. We couldn't yet drink it, but we could then do a much more thorough job of cleaning. The electricity came back on in ten days. When the power company came by to inform me, I asked them to stand by while I turned on the power. I was nervous about any invisible flood-induced electrical safety hazards. I turned all of the breakers off in my electrical panel and then threw the main switch on. So far so good. I flipped a breaker on and my test light came on. Then I turned each breaker on, one at a time. The electrical system seemed to be fine.

With the power back on, I could test the major appliances. The refrigerator was dead; its motor was ruined. Same with the dishwasher and the clothes washer and dryer. The electric water heater worked, to my surprise. It came on and heated right up! Regardless, it still went out to the street along with the other ruined appliances. Even if it worked at the moment, its lifespan was surely compromised.

Having power, once again, meant that I could run the air conditioner, which had not been reached by the floodwaters. I ran both the air conditioner and heater night and day, to help dry the floor, walls, and everything else that was still in the house. Gradually, it worked. However, as the floor dried, the wooden floorboards started to cup and buckle. Many boards warped up three or four inches. My hopes for saving the floor sank. We cleaned the floor as best we could and moved several things back inside the house to dry in the conditioned air.

Now I could pause and catch my breath before I began the tedious task of inventorying the damage to the house and possessions for insurance. There had been only minimal external damage to the roof. Only a few shingles and part of the ridge vent was gone. Thank goodness the storm was only a category two.

At this point, I got the hot tub fixed. Why then, I don't know; I was much too busy to get into it. It had been knocked off its foundations and its gazebo ruined. All of its internal parts had to be replaced, namely the pump, heater, and control panel. We drained the tub and moved it back onto its pad, replaced the parts, cleaned it, and filled it up. Good as new, one more thing checked off the list.

While working at the Oleanders, meals were unpretentious affairs, I lived mostly on canned food that I could fix and eat quickly. People occasionally came to my door, from church groups or scouting troops, with sandwiches or other food. I humbly accepted and appreciated these gifts being offered by strangers with no strings attached. I was touched by the warmth of human kindness.

One day a food trailer appeared a block away with a picnic table next to it. Hot meals began being served there daily, free to anybody who walked up. I was glad they were there. I wanted the more needy people to receive this blessing, but I went there one day for lunch, to see what they were serving. It was rice and beans with cornbread. Simple food—hot, filling, and wholesome—being provided by people who cared for those who were sad, hungry, hopeless, and in need.

At another aid point in San Leon, you could get free ice and MREs (meal ready to eat). One day I decided to try an MRE. Developed for our military, they were like a modern TV dinner, only fancier. The meals had a little heater inside to heat them up via a chemical reaction, once a little water was added. The MRE I got was chicken fajitas, complete with tortillas, Spanish rice, melted cheese, chips, and hot chocolate to drink. The heater actually generated enough heat to burn you if you weren't careful, and it got the food very hot. The meal was quite good. I noted that our troops were eating well. I imagine the cost to develop those meals was staggering. All of the locations around San Leon dispensing food and other aid stayed in operation for three or four months after the storm.

After two weeks, I was to a point where I could return to my job. Fixing the house became my second job to do on evenings and weekends. I had to perform this job, whether I wanted to or not. I didn't choose this job. Or did I? On closer examination, I realized that I *had* in fact accepted the risk of someday doing this, the day I decided to build a house near salt water.

I was still in a quandary about how much more of the house would have to be torn out and rebuilt due to black mold. The kitchen, bathroom, and interior walls were work enough, but would I also have to replace the exterior walls and the hardwood floor, as others had to do?

To check for the extent of this threat, I removed a couple of outside boards from the backside of the house. It was clean and dry underneath. It looked fine. I took out a few hardwood floorboards in the closet. It was clean and dry underneath them as well, just like the day I put it down. I used a hole saw to remove a couple of samples of the flooring in other parts of the house. Clean and dry there too. All of these test spots looked okay to me, but I needed a mold expert to render an opinion.

A friend of a friend named Mike had formerly been in the mold remediation business. He had seen plenty of houses with serious mold problems before and knew what to look for. He came out and examined the house as a favor. To my eternal joy, he pronounced it… fine! Mike said that the quick action of removing the interior walls helped prevent mold from getting a foothold.

I was so relieved I wanted to *hug* him! I suppose the eighteen inches of water the house took represented the crest of the flood. It had come up and then gone back down in a relatively short time. This might have kept the mold problem from being worse than it was.

"Put your house back together and move back in," Mike said.

Something to be truly thankful about!

Mike cautioned that I would still need to apply a mold-inhibiting solution to the interior wall cavities. This product was expensive—sixty dollars a gallon. Not only that, the product only came in five-gallon pails. That was *three hundred dollars*! Recoiling from this hit to my wallet, I got some and applied it to the open wall cavities, as well as the backs of the knotty pine wall boards.

When it was dry, I could put the interior walls back. I began with new insulation. Then I began putting the clean, mold-remediated bottom halves of the wallboards back. I went around the whole house, fitting boards and nailing them with a borrowed nail gun. It went smoothly except for a little consternation caused by a few unnumbered boards. I left them till last, and by matching up grains I was able to get every single board back up in its original place. *Woo-hoo!*

When the walls were put back, they looked good as new. I could begin to see real progress with the house, and it gave me hope. It felt good to see it returning from a state of ruin to a resemblance of how it looked originally. I began to feel better about things. Thanksgiving that year was indeed a joyous event. There was a lot to be thankful for. I utilized that weekend to keep working, and installed the new hot water heater. One step closer to normal.

The days rolled by. San Leon was by then in full recovery mode. It was slowly but surely coming back, and the whole town was a beehive of activity. Every day you could see and hear evidence of great industry. The daily *rip-rip-rip* of the debris-clearing chain saws was eventually replaced by the whine of circular saws. Construction sites started popping up everywhere.

FEMA had moved in and was doing what it could. Likewise, insurance adjustors, contractors, and debris removers. We heard rumors of all sorts of opportunists, some honest and some not. San Leon became overrun with them, like the carpetbaggers after the Civil War.

I worked almost every evening and weekend on the house. Christmas came and we paused just long enough to observe it with the reverence and gratitude that it deserved, and then got back to work.

We were yearning to get the house back to normal and couldn't wait to spend our first night back. This couldn't be until we replaced the mattress and box springs. When we did, it felt like a special occasion to stay overnight there. Another milestone on the road to recovery.

Up to this point, I hadn't done anything with the flooded record collection. What if the records could be somehow cleaned to the point that they could be played just one more time? If this were possible, they could be "recorded" onto my computer, where they could reside forevermore. Maybe my records weren't as "gone" as I first imagined. When I started researching this, I found that flood damaged records could indeed be cleaned enough to be played again. There was hope after all!

The music legacy thrives in my family. Two enthusiastic audiophiles stepped forward to help me with this task. How lucky can a guy get? They took the records away, and within a month, the first of my old LPs started coming back to me, in the form of CDs. Playing them brought water to my eyes. They were back from the dead. What I had feared was lost forever lived again.

The next big job to do in the house was to replace the cabinets in the kitchen and bathroom. The new cabinets needed to be custom-made, because they had to be able to slide under the countertops. There wasn't much margin for error. I selected a cabinet factory, and they came out to take measurements. I placed the order, and waited for them to be built. The new cabinets would be expensive, even though they were built out of plywood. Plywood in my mind would not fare much better in floodwater, but they were a step up from particle wood.

When they were delivered, I and a carpenter friend installed the cabinets in just one day, along with a new dishwasher. To my relief, the countertops were not damaged during the somewhat ticklish process. A weekend with the paintbrush had the kitchen looking good as new.

Now that the kitchen and bathroom were put back, I could get a new refrigerator and washer/dryer. These amenities made staying at the Oleanders much easier.

We couldn't put furniture and other furnishings back in the house until we got the floor refinished. When the floorboards had buckled after the storm, I assumed the floor was beyond repair. However, after a few weeks of drying the house out with the air conditioner, the floor actually laid back down, to my surprise. All it required was a light sanding and refinishing. That restored it to its former beauty. Some of the boards remained minorly cupped, but that was fine with me. Wood floors in old homes everywhere are like that. It gives them character. After the floor was done, I cut, stained, and installed new baseboards and wood trim. And the chair rail to hide the cut line in the wall.

That was it. The floor had been the last job. I pronounced the house *fixed.* The Oleanders was good as new!

We couldn't move in just yet though, for there were a couple of tasks to accomplish that were not construction related. The big palm tree rug that I thought was ruined had been rinsed off with the hose, dried, and rolled up on the front porch. It had been there since the storm. I didn't hold out much hope for it, but I contacted an upholstery cleaning business anyway to discuss the possibility of cleaning it. They claimed they could get it clean, and I decided to let them give it a go. The rug came back from them looking great. That emboldened me to try my hand at cleaning the smaller area rugs by hand. Most of them came out fine, too.

I could hardly wait to put the rugs down on the newly refinished and gleaming floor. Once we did, we could move the furniture back in. The furniture in the house had, of course, sat in water as well. Some of the pieces were antiques. The antiques didn't seem to mind the water at all. I only had to clean off the mud and rub them down with furniture polish to have them looking great. They don't make things like they used to!

What to do about the curtains? Their bottoms were muddy. I didn't think I could find the same patterns to buy new and I couldn't just throw them away. I got an idea from the method I'd used occasionally to wash sails. I put the curtains in the hot tub with detergent and let it run for an hour. Then I rinsed them with the hose and hung them up on rope clotheslines that I had strung all over the yard. It worked—the mud was gone!

There were other furniture and possessions that needed further attention in some way, but nothing that was needed immediately. They went into the shop to be fixed another day. I'd get around to them later. *Now* we could move in. The job was done. The ordeal was over! The Oleanders lived again. Brought back from ruin. One busy but joyous weekend in March we moved back in. It had been six months since the hurricane. The Oleanders was once again a place of tranquil mornings sipping coffee on the porch, planning Oleander parties, and planting palm trees. Thank God!

The yard had taken a big hit from the hurricane as well. Most of the trees around town showed damage. In addition to losing branches, many of the trees had lost every single leaf. They started growing new leaves right after the storm, even thought it was fall. They dropped these new leaves, as well, a short time later as it got cold. Thus, the trees in the area had two leaf drops that year. It was weird.

After the hurricane, we tried to help the plants at the Oleanders all we could. It was a mixed blessing that it didn't rain for a while. This was good in that we could put wet possessions outside to dry in the sun. However, there was a period of several weeks after the storm when we received no rain. The gardens could well have used some to wash the storm mud off and dilute the salty residue that had been left in the soil.

About two thirds of the plants survived the hurricane, the rest did not. Some plants seemed to *like* having been immersed in salt water for a few hours—they began blooming immediately afterward. The yard and the gardens eventually rallied, but it took a year or two for some plants to make it back.

Today, the Oleanders is again a place of lush, riotous, tropical beauty. This is due to the monitoring of plant sales at the nurseries and diligence with my shovel.

I recorded the following interesting note regarding fire ants: Before the storm, the Oleanders had its share of these ubiquitous and wretched creatures; the bane of gardeners everywhere in South Texas. After the storm, there were none. As a matter of fact, I didn't see a single one for about two years. While I am reticent to say anything good about hurricanes, this might be my one solitary exception. The fire ants eventually did return, however and reclaim what they obviously consider to be their place in God's kingdom, and mine.

After the rebuilding process was all over, I was glad, thankful, and sad. Glad for what we were able to save and thankful that the house was fixed—indeed, that it had been fixable at all. Many of my neighbors did not fare so well. I was sad for those who lost more, and for those whose own hurricane ordeals were not yet over. It was gratifying to know that, regardless of how good a carpenter I was or was not, the house that I had built withstood a hurricane.

I have never had to deal with major hurricane damage before. I am now initiated. Those who choose to live in coastal areas apparently have either a profound love for the sea or have deep roots there. Either of these things appear strong enough to override any fear of hurricanes. Yet I observe a slow but constant migration of people. A tide of those moving away from the coast, offset by new arrivals. People eagerly anticipating their turn to live by the sea. I was one of them, once upon a time.

I don't like hurricanes more than anyone else. But, just like others who live near the coast, I have had to come to terms with this threat. I have trained my mind to regard hurricanes not as a possibility, but a *probability*. And, just because we've had one doesn't mean that it can't happen again. Another hurricane in another year, the very next year, or even within the same year. Concerned about hurricanes I may be, but I can't live in a state of fear and worry. What would that do for one's happiness and serenity?

Consider Mt. Vesuvius, the volcano that buried the ancient city of Pompeii. It is still classified as an active volcano, yet today millions of people live in its shadow.

I choose to live on the coast. I've wanted to all of my life. I thoroughly enjoy all of the beauty and joy that living by the ocean has to offer, and I freely partake of the rich experiences to be found.

My hurricane strategy? Be prepared, run when the need arises, and maintain good insurance. They're just things…

Appendix 1
Flora 'E' Fauna

The Oleanders was named in the spirit of Bermuda. I wanted the Oleanders to reflect this in the yard. A few dozen hibiscus and as many palm trees and banana plants as the yard can hold, and about ten years' time ought to get me there. Or, at least get as close as it is possible to get to Bermuda in San Leon, Texas!

The fruits of my labors are already evident all around me. I am glad that I had taken the time to get some plants established here and there as I was building the cottage.

"We make happen the things that we want to happen."

One of the things that makes tropical places so, well, tropical, is the foliage, and the animal life. The flora and fauna.

The Oleanders of San Leon is a place of beauty and serenity. It is said to possess good karma. It wasn't always so. Prior to my arrival, it was a hopeless tangle of wild Texas coastal prairie. During the land clearing and building stages, the image of Bermuda was never far from my mind. Many of the plants contributing to Bermuda's lush tropical undergrowth (*indignant* to the area, remember?) would also grow here, but not all. Some would not be good choices because coastal Texas is at least one growing zone cooler than Bermuda. But, that is what makes Bermuda, Bermuda, and Texas, Texas. While I was building the cottage, I gladly accepted the occasional offers of hand-me-down plants or cast-offs from some botanically minded friend. I usually felt too guilty to take time away from construction to get them into the ground. Besides, I didn't have a clue where they should be planted. As soon as I had installed running water, I put all of the plants in one area under a tree where they would be protected from the sun, and where they could all be watered with one sprinkler. This area became known as the nursery. They would be fine there until such time as I could plant them. At one time this area contained nearly one hundred plants—a portable jungle. Every now and then when I'd get tired of building, I would take a break and plant something. Maybe I should have a gardening alter ego, named *Pete Moss*!

My personal taste in gardening might be described as "a combination of understated elegance and unbridled joy." I sought to create understated elegance by planting palms and other beautiful tropical plants that would one day grow to be big and majestic. The unbridled joy came by planting a lot of them! I believe that each and every plant that is planted elevates the *quality of life* by some definite but un-measurable amount.

I didn't really have a master gardening plan. When I got ready to plant something, I just arbitrarily picked a spot that seemed to need a palm tree, hibiscus, or elephant ear, so long as it met the plant's sun and water requirements. While I appreciate a beautiful and manicured garden, what I like better is a look where everything is all thrown in together, as it is in nature. This *avant-garde* strategy would one day make the Oleanders lush and beautiful. I still use this method. What works is encouraged and perpetuated. What doesn't work presents an opportunity for experimentation.

The soil in San Leon is not bad. Many years of falling leaves made for a nice rich growing medium in most spots. However, some parts of The Oleanders appear to be situated on an old oyster reef. That is, dig down in some places and you will hit solid oyster shells starting at a depth of only six inches.

Today, after all of these various botanical endeavors, the Oleanders is a fairly tropical place. It is a labor of love and a work in progress. I am never too busy to plant something new. I view the Oleanders as an artist's palette on which growing things are added to create a picture that is constantly evolving and changing.

There are many plants that look tropical and do well at the Oleanders. The following, in no particular order, is a rough overview of some of my favorites. First, I will share a wonderful discovery I have made:

Like elephant ears? I do! I love the big, tropical leaves they produce. The bigger the bulbs, the bigger the leaves. Large bulbs the size of a coconut produce huge leaves, but they are usually expensive in the nurseries. Not to worry, as the following story will tell.

Besides elephant ears, I like ethnic restaurants—Indian, Thai, Greek, Oriental, etc. This affinity led me, naturally, to ethnic grocery stores as well. One day I was visiting my favorite oriental supermarket. Walking in there is like stepping into the Far East without ever leaving home. Most of the labels are in languages I can't identify, and there's not usually anyone around who can speak English either.

I love a good adventure. On this day I was having a great time looking at the wide variety of produce, exotic seafood, and things that I still don't know the names of. I am always up for getting something I've never seen before to take home and try. Usually (but not always) I am pleasantly surprised. Something I saw that day gave me pause. They were large roots, and looked like elephant ear bulbs. Not a little, *exactly*. "Taro" was the name on the label. They were enormous, half the size of footballs.

I bought four of them and took them home to plant. What came up after three weeks was...Elephant ears! Big, luxuriant, floppy leaves—robust and healthy. I did a little reading and found that taro is a food staple in many parts of the world, like rice or potatoes. What is priced and sold proudly per bulb in the nurseries here in the U.S. is sold in bulk in an Asian supermarket like any other vegetable, and at a fraction of the cost. What a nice surprise! Many elephant ears (taro) now explode spectacularly each spring at the Oleanders.

Other things from the produce section of an ordinary American supermarket can be planted outdoors, too. One is fresh ginger root. There are many different varieties of ginger. They produce clusters of exotic and wonderfully scented flowers.

More favorites: not in the produce, but the floral department of a typical grocery store you will find the lowly pathos vine. These are common houseplants that can also be found in small pots on the desks of every secretary in the land. When planted in the ground and trained up a tree, they can in the right climate grow into vines several feet long with leaves up to twelve inches long.

Corn plants (not the edible vegetable) are another common office plant in America. They thrive outdoors too in this area, and even produce sweet-smelling flowers.

Many plants growing these days at the Oleanders are beautiful, some are unusual, and a few are just plain weird. Among the latter is the carrion plant, a succulent that produces one of the strangest "flowers" I've ever seen. The flower is oddly shaped and ugly brown. When it blooms, it produces an offensive odor, hence the name.

Four o'clocks are flowers that bloom each afternoon—at four o'clock! (One of mine blooms at three; it must be from a different time zone). The night-blooming cirrus does exactly that. Its blooms are fragile, beautiful, and wildly exotic. The evidence is usually beginning to wilt even as I head out for my morning walk.

Speaking of wildly exotic, some of the most beautiful flowers to be found at the Oleanders are passion flowers. Not many other flowers can compete when they are blooming. They are available in several colors.

Once while driving through rural Texas, I saw a big field of large white flowers with blood red centers. They looked for all the world like hibiscus. There were hundreds of them! The next time I passed through those parts I had a shovel with me. I collected a few samples and took them back and planted them. The flowers look exactly like hibiscus, but the stems do not, they are more weedy than woody.

A friend gave me a handful of castor beans, which I planted Jack and the Beanstalk style. They came up almost overnight. They feature large tropical green and red leaves, red stems and clusters of red seedpods. They are easy to grow, get big quickly, and look great.

Wild morning glory: these flowers are beautiful! There were some intertwined in all of the undergrowth when I first cleared the land. They occasionally pop up in the gardens. They are so beautiful that when they do, they usually get the Oleander Gold Star Award for beauty for that day.

• • •

When we had the Oleander Party, I tried a little trick I learned from my mother. Mom loved all growing things. While growing up, our house contained numerous pots of plants and the yard featured several gardens. In her day, she was the president of the local garden club. Her gardens were full of flowers and lovingly tended. It wasn't uncommon for cars to slow down for a look as they went by.

My mother never was one to have artificial plants around her. Artificial plants at the time looked it (artificial, that is). She needed living ones; nothing else would do. That is, until the manufacturers started finding out how to make artificial flowers that looked realistic. This technological breakthrough did not go unnoticed by my mother. One day she came home with a shopping bag full of them and proceeded to "plant" them out among her real flowers.

I rolled my eyes at this, whereupon Mom said, "Look how nice they look. Even the bees are fooled!"

She continued this practice from then on. One day when she happened to be looking outside the window, a passing car slowed down and then stopped. A woman got out and went over to some of the flowers for a closer look and smiled. Still smiling, she got back into her car and drove away!

Harkening back to Mom, I bought some fetching silk flowers and planted them at a few various and sundry places around the yard before the Oleander Party. At least in this case, the "bloom fell near the rose!"

The Oleander Farm and Ranch Report

The Oleanders, thanks to the diligence of the caretaker, is becoming quite a bit more luxuriant, aided and abetted by a steadfast faith in, and the vigorous application of, plant fertilizers. Orchids, bougainvillea, plumeria, and others have been added to the landscape, along with some edibles.

A. Produce

Banana crop: good. Many a bunch of ripe bananas (*Daylight come and me want to go home, day-o*). A call is pending to the Chiquita marketing rep. Did you know that banana flowers are edible?

Muscadine Grapes: one vine. Very sour if harvested too soon, delicious when fully ripened. Yield this year: twenty-five (grapes that is, not twenty-five quarts or pints or gallons; better luck next year.)

Peaches: zero, due to the demise of both trees. I still can't talk about it.

Grapefruit: tree not acknowledging any of the watering, fertilizing, and mulching I've done.

Lime: four young fruit on a five-foot tall tree. Very proud farmer.

Oranges: no fruit. Tree is either resting or waiting to be paid.

Figs: two trees, no figs yet. Farmer expectant.

Palms: a bunch. All growing. I buy them and they disappear into the landscape. I'd hate to guess how many there are now.

<u>Hibiscus</u>: many. I have low resistance at the garden center. Am currently enjoying them. The bugs are, too.

<u>Assorted herbs</u>: would have been good yield except for near-constant pilferage from the farmer.

<u>Marijuana</u>: (just seeing if you were paying attention.)

<u>Okry</u> (*okra*, if you are not from Arkansas): did you know okra is related to the hibiscus? Just look at an okra flower the next time you are in your vegetable garden and you will see that it is so.

<u>Tomatoes</u>: summer; bumper crop! Twelve tomato bushes put tomatoes on the table three times a day for a while. This is a good opportunity to make gazpacho soup.

Gazpacho soup was invented for the summer. Refreshingly cold on hot summer days, this adaption of the classic Spanish soup deliciously combines the best of summer vegetables. The best recipe I know of is my mother's, which I reprint, without her permission, because it's a good one. And, recipe or no recipe, it's fun to read.

• • •

Flossie's Gazpacho Soup

Go to the farmers' market. Leisurely stroll around and admire the day.
Sit on a bench and smile kindly on everyone. Finally, buy:

5 lbs. tomatoes
2 green peppers
2 medium cucumbers
1 medium red or white onion and
A few peaches for good measure.

Saunter home. That's the end of that. To horse! Time to spring into action!

Time to dice, chop, slice, hack, peel, and flail amongst the veggies. This takes me about two and a half to three hours.

> 4 lbs. tomatoes: dip in boiling water and rub off skins. Some people seed them, but not I. Your extra pound of tomatoes is for salad sometimes, or a BLT—or just admire them.
>
> 1 red onion. Or 1/2 the onion and the other 1/2 scallions with green tops.
>
> 3-4 ribs celery, leaves also if desired.
>
> 2 green peppers seeded.
>
> 2 medium cucumbers peeled and seeded (run spoon down middle)
>
> 4-6 tbsp. green hot or mild chilies or a 4 oz. can. Optional. I don't.
>
> 2-3 garlic cloves
>
> 1 can whole ripe olives, drained (chopped olives in can are chopped too small).
>
> 1 or 2 slices stale French bread, or regular bread in a pinch, crusts on or not.

Steel blade in food processor. Do *not* puree. Pulse veggies one group at a time to the size you like, starting with tomatoes—only because I say so. Check constantly. Drop whole peeled garlics down the chimney as you are chopping onions, as it chops them better. Process bread into crumbs. I put all this into a big Tupperware salad bowl as I go. Use your ulu, because it is so sharp, to chop the green onion tops into neat little rings. What, no ulu? The Indians and Eskimos use it to clean and scrape fresh salmon in Alaska. Well, all right, use your mezzaluna. What? No mezzaluna? Both of these are half-moon shaped blades you rock back and forth to cut. Very well, use a plain old knife, then. Back to the soup; add:

1/3 cup or more freshly chopped parsley. For this, wash 2 bunches of parsley briskly. Cut off about 1/2 inch of stems, take off rubber bands, sort through for wilted bits, cut off huge stems (will only be a few), and leave the rest of the stems. Wrap all in a towel or two, and leave in the fridge for the night to dry well. Next day process it, stems and all, in the processor with the steel blade, in 3 or 4 batches. Do *not* puree. You want nice little sprinkles. Put it all in a plastic container and keep in freezer. You will always have nicely chopped green parsley to put in whatever. You may already know this.

1-2 tsp. sugar or a couple of packages of Equal

2-3 c. tomato juice, depending on how soupy you want it

2-3 tbsp. good olive oil

Salt to taste. Start with about 2 teaspoons. I generally use about 4 teaspoons

Several grinds of pepper

Few dashes of Tabasco, up to 1 teaspoon

2 tsp. Wooster Cester Shire

2 ripe avocados. If you're mad about them, use 3. Cut into small pieces by hand and drop into mixture of:

1/4 c. red wine vinegar

1/4-1/3 c. freshly squeezed lime juice. This keeps the avocado from darkening. Don't put in soup; add at serving time.

Mix it all up gently, taste and ponder. When taste suits you, put in fridge to marry for at least 4 hours. This makes a bodacious amount that keeps well for several days. You have enough to share or you can hoard it all to yourself. Serve plain or put some croutons on top or a dollop of sour cream. Some put 1 cup of beef broth in place of 1 cup of tomato juice. Some add basil or cumin.

The peaches you bought? Enjoy in a cobbler or on your cereal. Delicious!

· · ·

B. Livestock

<u>Feral Cats</u>: several. Perhaps a feral dog could control this nuisance.

<u>Snakes</u>: Some, not many, none poisonous.

<u>Crawfish</u> (ditch lobsters): it is hard to establish numbers; they dig up mounds around the yard after a good rain. Never enough for a meal; farmer is ever hopeful.

<u>Tree Frogs</u>: not as musical as their Caribbean cousins, but welcome nonetheless. They stick to the wall around the porch light on a warm summer evening and eat insects in a dramatic way.

<u>Chameleons</u>: a healthy population at the Oleanders. They turn the color of whatever object they happen to be crouched on. Green is the prettiest. Brightly colored objects seem to throw them. In some parts of the world, geckos are commonly kept inside peoples' houses. A chameleon resides inside the Oleanders. It keeps the house bug-free. It is only slightly disconcerting to female company to see it dart under the furniture.

<u>Parrots</u>: one resident, numerous transients. When I first came to the Clear Lake area I was delighted to discover flocks of wild parrots flying thither and yon around Clear Lake. They are Quaker par-

rots. Quaker parrots are commonly sold through pet stores. They are about twice the size of parakeets and are brilliant, iridescent green with grey breasts.

No one knows for sure how the parrots got here. They may be escaped pets, or perhaps a shipment of parrots intended for a pet store got loose from the airport. Whatever the case, the climate is mild enough in the area that they can survive. There are several local colonies which are thriving and growing. My compendium on parrots tells me that Quaker parrots are native to South America, although populations exist in Puerto Rico and other areas of the United States.

The wild parrots fly over the Oleanders every day. I am not bothered in the least with their cheerful screeching. Perhaps I can attract some by building a nesting platform. Any parrots that took up residence in *my* yard would be safe. Maybe I could come across some orphaned babies, or injured adults, to nurse back to health…

• • •

Hummingbirds: many, in season. One day while working on the patio, I thought I saw a hummingbird flit by. Then I saw it again, clearly. It hovered over a flower for an instant in a shaft of sunlight that reflected brilliantly off of its iridescent green feathers. Then, in a flash, it was gone. That was all I needed. The next time I was out, I got a hummingbird feeder.

Soon, I had hummingbirds visiting at odd times, all day long. They were tiny and beautiful, and it was fun to watch their antics.

It became apparent that some hummingbirds had Napoleon complexes. That is, a pint-sized "Type A" personality would try to control the feeder and not let any others around. It was comical and entertaining to watch these miniature aerial dogfights. It was funny to think that such a miniscule creature felt the need to dominate, to own, or to protect…*something*.

It made me smile to imagine one hummingbird yelling in a very high-pitched voice, "I'm gonna kick your butt!"

And another one yelling back, "No, I'm gonna kick *your* butt!"

And all the time, while the hummingbird attempting to dominate the feeder is off chasing another one away, a third humming bird has landed on the feeder and is leisurely having its fill.

I had been told that the hummingbird feeder mixture should be refreshed periodically lest it ferment. This led to thoughts of it sitting there in the hot Texas sun day after day and turning into a red, intoxicating elixir, resulting in clouds of inebriated hummers flying around sloppily, crashing into windows and people's faces. And then possibly me coming home one day to find a tiny sign attached to the hummingbird feeder, printed in very small kindergarten prose, reading:

> Dear Andy—
> Please ferment *before* filling.
> Thanks,
> The Oleanders of San Leon Hummingbirds

A friend dropped by one day when I happened to be mixing up a batch of sugar, water, and food coloring for the hummingbird feeder. She was a health-conscious person who evidently wasn't familiar with the ways of hummingbirds. She became aghast at the amount of sugar I had just measured out.

"My *God*, that's *way* too much sugar," she exclaimed. "It's so bad for them—they'd *never* be able to fly if they ate this stuff every day! And just think of all of the health risks…"

She then tried to talk me into making up a new batch using a low-cal sugar substitute, and I might have done so if not for another alert friend who gently informed me that sugar substitutes were in fact *dangerous* for hummingbirds.

They need real sugar, such as what is in the hummingbird feeder mix packages. I reckoned I'd just have to risk flocks of obese, drunk, hummingbirds flying around overhead, imperiling people's safety.

Mystery, Anyone?

I discovered something odd. There is a natural drain in the yard. Once after a long hard rain, the yard was left with a few inches of standing rainwater. When I was walking around afterward, I noticed water running into a small hole maybe an inch and a half across. Supposing it to be a crawfish hole I watched for several minutes to see if it would fill up. It didn't. The next morning as I was walking the grounds again, what was left of the rainwater was *still* draining into the hole.

That couldn't be right! Even a big crawdad hole would fill up eventually. Where was all that water going? What was down there? Could there be a buried room containing a cache of Spanish gold? Perhaps an elaborate burial chamber of the fierce and proud Karankawa Indians who once lived in this area? Maybe an undiscovered subterranean cave that leads to the sea? These meandering thoughts meandered into my meandering mind.

There are several sites where treasure has been discovered along the Texas coast, including Galveston. Pirates such as Jean Lafitte were active here. Gold, silver, coins, and other rare and valuable artifacts have been recovered all up and down the Texas coastline. I read in the newspaper a few years ago that city workers repairing a storm drain in Corpus Christi accidentally stumbled upon a treasure of old coins that were found to be Spanish in origin. It prompted a three-way grab for ownership between the city, the workers, and the state.

There are lots of stories of buried treasure around the world. Even today, someone digging a road in England occasionally comes upon a cache of coins dating back to the Roman Empire. And then there is the fascinating story of a wild, far-fetched treasure hunt on an island in Nova Scotia, Canada, called Oak Island.

Oak Island

Oak Island is the setting for numerous hunts for a treasure that many believe to be buried there. It has quite a history. It began in the late 1700s when some local boys discovered a curious round depression in the ground in a clearing on the island. Next to it was a large tree with an old pulley hanging from a branch over the depression. It had long been suspected that there had been pirate activity in the area, and that buried treasure could likely be nearby.

The boys began to dig in the center of the depression. They came to a layer of flagstones a few feet down. Digging deeper, they came to a layer of logs, like a platform. This caused much excitement and raised their curiosity, but after clearing the logs out of the way, there was nothing but more dirt. They resumed digging and presently came to another layer of logs. Again, nothing significant lay beneath the logs. They kept digging and came to a third platform. After finding nothing of value there either, they gave up.

Word of this curiosity spread. Others took up the digging, but they too found nothing. The earth was said to be softer than the surrounding dirt, suggesting that a hole had been dug there before. Markings, possibly from previous digging, were supposedly evident on the walls.

The story of the site continued to spread and sporadic digging in the area continued. In the early 1800s a mining company arrived at Oak Island to do some exploration of its own. They began digging in the same spot. They found more layers of logs as well as layers of charcoal and coconut fiber. At a depth of ninety feet they unearthed a stone with symbols of unknown origin on it. As they were preparing to go deeper, the pit unexpectedly flooded. Attempts to remove the water failed and the company gave up on the hole that was to become known as the Money Pit.

Comprehensive efforts were made by others to unravel the mystery of the Oak Island Money Pit. Subsequent diggings produced more wood, bits of metal, and other items. The digging there has continued off and on, right up to modern times. More tantalizing objects have allegedly been found. Today, for all the digging, no treasure has ever been found at Oak Island. But then the mystery about what has been found there has never been satisfactorily explained, either.

• • •

Mysteries like this drive me wild! The truth about the Money Pit may never be revealed to us. I may, likewise, never know where the water draining into the ground at the Oleanders goes. It will take a backhoe to find out.

God Talking

God spoke to me directly last night. I was mowing the lawn and had just gotten to the part where I had seen small poison ivy sprigs growing. Roundup had not been completely effective.

The rest of the grass in the yard was knee high, prompting Ivan to one day ask me if my lawn mower was broken. Ignoring his sarcasm, I replied that I was waiting for gasoline prices to go down, and then asked him if he knew where I could buy a diesel lawn mower.

"And anyway," I added, "There's no sense in scalping the lawn too early (it was mid-summer) and damaging the tender young shoots."

However, the inevitable day arrived when there was nothing more pressing to do and I resigned myself to the fact that I was going to have to mow the yard. I got started. I became nervous as I got near the area where I had seen poison ivy. I offered a half-serious prayer to God as I plunged in:

"Dear God, I am just the lonely caretaker of your garden.
I am attempting to keep my little portion of it beautiful. I
don't deserve to get poison ivy this time. Might I be spared?"

The ground shook. They sky, which had been clear, clouded up. The wind started to blow. God was present, and he spoke thus:

"If you choose to ignore my leaves of three, Misery will accompany thee."

"But God," I opined. "My heart is pure; can't you give me a break? I wish to mow, but not to ache."
God spoke as before:

"Dear child: Why dost thou think you deserve special favors; To be granted to you, but not to your brothers?"

And with that he sent one hundred ants down upon my ankles.

Once again spoke I to the Lord: "You're right, my Lord. If you I ignore, I'll get what I deserve, and my limbs will be sore!"

And thus it went.

Resigned to my fate, I pointed my lawn mower at Poison Ivy Hell and mowed slowly forth. The mowing was followed by an immediate and earnest cleansing, body, not soul, in an attempt to thwart the inevitable.

The next morning, I arose and discovered not a single poison ivy bump. And it was in that sublime, itch-free moment I realized that God had spoken to me yet again!

About the Author

Andy Upchurch was born in Amarillo, Texas, in 1954. The family moved to Fayetteville, Arkansas, when he was an infant where he lived until high school graduation. He attended the University of Arkansas for one year and then transferred to North Texas State University in Denton, Texas, where he graduated in 1978 with a degree in music education. He lived in the Dallas area for around fifteen years prior to moving to the Clear Lake, Texas area.

He has a deep-seated affinity for salt water and the Texas coast. He still lives there today, at the Oleanders of San Leon.

(theoleandersofsanleon.com)

Endnotes

1. Eggenberger, Richard and Mary Helen, *The Handbook On Oleanders* (Cleveland:Tropical Plant Specialists, 1996).

2. Gallaway, Alecya, *The History of San Leon, Volume 1* (San Leon:Scalare Creations, 2001).

3. Merle Travis. *Sixteen Tons*. From *Folksongs of the Hills*. Capitol Records T-891. 1946. LP.

4. Clark, Guy. *Blowin' like a bandit*. From *Homegrown Tomatoes*. W B Records 1-23880. 1983. LP.